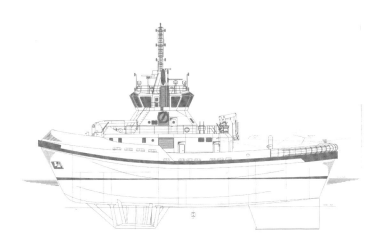

UNDER TOW

UNDER TOW

A CANADIAN HISTORY
OF TUGS AND TOWING

DONAL M. BAIRD

Vanwell Publishing Limited
St. Catharines, Ontario

Vanwell Publishing acknowledges the financial support of the Government of Canada through the Book Publishing Industry Development Program for our publishing activities.

Vanwell Publishing acknowledges the Government of Ontario through the Ontario Media Development Corporation's Book Initiative.

Design: Linda Moroz-Irvine
Cover photograph courtesy of Don Macmillan

Vanwell Publishing Limited
1 Northrup Crescent
P.O. Box 2131
St. Catharines, Ontario L2R 7S2
sales@vanwell.com
1-800-661-6136
fax 905-937-1760

In the United States:
P.O. Box 1207
Lewiston, NY 14092
USA

Printed in Canada

National Library of Canada Cataloguing in Publication

Baird, Donal M.
       Under tow : a Canadian history of tugs and towing / Donal Baird.

Includes bibliographical references and index.
ISBN 1-55125-076-4

       1. Towing--History. 2. Tugboats--Canada--History. 3. Towboats--Canada--History. I. Title.

VM464.B33 2003   387.2'32'0971   C2003-902161-0

TABLE OF CONTENTS

WE ALL CARRY THE IMAGE OF THE SAUCY, fussing, self-important little vessels called "tugs," or "towboats," but few people know them well. They are taken for granted and are not of direct concern in our lives. However, touched by the romance that attaches to anything that sails on the sea, tugs have a story worth telling.

The many among us who pursue an interest in ships and the sea seem always to have our own personal areas of interest. Some have a particular attraction to tugs. What other vessel has such evident personality? Who else gets to push the big guys around and get thanked for it?

The value of steam-powered vessels for towing and otherwise assisting other vessels was recognized right from the beginning. Eventually, a highly specialized design evolved for this purpose. It is hoped that this book will show that the role of tugs in waterborne commerce has been both interesting and important, ranging as it does from the humdrum moving of mud scows to heroic high seas rescues.

I thought I knew quite a lot about the subject from my many years of haunting waterfronts. Now my eyes have been opened to the great diversity of the tugs' applications and their key significance in some areas of commerce, such as the great age of the world-girdling, square-rigged sailing ship. A surprise was the degree to which the little tugs, all through their history, boldly made their way all over the world, and through every sea.

As in any area of special interest, there are those who would like minute detail and a record of every tug that ever existed. This is, of course, impractical, calling instead for a selective approach. Another problem is that of terminology. In this work a compromise was struck, with a leaning towards the traditional. Although Americans and many West Coast Canadians refer to them as "towboats," the more universal "tug" is used here. Boats and ships are traditionally feminine in gender and are often referred to as "she." The definite article before vessels' names has been omitted in deference to the tradition of giving them personality, something this book ought to do. On the technical side, there is a problem with horsepower, there having been a number of kinds, not always transposable. The solution has been to quote what is available. Brake horsepower (bhp) is preferred today and the use of Bollard Pull is a more accurate description of a tug's total applicable power, combining all the factors of hull shape, propellor design and power transmission into one figure.

THE AUTHOR WISHES TO NOTE WITH APPRECIATION the interest and help of many people in the preparation of this history of tugs. Prominent among these were the major tug-operating companies and personnel, some of the latter regrettably no longer with us, this book having been long in gestation. These sources provided data, pictures and opportunities to see their tugs at work, notably Seaspan International and their corporate communications officer, Debbie Tardiff in North Vancouver; Donal McAllister, late president of McAllister Towing and Salvage, Montreal; John Kavanaugh, late president of Eastern Canada Towing, Halifax; Leland Carpenter of Atlantic Towing in Saint John and Evans McKeil of McKeil Marine, Hamilton.

The various maritime museums have been helpful over a period of years with pictures and historical data, in particular the Maritime Museum of the Atlantic, through their then librarian, Mary Blackford, and the Maritime Museum of the Great Lakes through the late Don Page, honorary curator.

Knowledgeable tug enthusiasts who should be singled out for supplying encouragement, pictures and information are Mac Mackay in Halifax, John Weeks in Saint John, the late Commodore O.C.S. Robertson, RCN, GM, of Oakville, Ont., members of the Pacific Coast Tug Society, Vancouver, and the late Ernest Bustard, naval architect, of Oakville.

Only two years after Robert Fulton's success, John Molson of Montreal started regular St. Lawrence River service between Montreal and Quebec with his all Canadian built *Accommodation* in 1809. It was the beginning of a large and prosperous river shipping line that included towing. (Molson Archives Collection, NAC C111285)

Vessels Without Sails

THE FIRST STEAMBOATS were put into service to carry people and goods. It was quickly seen, however, that there would be opportunities for greater exploitation and versatility of the invention by adding towing to its uses. Not only humble barges and rafts of logs, but the glamorous world-circling packets and clippers, pressed to show their speed of passage, wanted the benefits of this wind-and tide-defying power when sails failed them.

At the beginning of the nineteenth century, the Industrial Revolution in Europe stimulated trade around the world. There was also a push of European immigration into the relatively untracked interiors of other continents such as North America. Both of these developments exerted new pressures for more efficient waterborne commerce. The steam railway would help carry the raw materials and finished goods overland, but floating freight over water in the bottoms of vessels was still the most effective means of transportation. In many respects it still is today.

More certain and speedier means of transport would be needed than horses pulling barges on canal towpaths, or using manual capstans and kedging with anchors to move sailing ships in and out of harbours, to say nothing of tacking vainly against adverse winds. Great rivers and estuaries on many coasts could not be effectively utilized because of narrow and tortuous channels, strong currents and treacherous entrance bars. These barriers frequently required ocean ships to transfer their cargos to small vessels. The discovery of a capability for ships to cross seas from river port to river port was very valuable to the development of commerce and industry. This knowledge was applied on the short seas of Northern Europe, and the major estuaries and rivers of Britain, Europe and other continents.

The power of steam was a vital element in running the mines and factories of the Industrial Revolution. It is no wonder that its capacity to overcome the limitations of wind-powered sails was soon pursued. However, there was a surprising amount of trouble with the technology of applying the still primitive steam engine to the propulsion of a boat or ship. A number of would-be inventors saw the steam-powered vessel as useful for specific applications. Speedy and reliable carriage of passengers seems to have been predominant, although towing barges and carrying freight were also considered from the start.

Navies were a little slower than commercial enterprise, but, once convinced, saw that the same attributes of movement through confined waterways and independence from wind and currents were of potentially great tactical value. Gaining the wind gauge on an enemy would no longer mean so much.

A proposal to put the pioneering Newcomen atmospheric steam engine in a boat for the purpose of driving stern paddles was put forward as early as 1736 by Jonathan Hull in England. It seems probable that the cumbersome steam engine of that time would probably have sunk any boat it could propel and the idea was not put to the test. Not all inventors thought of using the paddle wheel with the steam engine, even though paddles had been around since the early Egyptians. Struggling with a system of vertical paddles that imitated the human canoeist, the American John Fitch actually had a boat running commercially on the Delaware River for the summer season of 1790. However, it ended there. Apparently it worked, but not well enough. Fitch can hardly be blamed for his frustration at failing to gain credit for the invention of the steamboat.

CHAPTER 1

Development of the Steamboat

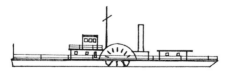

Magnet (Author's sketch)

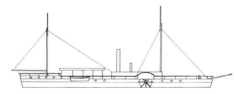

Clermont (Author's sketch)

A mid-nineteenth century Montreal Harbour scene includes raftsmen on their way through to Quebec, a towboat bringing a sailing vessel in through St. Mary's Current and an ocean steamer heading downriver. (Drawing by James Duncan NAC C121143)

Who did invent the steamboat? Who harnessed the steam engine to a propulsion system so that it became an established, workable transportation system? Various people independently tackled the problem on both sides of the Atlantic and produced boats that worked; but these boats were commercial failures and were abandoned because of poor speed, power, reliability or, that common problem of inventors, rejection by established interests. The first of these boats after that of John Fitch was designed as a towing vessel. It was named *Charlotte Dundas*, and was the result of an inspiration by one Patrick Miller and engineering by William Symington, both working on behalf of Lord Dundas of Kerse. This peer was a governor of the Forth and Clyde Canal Company in Scotland and wanted to tow coal barges on the canal. Built in 1802, Symington's boat had a single paddle wheel mounted within a slot in the hull; it was sort of an internal stern wheel.

Charlotte Dundas successfully towed two 70-ton barges, but this pioneer steamer's life was short. Lord Dundas received an order to build a number of these towing vessels from the great pioneer canal builder, the Duke of Bridgewater. Unfortunately, the Duke soon died and with him, interest in steam towing. Canal authorities feared that damage would be caused to the canal banks by the boat's wake and there was no one in a strong position to fight for the towboat's

continuation. *Charlotte Dundas* was laid up and what could have been the solid establishment of the steam vessel in the form of canal tugs thus died. An unknown benefit was passed on, however, in the development of this steamer. The American Robert Fulton examined the pioneer paddler and possibly had a demonstration of its operation before going on to build his own successful steamboat.

Americans, nevertheless, insist on calling Fulton the inventor of the steamboat for his Hudson River passenger boat, which was put in service in 1807. This boat is established in popular history and well known to every American as *Clermont*, though technically its real and original name was *North River Ferry*. Giving the credit to Fulton is justified by historian James Thomas Flexner on the basis of Fulton's having established the steam-propelled vessel as viable and of commercial value. By this reasoning, the death of Lord Bridgewater and the reactionary attitude of canal operators deprived Symington of this honor for his work. In any event, as Flexner points out, the operation of steam-powered vessels was continuous from the time of Fulton's first commercially viable boat on the Hudson River.

With primitive roads and great distances to be covered, the need to expand commerce into the interior of the continent gave American and Canadian entrepreneurs the motivation to achieve

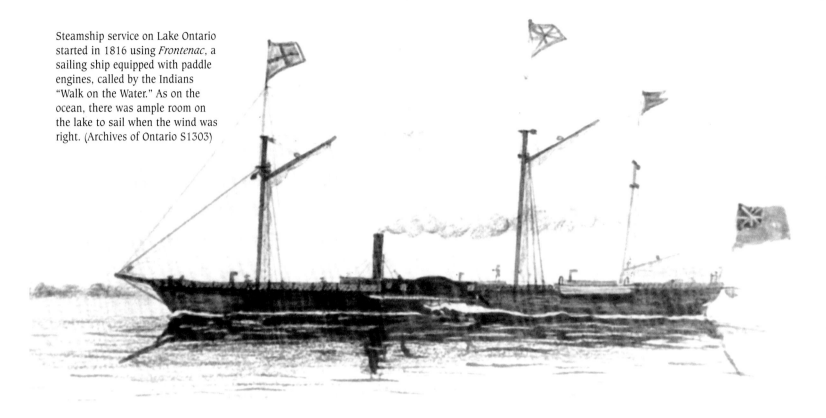

Steamship service on Lake Ontario started in 1816 using *Frontenac*, a sailing ship equipped with paddle engines, called by the Indians "Walk on the Water." As on the ocean, there was ample room on the lake to sail when the wind was right. (Archives of Ontario S1303)

practical navigation on their great rivers and lakes. The existing sailing, barge-poling and towpath methods were not adequate for the long distances and complexities of inland transportation. A number of American inventors were working on steam propulsion in the latter part of the seventeenth century. They lacked the scientific, engineering and industrial resources of Britain and, unfortunately, persisted in trying to reinvent what was already established—the basic steam engine. Devising a means of propulsion should have been a considerable enough challenge.

In 1788, seventeen years before Robert Fulton's widely accepted invention of the steamboat, two Americans, John Fitch and James Rumsey, were in intense competition over the claim to have invented the steam-powered vessel. In fact, neither was particularly successful at that point. Fitch finally produced his boat on the Delaware River. It was equipped with a series of stern-mounted vertical paddles, simulating a human paddling motion and driven by a steam engine through a system of levers. It was a crude mechanism, but the boat steamed along at a speed of six to eight miles per hour while carrying passengers along the Delaware. Fitch's boat logged thousands of miles during its one season. Customers were too few, Fitch's boat was not a financial success and it did not sail

after that year. His competitor, Rumsey, produced a water-pump jet-type of propulsion that proved very inefficient and uncompetitive.

Fulton was a more sophisticated inventor and entrepreneur than either Fitch or Rumsey. He regarded the proven British engines as superior power sources. While traveling abroad he thoroughly studied *Charlotte Dundas* and later built a small steam-powered vessel on the River Seine at Paris in 1803. This boat towed two barges at an unremarkable speed of two to three miles per hour, but sank in a storm before final completion.

Fulton later acquired a Boulton and Watt engine in Britain and built his commercially viable steamboat, connecting the rotary motion of the engine to a pair of paddle wheels, one on either side of the vessel. It was a very elementary concept and the component elements were all already in existence. Fulton's major original contribution seems to have been the side paddle wheels.

With other North American hopefuls such as John Fitch and the Canadian John Molson, Fulton saw the steamboat primarily as a passenger carrier. It would be infinitely more comfortable than a stagecoach bumping over what passed for roads. Fulton's boat plied the Hudson River in 1807 as *North River Ferry* and was immediately accepted by the public in commercial service, running on a

A rudimentary sternwheeler from a later period shows the essential form of the early river vessels of this type, such as appeared early on the Saint John River both for passengers, freight and towing. (Archives of Ontario 23983A)

schedule from New York to Albany, some 150 miles away. *North River*, as it soon became known (but going down in history simply as *Clermont*), broke down frequently and was modified extensively by Fulton, so that the service was maintained.

Business thrived for Fulton, who provided the paying public with a comfortable and fairly certain mode of travel between New York and Albany. He built up a fleet of more than twenty boats in his lifetime, but he also spent a lot of his energy and money in battles to preserve his state-granted monopoly on the Hudson River service. The potential for steamer traffic on the mighty Mississippi system also interested Fulton and he provided pioneering vessels there as well.

A few years after Fulton's Hudson River Line, and quite independent of his example, another pioneering steamboat line was born in North America, the commercial fleet established by John Molson on the St. Lawrence River.

Steam on the St. Lawrence

In sparsely populated British North America at the beginning of the nineteenth century, the St. Lawrence River-Great Lakes system was the principal means of long distance transportation, a great highway to the interior of the continent. Roads between the principal cities of Montreal and Quebec were muddy cart tracks. There was no road onward to York (Toronto) and Niagara. For sailing vessels there were major obstacles in the form of strong currents and tides in the lower river, with rapids and confined searoom farther upstream.

Quebec was reasonably accessible from the sea and was thus the major port of entry. The larger sailing ships from overseas stopped at Quebec, where passengers and freight were transshipped via smaller vessels. To sail on up river to Montreal, vessels were faced with tides, currents, shallows and, just before the port of Montreal, the swift St. Mary's Current. Vessels had to wait for a strong east wind to push them into the port, or be helped by oxen pulling along a towpath. These hazards kept Montreal, the burgeoning centre of trade and commerce in Canada, from becoming an effective seaport. Just above Montreal a series of rapids obstructed passage to the Ottawa River and Lake Ontario.

John Molson, a successful Montreal entrepreneur in breweries, banking and lumber, had seen the steam engines of James Watt in use at breweries in England. In 1808 he decided to use the power of the steam engine to propel a ship on the St. Lawrence River. Rather than purchase Watt's well proven engine, he elected to build both boat and engine in Canada.

The Forges de Saint Maurice at Trois Rivières had been established during the French régime in 1733 using local iron, and were capable of casting the main engine components. These were to be finished by local Montreal craftsmen. A shipwright and an engineer were brought from England to help. The keel for Molson's boat was laid at the recently established Munn's Shipyard in Montreal, in March 1809.

Fitted out at Molson's own wharf, the result was a wooden vessel, long and low in the fashion of inland sailing vessels, but equipped with a six-horsepower boiler, low pressure steam engine and side paddle wheels. Molson named her *Accommodation*. After trials and some engine modifications, *Accommodation* made a splendid run downriver to Quebec on the first of November 1809, under Captain John Jackson, with Amable Laviolette as pilot. John Bruce, Molson's Scottish consultant, was engineer. There were ten passengers on the 36-hour trip, which included 30 hours at anchor along the way.

Molson laid out the sum of £2000 for *Accommodation*. He charged fares of $9.00 or $8.00, depending upon whether the trip was up or down the river, the current making a difference in the time of passage. This first powered vessel on the St. Lawrence was 85 feet long and had sleeping berths for twenty, but was a commercial failure. It may have been due to a combination of mechanical inefficiency and dependence primarily upon passengers for revenue. The following year, Molson's son, John Jr, refitted the boat with a more powerful boiler and continued service for the 1810 navigation season. The operation still lost money.

Nevertheless, trade that was useful to the various Molson enterprises encouraged the river navigation pioneers to persist. The fourth commercial steam vessel in the world, powered by what was apparently the first successful marine engine built outside Great Britain, *Accommodation* served an important purpose. It led her owner to build a replacement in the hope of greater efficiency in performance.

Molson went to New York to consult Fulton on designing and building a bigger, better steamer. Fulton recommended the British Boulton and Watt engine he used in his own vessels and offered to help Molson get a government monopoly for service on the St. Lawrence. He also offered to design a passenger steamer that would make four to five mph, but Molson found the price, which included a ten percent share of net profits, too steep. He did take

Fulton's advice, unfortunately, and applied for a monopoly. After a long drawn-out campaign, he was turned down.

During this period, in 1811, Molson went to England where he made friends with James Watt, ordering two steam engines for a new boat laid down at Logan's shipyard in Montreal. At 400 tons, this was to be the largest steamer in the world. Launched as *Swiftsure* the following August, she steamed to Quebec and back on her maiden voyage, true to her name, without any problems.

Regular service was established and the new boat was utilized at times to transport troops during the War of 1812, on one trip carrying 600 soldiers. It was a very early use of a steamship for war purposes. Fulton had built a steam warship at this time but it was too late to see service in the conflict.

In 1814, Molson was encouraged to launch *Malsham*, a larger, faster vessel having both cabin and steerage classes. Cabin class passengers in those times rode in the cabin. Steerage class meant riding amongst the freight on deck. Later an immigrant rate of fourpence gave passage from Quebec City to Montreal in an open scow that was towed behind. Many in the vast waves of Irish and other immigrants in the first half of the nineteenth century came into the continent this way.

It was a good time to build a new river transportation system, with the influx of immigrants just beginning and the timber export trade expanding as Napoleon closed the Baltic Sea to the British. The John Molsons, father and son, apparently captained their two river steamers themselves, competing and even racing against each other. The business became very profitable in both passengers and freight, but it seems strange that these two could be off sailing the great river when there were various other important business enterprises to be managed as well. Part of the picture was, of course, the value of the steamboat service in carrying Molson's ales to new markets and in faster bank clearing-house operations between Montreal and Quebec. Perhaps there was as much management business for the Molsons in Quebec as in Montreal, the former being the capital.

Since Molson had lost his bid for a monopoly on the river, competition was inevitable. One of Montreal's other Scottish entrepreneurs, Thomas Torrance, built his *Car of Commerce* to outclass the Molsons, who responded with a still bigger vessel, *Lady Sherbrooke*. These two larger boats utilized the same model of engine from Watt's Soho engineering works. *Lady Sherbrooke* was 170 feet long, with a 34-foot beam and a 63-hp, side-lever engine. All these St. Lawrence River vessels were sidewheelers.

The Glasier Company's sidewheeler *Hero* of 1889 tows a raft of logs on the slow moving Saint John River, where steam towing came as a Godsend. Only in spring were there currents strong enough for rafts to float down to the river's mouth on their own. The 128-ton *Hero* carries a large load of cordwood for fuel. (Provincial Archives New Brunswick P13-60)

In 1817 the Molsons went ashore, leaving the increasingly competitive sailing to professional captains; but they absorbed several rival steamboat syndicates, forming the St. Lawrence Steamboat Company, generally known as the Molson Line. Competition was still stiff, however, as others came into the fray. There was an undercutting of rates and several collisions occurred between the racing boats. Thomas Torrance failed to keep up, but his son John, a tea importer, entered the lists with a newly purchased boat called *Hercules*. The design of this vessel recognised that there was a great advantage in being able to tow as well as carry payloads. *Hercules* was built with a very powerful engine for just this purpose and Torrance operated her under the name of The Towboat Company.

Hercules must have been the first towboat, or tug, in Canada. In May 1826 she towed an ocean ship up through St. Mary's Current, right into the Port of Montreal. This significant event signalled the coming end of Quebec's dominance as the transatlantic shipping terminus for Canada. Montreal became a Port of Entry in 1832, spurring government projects to improve the port and wharves, thereby setting it up to flourish as the country's major east coast port for nearly a century and a half. The construction of the St. Lawrence Seaway from Montreal to Lake Ontario and the advent of container ships would finally break this hold.

John Torrance had the misfortune to have his mighty *Hercules* ram the Molson steamer *New Swiftsure* in 1826. With heavy damages awarded to them, the Molsons were able acquire a new boat to outclass *Hercules*. Named *John Molson*, she carried 60 cabin class passengers. Torrance entered his *St. George* and *Britannia* in competition by 1833, but later that year he abruptly gave up the fight, merging with the Molson Line.

Molson went on to take over the Ottawa Steamboat Company, thereby gaining a monopoly on the Ottawa River and eventually the Rideau Canal. He dominated traffic on the river system from Kingston to Quebec for a decade. His big and luxurious, 182-foot *John Bull*, with two 85hp engines, had trumped Torrance's fast *St. George*, although she was expensive to run. But Molson, now a tycoon of diverse interests, had great financial stamina and dominated the pack. Steamers were now busy carrying passengers, freight and mails, as well as towing barges and timber rafts.

The adventurous entrepreneurs in commercial steamboating had come to the realization that providing a comfortable alternative to the crude roads and stagecoaches for human passengers was only a small part of what was now possible. A clear indication of this was shown when *John Bull* steamed upriver from Quebec pulling six barges carrying at once 1800 people and 2600 tons of freight. The first vessels that could be called tugs, like *Hercules* and *John Bull,* were not specialized in towing alone. They were sufficiently commodious that there was room for passengers and some freight. *John Bull* was considered luxurious in her cabin appointments. It was thus possible for these vessels to be very flexible in meeting the traffic demands, whether fast express service or heavy loads.

There were numerous other steamers and their owners on the St. Lawrence in the early 1830s; one shipyard in Montreal turned out nine vessels between 1829 and 1833. By the mid-1840s there was a commercial slump and the timber trade fell off sharply. John

Unidentified tug. (Maritime Museum of the Atlantic)

Molson had turned to an interest in steam railways before he died in 1838. It seems as though the family then lost active interest in steamboating. *John Bull* came to a sorry end, as was all too common in those times, burning on the river in June 1839 with considerable loss of life.

Other areas of Eastern Canada were quick to recognise the value of steam transportation on lakes and rivers when roads and railways were almost nonexistent. *General* was plying the Saint John River in New Brunswick in 1816, as was *Frontenac* on Lake Ontario. The 1820s saw what the Indians dubbed "fire canoes" increasing in number on these eastern lake and river systems. The original concept of carrying passengers and freight was very quickly overshadowed by the towing idea.

Comet was possibly the first successful commercial steam passenger vessel to prove her viability in Britain, in 1812. She had tiller steering and unique, tandem, four-bladed paddles. (National Maritime Museum, Greenwich 2432)

Origin of the Tug

THE EGYPTIANS EMPLOYED GALLEYS WITH OARS to tow barges loaded with stone in the building of the pyramids, so the concept of towing vessels may be said to be almost as old as history. The Romans used oar-powered boats to manoeuver larger, sailing vessels, as did the British Royal Navy centuries later. The great, ungainly line-of-battle ships of Nelson's day were often manoeuvered when becalmed and in the confined waters of ports by towing with the ship's own boats. This was more practical in the case of a man-o'-war than a merchant vessel, since the former had large numbers of men and large boats available.

It is not surprising, then, that the idea of utilizing a steam-powered vessel to tow sailing ships and barges occurred independently in many quarters. In fact, the idea of steam propulsion was sometimes put forward with towing as the primary objective, especially in Britain. This was the case with Symington's *Charlotte Dundas*. Jonathan Hulls proposed a steam-powered boat for towing, but did not bring the idea to fruition. Richard Trevithick, the railway pioneer, conceived a plan for a towboat to pull a fireship in amongst the ships of the French navy poised for an invasion of England at Boulogne. However, the fleet moved away and he converted his scheme to a tug that would move ships around the London docks. It would also carry a steam crane and a fire pump, making it the first powered fireboat. All this potential capability was too much for the river and dock workers, whose heavy opposition forced him to quit his efforts.

The North Americans, on the other hand, looked first at vessels that would carry passengers and some freight as an alternative to crude or nonexistent roads. The economics of steam-powered commerce with low efficiency engines and small carrying capacity soon gave them the notion of towing as the main profit centre. Sailing ship masters and timber raft operators quickly realized the advantage of being able to purchase a tow to maintain schedules.

After the brief appearance of *Charlotte Dundas* in 1802, it was left to the American Robert Fulton and the Canadian John Molson to build and operate successful steamboats, while a British carpenter struggled to promote and gain capital for his vessel. After a dozen years, Henry Bell got his passenger boat *Comet* operating in 1812. She was built by John Wood of Glasgow with engines by John Robertson. *Comet* also proved the steam vessel was practical, operating commercially between Glasgow and Greenock on the Clyde, until she was wrecked eight years later.

A little behind the North Americans in utilizing steam propulsion commercially, the British appear to have been quicker in developing the idea of the tug itself. There were conflicting claims to first place, but the earliest towing jobs were performed by small vessels designed for short passenger, baggage and freight runs. In 1814, the steamboat *Industry* was put into service on the Firth of Clyde to carry passengers between Glasgow and Port Glasgow. Soon she took over the work of lighters and packhorses used for carrying luggage to the port. Later this little 83-ton side wheeler was towing barges to increase her load factor, and has since been put forward for honours as the first tug.

However, in the same year on the River Tyne, another small steamer with the unimaginative name *Tyne Steamboat* began carrying commercial traffic on that river. She was joined by *Eagle*, but they were not a commercial success until 1818. This came when their operators saw there could be a profit for all concerned in towing incoming ships over the bar at

CHAPTER 2

The Towing Idea

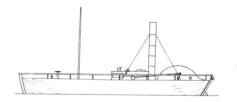

Charlotte Dundas (Author's sketch)

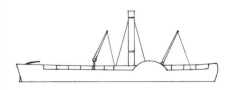

Industry (Author's sketch)

Royal William demonstrated transatlantic steamer capabilities in 1833 when she made the crossing entirely with her paddles, the first vessel to do so. Built in 1831 at Quebec, she had a chequered career that included some time as a seeking tug on the St. Lawrence River. (CP Rail Corporate Archives 19799)

the river mouth and up the tricky, shallow channel to Newcastle. This not only made a viable business of towing, but allowed larger seagoing vessels to go up to Newcastle, thus making it an ocean port. The heavy coal traffic from Newcastle to London became much more reliable and prices more stable. The Tyne thus became a base for building numerous steam vessels designed, built for and used largely in towing.

The case of the River Tyne set the pattern for many other rivers or their estuaries. The help of steam towing to incoming and outgoing ocean and coastal sailing vessels expedited trade and, in many cases, turned local river ports into important ocean ports. It helped to provide the sinews of the Industrial Revolution, moving volumes of cargo on reliable schedules on the River Rhine, across the short seas of Western Europe and into the heartland of North America. It brought more certain and economical transportation on the Rivers Forth, Mersey, Thames, Hudson, Mississippi, St. Lawrence, Hoogly, Volga, Yangtse, de la Plata and others.

Many of the very early British and some Canadian tugs started first as ferries, carrying passengers. Towing cut very quickly into the service to passengers. Uniquely in Britain, tugs that also carried passengers both on local outings and to and from passenger ships anchored offshore existed into the middle of the twentieth century. The first ferries between Quebec and Lévis on the St. Lawrence River suffered from the same confusion of purpose, as did those of New York.

When it comes to a claim for the title of "first tug," there is a special argument for one particular candidate. This was a steamboat built in 1816 at Leith, Scotland, and its claim can be based on the fact that its name was *Tug*. There is no indication of this word being associated particularly with towing vessels previous to that time. *Tug* was built expressly for towing between Leith and Grangemouth, continuing until 1838 when she was converted into a sailing vessel.

The Thames, leading as it does to London, was naturally a great avenue of waterborne commerce in spite of the dictates of powerful tides. Before steam, sailing barges and keelboats powered by a sweep oar were utilized on the river and the connecting canals. These were skilfully handled to take best advantage of tides, winds and currents. Horses pulled them along from adjacent towpaths in the narrow stretches. It is surprising that steam towing did not appear on the Thames until 1832, when two tugs were brought in, probably from the Tyne. These first tugs were weak in power and had trouble working against the strong tide. The next year, William

Watkins of London went to the Tyne to order construction of the 64-foot paddler *Monarch*, which he put in service on the Thames. This tug of greater power was the first in a long line of Watkins tugs to serve in those parts. *Monarch* is the tug depicted in the famous Turner painting *Fighting Temeraire*.

It was said that Queen Victoria's consort, Prince Albert, encouraged the steam tug idea because he was bothered by the clop of horses' hooves on the towpath outside Windsor Castle. Before long, little tugs were pulling tows of as many as ten barges, formerly operated separately along Britain's well developed canal systems. On the Thames, lighters were towed close-up behind the tug in trains of several tied together.

There was very little to these early British tugs. Nothing showed above the bulwarks of the hull but a mast, funnel, steering wheel or tiller and the engine signal bell-pull. There was no deckhouse and the boiler top was open to the weather. Hinged masts and funnels were needed for passing under low bridges. The side paddle wheels were driven on a common shaft by one single-cylinder engine at first, but two engines, one for each paddle wheel, soon came into use.

In addition to more power, the dual power plant improved turning capability, since each paddle ran on its own engine and could turn independently. The wooden hull was built along the customary lines of a small sailing vessel, narrow and with a raked bow, frequently with a gaff and sails. A vestigial bowsprit was quickly abandoned in the rough and tumble of tug operation. The early boats ran from 50 to 70 feet in length.

Most of the early tugs were operated as individual enterprises until commercial success resulted in fleets under one ownership coming into existence in the 1840s. William Watkins became a fleet owner and the Watkins name was prominent on the Thames for more than a century. The towing of sailing vessels in and out of rivers and harbours spread quickly as a normal part of shipping routine. However, the actual manoeuvering of large vessels in and out of docks was still accomplished largely by hand capstan warping. The towing business took some time to develop as a full-time occupation for the steam vessel, though, many having to continue as ferries and carry freight as well.

Very early in the era of the steamboat, samples of the British product paddled off to other countries. One vessel sailed to Petrograd to provide services on the Neva, the tug *Hercules* went to Rotterdam in 1825 and *Enterprise* voyaged as far as India. Tugs and other small vessels were needed everywhere that British sail-

The experimental Leary raft rounds Partridge Island on departure from Saint John under tow for New York in 1890. This was one of several pioneering attempts to find economical ways to transport logs on the open sea. (National Archives Canada NAC C371)

A view of the simple layout of the early British paddle tug. The Captain on the bridge of *Vulcan* calls orders to the engineer, standing at his position directly over the engine between the paddle boxes. The boiler is behind the engine. (East Kent Maritime Museum, Ramsgate)

ing ships plied their trade. Built by skilled craftsmen in Britain, they were delivered under their own power. The first steamer on the Pacific Ocean was *Rising Star*, built by Maudeslay in 1821. She was a full-rigged sailing ship with a 45hp engine. Probably as an "occasional paddler," she went round the Horn to take part in a South American revolution that was over when she got there. In the 1830s, not so long after the first steamboats ventured outside a harbour's mouth, the little steamer *Enterprise* travelled from the United Kingdom to India. The voyage was 13,000 miles, taking 64 days under steam, 39 days under sail and 10 days in ports along the way. *Enterprise's* 15-foot diameter paddle wheels were turned by two side-lever engines producing 120hp from a copper flue type boiler operating at three pounds pressure(psi).

Towing Comes to North America

Fulton and the Molsons had made a good business of steam driven passenger and freight packets, drifting into towing as an extra benefit. Some of the very first Canadian vessels were rated as tugs, but pursued any trade presented. The British were to become the world leaders in the technology of powered vessels, but North Americans carried out their own development in their own way, satisfying their particular needs.

In New York, Boston and Philadelphia, ferries began helping sailing ships in and out of port. In New York this often involved a 17-mile tow to searoom at Sandy Hook. The first New York tug has been represented as *Nautilus* in 1818, but she was a bay steamer pressed into service to clear a way through ice. The first purpose-built tug was *Rufus King* in 1825. These were all side paddlers. The first screw tug was *Robert Stockton*, with an Ericcson screw propeller, built in Birkenhead in 1838 and sailed across the Atlantic under a schooner rig. The Erie Canal first saw steam around 1830, with three towing companies using old steam vessels from the Hudson River.

In Canada there is little of the rich record of early tugs found in Britain. However, there appears to have been a long evolution to the specialized tug design by way of a gradually changing, general purpose vessel. There seems to have been a prolonged clinging to some accommodation for freight. As we will see, towing in North America developed as an essential component of internal transportation along great waterways such as the St. Lawrence, Hudson, and Mississippi Rivers, the Great Lakes and the sheltered coastal passages of the West Coast. The vessels handled great rafts of timber and barges carrying essential supplies and materials for which there was no alternative route.

There was a cross-fertilization of ideas over the great Western Ocean nevertheless. The speculative, Quebec-built *Royal William* and Samuel Cunard's vessels demonstrated the transatlantic steam packet's possibilities, while the British engines and a few earlier steam vessels came out to serve in North American trades. The Scots became the experts in building reliable and efficient marine engines after the original work of James Watt, led by the perfectionist craftsman Robert Napier. This Scot's work was a significant element in the early establishment of Samuel Cunard's name as the standard of reliability in steamship service on the Atlantic, Napier building and engining all of that Halifax entrepreneur's early ships. For the next century, the British built and ran the engines of many of the world's ships.

The Canadian *Royal William* was an interesting case. This famous vessel was not designed to demonstrate the ability of steam driven paddle wheelers to cross the Atlantic. The intention was to provide a passenger service between Quebec and the Maritime Provinces. She was built at Quebec City in 1831 by John Goudie and engined by Bennett and Henderson of Montreal. Only the crankshaft was imported, from Napier in Glasgow. Bennett had worked for James Watt and came out to Montreal to install Boulton and Watt engines in Molson's early boats. The unfinished ship was towed to Quebec by the steamer *British America* for the installation of the 200hp side-lever engines that would drive her paddles.

On her first trip *Royal William* steamed from Quebec to the Miramichi River in New Brunswick and around to Halifax in six days. Then, financial misfortune struck from an unexpected quarter when she was quarantined in the great cholera epidemic of 1832, first at Miramichi, then Halifax. Taken off the intended run and laid up for a time, she was put to work the next year as a towboat for sailing packets, moving them between Quebec and the quarantine station down river at Grosse Isle. After a tentative trip to Boston yielded no useful profit, the shareholders decided to sell Goudie's vessel.

At this point *Royal William* steamed off on her history making voyage—first across the Atlantic solely under steam—a far more impressive performance than that of the American *Savannah* in 1818, a part-time paddler. This was done to demonstrate fully the ship's steaming capabilities. In fact, one paddle wheel was damaged in a storm off Newfoundland and she limped, without using her sails, the rest of the way to Cowes on one wheel in a slow 25

One of the last working British steam paddlers, *Eppleton Hall*, lies at San Francisco awaiting restoration after a long sea voyage following her retirement in Britain. (Peter Baird)

One of the huge, shallow draft Rhine River paddle-tugs that handled barge traffic through Europe before the switch to diesel engines, *Koln* has boilers both fore and aft of her engine room, a common design for big paddle wheelers. (Jane Kennedy)

A personification of the saucy little tug, the 1895 210hp *Mathilda*, in Sincennes McNaughton colors, steams down Montreal Harbour in the late 1950s. (Author's Collection)

The wooden steam tug *Master* (1932, 330hp) still steams around Vancouver, lovingly maintained by local enthusiasts of the SS *Master* Society. Steam power in tugs largely disappeared early on the Pacific Coast. (Ron Mitchell)

Manoir (1930, 640hp) of the Davie Shipbuilding Company harbour fleet working a passenger ship at Quebec. She was built in their yard at nearby Lauzon. (Mac Mackay)

Toronto Harbour Commission's well-known *Ned Hanlan* (1932, 280hp) sometimes had to double as an icebreaker and ferry. Now she is enshrined on land as a museum artifact. (Author's Collection)

One of the splendid big South African Railway tugs steams out Capetown harbour under Table Mountain in 1960. High winds and strong currents around the Cape demanded big tugs. (Author's Collection)

Maarten is a restored Dutch steam tug of 1926 vintage, still operating at old steamer musters in Europe. Her folding funnel and mast identify her as a river and canal tug able to pass under low bridges. There is little superstructure, the boiler is enclosed in the black boiler casing and the engine casing under the lifeboat. (Don Macmillan)

Head-on view of *Master*, the restored veteran steam tug of the SS *Master* Society in Vancouver. This 1932 wooden vessel gets under way several times a year for various outings. (SS *Master* Society)

Built in 1912 at Quebec as *Margaret Hackett* for barge towing on the St. Lawrence, the 155-ton *Ocean Hawk* (560hp compound engine) spent most of her days berthing ships at Saint John, New Brunswick. Here she helps *Princess Helene* get off on her daily run across the Bay of Fundy, about 1960. (Author's Collection)

Ocean Osprey, a 1000bhp Empire class tug built for war service in Britain, lies peacefully in Courtenay Bay, Saint John, around 1960, her boiler on simmer, awaiting the call for another ship movement job. (Author's Collection)

The long-lived paddle tug *United Service* of Yarmouth, England, picked up added revenue with short excursions for the sea loving English in summer. The combination of towing and passenger carriage was quite common for tug operators in Britain for over a century. (National Maritime Museum, Greenwich P19990)

days. Repaired there, the doughty little ship paddled triumphantly on to Gravesend. *Royal William* carried out charters to Portugal where there was a war in progress over succession to the throne. She attracted the attention of the Spanish, who bought her to become the first steam warship. She was the first such warship to fire a shot in anger, too, in 1836. Her hull rotted out in ten years' time, but the Montreal-built engines puffed on in another hull for a further twenty years.

On the important river systems of Canada in the first half of the nineteenth century, the St. Lawrence, Ottawa and Saint John, steamboats were first used successfully for carrying passengers and freight, then started towing when it proved advantageous. These towing vessels normally did not carry auxiliary sails, as did many tugs on coastal voyages. The tug built on a hull designed specifically for the purpose came slowly.

On the Saint John River

The Saint John River rises in the State of Maine and meanders pastorally over 500 miles along the border with and through New Brunswick before squeezing through a narrow gorge into Saint John Harbour and the sea. From early days it was an important route for timber traffic. Large rafts of pine logs and scowloads of lumber passed through the port of Saint John headed for Britain. As elsewhere, rafts were floated on the slow current with the aid of steering sweeps. Small woodboats carried sawn lumber under sail. Great log drives were staged in the spring on the upper river, usually to be retrieved and either sawn or harnessed into rafts at Fredericton.

The steamboat arrived on the Saint John very early, in 1816, in the form of the passenger side wheeler *General Smith*. She had a 20hp Scottish-built engine and boiler and was a long shallow boat

Typical of the river steamer not yet evolved into a specialized tug form is the 162-ton *Hope*, seen straining on towlines to a raft on the Saint John River. The rocking beam connecting the steam cylinder to the paddle crank of the American style engine is plainly visible. (Public Archives New Brunswick P21-10)

with very little freeboard. On her maiden voyage she carried sixty passengers from Saint John to Fredericton, a distance of almost 100 miles. *General Smith* seems to have served a need for passenger packet traffic and was alone on the river for some time.

It was not until the 1830s that the number of steamers began to increase. The similar boats *Woodstock*, *John Ward* and *St. George* appeared in the early thirties and, while running on passenger and freight schedules, also found it profitable to do some towing. It did not take much imagination to see the possibilities in towing when rafts of timber were being negotiated around the bends of the river with the aid of a very sluggish current and dozens of men labouring on long sweeps. *Woodstock* was a 91-foot vessel of 74 tons. She towed lumber scows between Oromocto, near Fredericton, and Saint John. All of these early boats were side wheelers and the American-style, overhead walking-beam, vertical piston engine became standard.

There is little mention of tugs in the records in the first half of the century. It seems that any steamboat might be used to tow at will. By mid century, however, some passenger and freight boats were converted for towing service exclusively, and some even made the change in the other direction. From then on, the long, low hull designs became shorter and more manoeuverable, and a distinctive tug hull developed.

Shallow draft boats operated on the upper river between Fredericton and Woodstock, but in the low water period of mid-summer had to retire to the lower river. Not having regular passenger and freight runs there, they were often employed in towing. Tows on the river included log rafts, three-masted schooners destined for coastal voyages loaded with Grand Lake coal and scows or woodboats loaded with sawn lumber. The tug *Magnet*, built in 1855, was soon refitted to carry passengers and freight, too. Apparently, people were accustomed to hitching rides on tugs

Top: A large raft of logs moving under sail power on Lake Manitoba, complete with bunkhouse and cook shanty. Progress must have been chancy on open waters without the help of steam power or the steady currents normal on rivers. (Manitoba Provincial Archives Transp Boats 5)

Bottom: With steam towing power, bag booms became common where waters were wide enough. Here is one passing down the Restigouche River at Matapedia, Quebec, in 1930. Speed was two or three knots. (NAC PA 89633)

Towed barges, often converted old sailing ships, eventually replaced much coastal sailing ship traffic. American companies utilized very long low-lying tugs like *Gypsum King*, which worked in the gypsum trade from Windsor, Nova Scotia to New York. (Maritime Museum of the Atlantic N-11 876)

to travel up and down the river when passenger vessels were not available, especially on the upper river. Eventually *Magnet* was sold to the Glasiers, the timber barons of the river, probably spending her days towing logs and lumber until, one day, her boiler blew up.

An unusual vessel was launched near Fredericton in 1845. *Reindeer* was fitted with sponsons on each side to allow a speedy hull form with shallow draft when loaded. She was 130 feet long and had a compound beam engine. She was fast and economical. Her designer was Benjamin Tibbets, who appears to have claimed

that he made the successful compound engine possible with his patented steam chest located between two cylinders, one high and one low pressure. He fought a losing battle over the patents, other successful builders pointing out that they did not have such a chamber and obviously did not need one.

Tibbets went to Quebec City where he and his brother, Henry, were involved in building steamboats. In 1855, they brought their *B.F. Tibbets*, a 124-foot side wheeler with a Tibbets compound engine, to the Saint John River for work towing log rafts from Grand Lake to Saint John. Before long this towboat caught fire on Grand Lake, the crew abandoning her as she steamed full ahead toward shore.

The Tibbets compound engine from *Reindeer* was subsequently used in another upper-river fast passenger boat, *Antelope*, in 1861. Eight years later *Antelope* was sold to the Glasiers for work towing lumber, but was used as well for the occasional excursion or picnic outing. Specialization as to types of service was evidently not a vital matter in those times. After ten more years, this same Tibbets beam engine was installed in a new Glasier tug named *Admiral*, and was still busy working more than forty years later. Paddle engines turned over slowly and never wore out, but the wooden hulls took much abuse and did not last very long.

The Saint John River was an ideal broad highway for carrying the steady stream of raw and finished timber from the interior of New Brunswick to the seaport of Saint John in the booming first half of the nineteenth century. The one major drawback for transportation was a bottleneck for the waters of the river, the Reversing Falls Gorge where the river empties into the harbour of Saint John. When the mighty tides on the Bay of Fundy, with a range of more than 20 feet at Saint John, are low, the river plunges through the gorge in a furious maelstrom—almost certain death for any vessel. However, twice a day when the tide is high, the sea pushes the river back through the gorge in rapids now pouring upstream. Between the two rough water spectacles there are short periods when the two powerful forces are in balance. There are thus four brief chances each day for vessels to pass through the bottleneck in safety, a splendid situation for tugs.

Traffic between harbour and river has always been governed by the rigid timetable of the tides. Tugs would be busy during the periods of slack water, taking scows and sailing vessels through. The master of a harbour tug taking a tow upstream would be anxious to get back down again without being stuck upriver until the next slack tide. Tug operators became astute at coordinating their operations. To get the jobs, it was necessary to be in the harbour to handle incoming ships on the flood tide and outgoing ships on the ebb. In between, there were the forays up and down through the gorge.

The tides called the schedule and this changed by about an hour every day. There have been miscalculations, tugs and their charges coming to grief, even though, when the timing is right, a canoe may be paddled through. In the heyday of river traffic, for its convenience, Saint John had a busy little port above the Reversing Falls at Indiantown in the city's north end. This was an important base for the river tugs and passenger packets. The first steamer built expressly as a tug at Saint John was said to have been built by the Vulcan Foundry as late as 1846. It soon blew up, a not unexpected occurrence with early tugs. The casualty rate was high due to boiler explosions, fire and the running aground of the flimsy wooden hulls.

Long hauls on the river system were the impetus for early steamers and towing. Harbours without such a demand for river traffic, such as Halifax or St. John's, Newfoundland, do not appear to have had these very early steam vessels. Engine-powered coasters plying the unforgiving shores of eastern Canada, especially any involving towing, developed later.

The 1898 *Flying Scotsman* was a later seeking tug with steel hull, but still favouring the high manoeuverability of paddle wheels. The paddles were not so desirable on the open sea, however, and the screw tug took over that area. (National Maritime Museum, Greenwich P 19834)

A Lucrative Trade

OVER MANY CENTURIES THE WORLD'S SEAS were explored, great naval campaigns fought and commerce on a global scale carried on under the power of sails driven by the wind. But the vagaries of this source of propulsion made timing uncertain to say the least. On the broad oceans, days or weeks could be lost beating against headwinds or idling in the doldrums. Vessels zigzagged about the oceans in a roundabout fashion, following the most favourable currents and the prevailing, or trade, winds to make the best time. The fastest way from the Straits of Magellan to San Francisco was by way of the Hawaiian Islands, a detour far into the Pacific. It was worse in channels, estuaries and rivers. The dangers of lee shores were added to the delays of waiting for a favourable conjunction of wind and tide to run in over an entrance bar. A long ocean voyage might be made in reasonable time, only to finish with weeks of tacking back and forth in and out of sight of land, a few miles short of the goal. Worse, a miscalculation could leave the ship smashed to pieces on a hostile shore such as the coast of Cornwall or the infamous Cape Flattery at the entrance to Juan de Fuca Strait.

No wonder, then, that the wind and tide defying power of a steam engine propelled vessel was seen as the answer to a master's prayer at the beginning and ending of his voyage. Even the most reactionary windship captain could see it that way. Instead of costly, time consuming delays beating about in sight of port, a bit of cash to an enterprising steam tug master could have him and his ship safely moored in harbour in a few hours, ready to discharge cargo.

Going out a few miles to fetch in a windjammer was quick cash for the tug operator. Many a steam vessel, built for ferry service on rivers and estuaries, soon became at least a part-time tug. In the early days, tugs were not a highly specialized design that differed significantly from other vessels. On the mighty St. Lawrence River, where it narrows just before Quebec City, several ferry operators became notorious for leaving passengers waiting on the wharf, or even carrying them off down river, because a chance to obtain the tow of a sailing ship had turned up.

As in most profitable trades, competition was keen in the towing of ships from a position warped off from a pier to a spot clear of the coast where there was safe room to catch a breeze and a good slant to the wind. Obtaining the nod from the shipping agent to take a ship to sea was a straight business proposition, based on service and the asking price. It was another game with incoming vessels.

A sailing ship's arrival off a port was seldom announced in advance with any accuracy. A steamer or a faster sailing ship might report the imminent arrival of a vessel heading into port behind it, but there was generally little indication as to when a tug might find a ship wanting a tow in. Some ports had watch stations on prominent headlands from which flag or telegraph signals advised of approaching ships still a few hours out. Halifax's famed Sambro station and Liverpool's Bidston Hill are examples. But, for many ports, the tow was needed from many miles at sea or far downriver. The towing distance might be 50 or 100 miles, or more than a day's haul.

To snatch up such incoming business in the face of competition, tugs began to venture farther and farther out to sea along the incoming shipping lanes. There they would linger athwart the track to intercept a likely quarry, far out of sight of land. Of course, they often found themselves in these areas anyway after dropping an outgoing ship. A paying trip both ways was naturally much to be desired.

CHAPTER 3

The Seekers

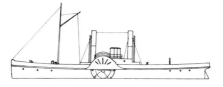

Conqueror (Author's sketch)

Cruizer -Flying Buzzard (Author's sketch)

Typical British paddlewheel tug
(Author's sketch)

Built very late in the era of seeking, the Watkins tug
Java of 1905 worked the Thames and English Channel.
She had a triple expansion engine and lasted until
1965, serving through two world wars. Like many
other British coastal tugs, she had no enclosed
wheelhouse.
(National Maritime Museum, Greenwich P 29274)

Working on tips and clues gleaned from shipping industry contacts and newspaper shipping notes, the tug master, usually the owner or a shareholder in his tug, formulated his strategy. Then he slipped to sea to lurk off the headlands where he thought a customer might appear. Certainly, he was not keen on tipping off a competitor, and might slink off at night without showing his navigating lights.

Because of such furtiveness, tugs in this line were once known as "dodgers," but the general term for the fraternity at large made them "seekers." Seeking was a century-long trade, from very early in the lifetime of the steam vessel, about 1830, until the end of global sailing ship commerce between the World Wars. Many tugs were designed and built as seekers, featuring long, lean, fast lines, large coal bunkers and raked funnels to impress potential clients with their power and speed.

Large, long distance seeking tugs thrived in many parts of the world: in the English Channel, on all the great river estuaries from the Hoogly and Yangtse to the St. Lawrence, Mississippi, and Hudson as well as coastal passages like the Strait of Juan de Fuca. Even far inland, large seekers plied the Detroit River currents. New York's first tug, *Nautilus*, was profitably engaged in seeking in the Lower Bay.

From the famous Clyde fleet of long distance seeking tugs, *Flying Buzzard* of 1895 was renamed *Cruizer* and taken to Nova Scotia by Canadian Pacific Railways. The single-screw, 380-tonner worked out of Sydney for many years. (Wallace Collection, Maritime Museum of the Atlantic MP23.2.1)

As the seeking tugs ran farther to sea to intercept ships, they needed much larger coal bunkers and usually carried sails to economize on fuel consumption. Seeking called for endurance and seaworthiness. It became an easy step from such enterprise to ventures in long distance port-to-port towing. The lure of the monetary rewards in both of these areas led to enterprise, risks and, all too often, disaster. Nevertheless, before long these vessels, very small from an ocean voyage point of view, began regularly to ply the oceans of the world.

For the captain of a sailing ship, the service of a seeking tug was a blessing, particularly in tricky waters, and might easily cut a week from the duration of his voyage. For the early tea clipper or passenger vessel, this factor could be critical. It was also a test of the master's judgement. The cost of "taking steam," as it was called, depended upon how far out he decided to take a tow and also his bargaining skill. If the wind and tide were favourable, the captain might resist the blandishments of the seeker until he was close in to port and, thus, get a low price. On the other hand, the seeker might give up and go off in disgust to look for another tow. This might leave the sailing vessel at the whim of a failing wind, a turning tide and a rocky lee shore. The asking price went down as they approached port, but might go up if the ship appeared to be getting into a deteriorating situation.

There was an accepted rule among the seekers that whoever was first to get within hailing distance of a prospective tow was left alone to bargain with her captain. Only when this tug gave up could another come forward to make an offer. The bargaining could go on for a long stretch, the tug captain sociably briefing his oppo-

A local river tug on the Miramichi River, a major lumbering route in New Brunswick, moves out a barkentine loaded with lumber for the tow to the Gulf of St. Lawrence. (Provincial Archives of New Brunswick P6-255)

site number on the latest news of the world. The calculating ship's master meanwhile was assessing the likelihood of either an improvement or deterioration in the weather. The longer he kept the tug waiting, the more chance of driving a hard bargain, unless the weather turned sour. It was a game of poker and in the end the stakes sometimes included the lives of the ship and her crew.

Seeking began in the British port approaches like the River Tyne, where tides, shallows and rough waters over an entrance bar caused great difficulties for vessels under sail. The port of Newcastle prospered on the benefits brought by tugs. The great tidal estuaries of Britain, the Clyde, Forth, Mersey, Humber, Thames and the Bristol Channel became important seeking territories. They experienced burgeoning traffic to new ports around the world that could only

compete once ships were no longer stymied by adverse tides and winds. In North America, Montreal and New Orleans were each able to become a terminus for ocean vessels, and the export of coal and timber from British Columbia ports to the world became profitable on a large scale. Notorious tidal turbulence on shallow bars off San Francisco's Golden Gate and the mouth of the Columbia River could be less hazardous if transited with the aid of a tug.

The Port of London was an outstanding example of where the seeking tug was a vital element in the growth of seaborne commerce throughout the nineteenth century and still essential for the few square-riggers that remained on into the twentieth. The sea links of the far-flung British Empire homed in principally on Liverpool or London from the Atlantic Ocean by way of the Irish

A Great Lakes schooner gets help through the St. Clair River between Lakes Erie and Huron from the diminutive (1890) steam tug *Nellie Blye*. (Archives of Ontario S13603)

Sea, the English Channel and the Thames Estuary. Ships fought their way up the narrowing English Channel against tides and winds coming down from the North Sea, nervously worked past the deadly trap of the Goodwin Sands, rounded the coast of Kent and made their way up the long tidal Thames Estuary in steadily narrowing waters.

It was very early, in August 1816, that the primitive steamer *Majestic* appeared on the Thames to help ships in and out of London. She was claimed to have been the first powered vessel to engage in the towing of ocean ships. Liverpool's *Charlotte*, built as a ferry, was also towing ships on the Mersey from October of that year.

Farther and Farther to Sea

As tugs and ships grew in size and commerce demanded tighter shipping schedules, the Thames tugs towed their charges farther and farther down the estuary. Consequently, they were greater dis-

tances at sea when it came to looking around for an incoming ship to tow back up to London. More and more boldly they ventured out, sometimes too far, getting into difficulties because of their low power. Often, they would be unable to control a tow in heavy weather, having to drop it to save themselves. That left the ship to fend for itself, frequently with fatal results. Her sails might have been stowed already in anticipation of arrival in port. The paddlers were not really well suited to open seas, but avarice took them there often.

The tugs grew larger, and soon employed two boilers, each with its own funnel. Two stacks were a sales advantage, denoting greater power to impress the customer, just as the four stacks of a *Mauretania* or *Olympic* later indicated speed to the intending transatlantic passenger. The tugs were still side-wheel paddlers, but now most had a separate engine for each paddle wheel, giving them greater power, manoeuverability and reliability.

With the graceful lines of the big, wooden coastal waterway and seeking tugs of the Pacific Northwest, *Commodore* was built at the Moodyville sawmill at Vancouver in 1907. She brought sailing ships into lumber and coal ports of the Strait of Georgia and Puget Sound, serving 48 years. (Vancouver City Archives)

London tugs were working right around the coast of Kent and down the English Channel by about 1860. Eventually, seeking tugs were dropping outbound ships anywhere from The Downs to the Isle of Wight, according to the state of the winds and how anxious the ship's master was to get to open sea. The seekers congregated along the coast from The Downs to Dungeness, even to Falmouth, looking for incoming traffic and a paying trip home. Some tug masters had spotters on the heights of land on the Isle of Wight and on the Scilly Islands. At Falmouth, the London seeking tugs met those of the west coast, down from Liverpool, or even a few from continental ports.

The Australian gold rush, starting in 1851, caused a demand for fast passages by immigrants. Those ships advertising that they would be "taking steam" down the Thames Estuary, were looked upon as likely to aim for a fast passage all the way. It meant a boom for the tug owners and there were sixty-eight tugs based on London in the 1850s. Similarly the Crimean War in that same decade caused a big demand for tug services as fleets of transports hurried from the Thames for the Black Sea.

William Watkins and the Caledonian Steam Towing Company were the big names among British seeking tug owners in the latter part of the century. Typifying the ultimate in Thames seekers was Watkins' screw-driven *Simla*, built in 1898. Lean and fast, with big coal bunkers and a full set of fore-and-aft sails, she was 144 gross tons and powered by a 99 net hp compound engine. Like most London seekers, she was built to tow sailing ships between London and the English Channel. *Simla* steamed for sixty-six years, including service in two world wars, with action in the evacuation of Dunkirk in 1940.

Seeking ended with the loss of most of the remaining ocean sailing ships in the First World War and the depression of the 1930s. Among the last of the British tugs built as seekers was *Java*, built in 1905 and serving through both world wars, till scrapped in 1965. The last serving seeker was *Cervia*, which went out to meet the proud windjammer *Pamir* off Dover as late as 1948. This celebrated square-rigger of the sunset of sail had been taken out Juan de Fuca Strait to the Pacific off Cape Flattery on her last departure from British Columbia, in 1946, by *Island Commander*, a famous tug in that territory.

In the latter part of the nineteenth century, tugs were being designed for the dual function of seeking and long distance, coastwise towing. Any distinction between the two was becoming blurred, by jobs such as moving a ship from Falmouth to Rotterdam, Sydney to Newcastle in Australia, or Victoria to Nanaimo, British Columbia. One of the fleets most famous for such tugs belonged to the Clyde Shipping Company, whose boats carried the prefix "Flying" in their names. Most were twin-screw vessels and rigged with sails to conserve coal, although they often had a

hold forward, suitable for use as an auxiliary coal bunker on long trips. It was more often used to carry fish, as these tugs were sometimes contracted to carry catches ashore for the trawler fleets.

The biggest of the Clyde tugs was *Flying Buzzard* of 1895, a 380-tonner with only a single screw, a low lying vessel having a long deckhouse and tall thin funnel. She worked the Firth of Clyde for a time under a series of owners and had an early change of name to *Cruizer*. But most of her more than half a century afloat was spent in eastern Canadian waters under Canadian Pacific Steamships (CPS) ownership. She performed yeoman service out of Sydney, Nova Scotia, through the Second World War.

As the improving speed and regularity of steamship schedules gradually reduced the sailing ship's share of cargoes, mainly bulk materials such as grain, coal, wool and lumber, the last square-rig-

The large steel windjammers of the Erikson fleet still operated in the grain trade in the 1930s, still needing seeking services. The famous Dutch long distance tug *Zwarte Zee* passes a line to *Pamir*. (John Weeks Collection)

gers fought back with the advantage of wind as a very economical fuel. They also used tugs increasingly in the channels and short seas. Thus, it became common for a ship to load part of her cargo in one port, then take a tow for fifty or a hundred miles to another port to "top up." Or, on arriving from a transoceanic voyage, she might sign off most of her hands, unload and be taken by a tug with only a skeleton crew aboard to another port before beginning a new voyage. Tugs towed ships in this way between Irish, Welsh, English, French and Low Countries ports. The famous expression "to Falmouth for orders" was frequently the start of this kind of round for ships coming from long voyages.

At the start of the twentieth century, the majestic full-rigged ship was still competing in selected trades on the power of the wind. However, it was clearly a case of wind power on the long ocean passages, but steam at both ends. This routine was the one that had helped sail to compete with steam all through the golden age of the fast clippers. It might start with the ship warping herself by her crew's muscle power on the capstan from her berth in a London wet dock to the gates leading into the River Thames. Here the appointed tug takes her under tow and down into the estuary, taking advantage of the tide as it turns and helps them along. On down to open waters and around the North Foreland on the coast of Kent they steam.

The ship's crew enjoys the easy routine of preparation for sea without yet setting any sail. From Ramsgate onward they watch closely to see when the captain will decide to drop the tug for a down channel breeze. With sufficient searoom and a respectable wind, the gaskets are cast off and some sail is set. Released as the ship gains way, the tug comes around to take off the pilot and disappears shoreward in a smudge of smoke. So commences the usual voyage of a windjammer, with perhaps a hundred lonely days of open ocean ahead.

Nearing the end of her journey, still almost out of sight of land, the ship meets her first contact from the land. A tug appears out of the morning mists to pass the tow, her crew greeting the mariners in Australian or American accents. Now the seamen can stow their sails for the harbour sojourn. This may include trips among several ports up and down the coast, unloading and loading, just as at home. Eventually, there will come the tug that will take them to sea again off Sydney Heads, Sandy Hook, the Yangtse or Cape Flattery.

On the other side of the world our windjammer charges up the English Channel again, a fresh breeze on her quarter. Entering the seeking grounds below the Isle of Wight one morning, her crew sees a tug heave into sight and come near to welcome the captain home, hand over a newspaper and offer a towline. "How much," asks the captain. "Only 50 Pounds," is the reply, bringing a quick rejoinder, "What do you take me for, a philanthropist?," and the crew gather round for the entertainment.

The sailing ship may have rounded the globe, sailing 30,000 miles. But steam power through the services of tugs took much of the chance and delay out of the voyage. The advantages of a powered vessel were utilized at the points where they were most needed, then dropped in between. The stories of the great tea clipper races from China to London are the epitome of the age of sail. The fastest ships often arrived in the English Channel within a few hours of one another. Careful notice of the role played by the tugs at each end of the voyage shows that they may well have been decisive in the results. Before the invention of modern, built-in manoeuvering devices, even the great turbine-powered passenger liners depended heavily upon tugs in the confines of harbours, canals and docks.

The British Lead

HAVING PIONEERED TUGS and ventured both across and down the English Channel as far as the open sea, the British tug operators easily pushed their horizons farther and farther afield. The British tugs developed and commanded the deep sea towing business from its inception, about 1850. This was in the form of long tows to bring home crippled steamships to their builder's repair yards and delivering new vessels not suitable for making their own way to their destinations. The Watkins tugs of London were prominent in the latter type of work.

The early ocean steamships frequently broke down mechanically. Having only one engine, propeller and rudder, they were required to carry auxiliary sails, but did not sail well. If crippled in remote places, they might sail to a convenient port or wait to be spotted by another vessel that would tow them in. However, most of the ports of the world were unable, in the middle of the nineteenth century, to provide repair facilities. The Alexandra Towing Company of Liverpool specialized in the recovery of broken down steamers from such primitive ports, as well as the rescue of cripples on the high seas. The latter involved a great deal of guesswork and searching in the days before wireless radio communication. The searching tug master had to estimate where a ship might have drifted since last seen, possibly weeks before.

From mid century, larger and larger ships were sailing to newly developing ports all over the world. Harbours and river channels had to be dredged to handle them in the new trade being generated by the industrial age. Before Holland took command of the market, dredges and their hopper barges were very much a British product. The inefficiency of trying to ship the component parts of a dredge to a remote country, then reassemble it in difficult conditions was soon learned. Towing of completed dredges, barges, floating cranes, floating drydocks and even lock gates over great distances and across oceans became a necessity.

William Watkins, with a fleet of big seeking paddle-tugs working down the English Channel, picked up much of the early business and acquired the pioneering expertise. Watkins started with some shorter runs, then became bolder. The big bucket dredgers were top-heavy, hence were not noted for seaworthiness or docility under tow. His son John, operating on the west coast where tugs were generally bigger, turned over to his father his 219-ton *Victor* from his Liverpool fleet. In 1860, the tug was used to tow a dredger from Gravesend to Cadiz for £752. This event can be considered the start of major ocean towing.

There were earlier tows that were longer, but they were easier. In 1854, both the Royal Navy's steam warships and private commercial tugs had delivered various tows to the Crimea on the Black Sea. They were never too far from a coaling port in the Mediterranean and had lighter or more amenable tows. British-built paddle-tugs and other steamers were themselves delivered all over the world to work in new ports and old. Because of their limited coal bunker capacity, these tugs generally went much of the way by sail if frequent bunkering ports were not available. The 60-horsepower, 140-ton tug *Surprise* made her way around the world to Tasmania under sail in 1834. The Hudson's Bay Company steamer *Beaver* sailed all the way to the west coast of North America in 1835, carrying her paddle wheels stowed on board, to bring towing to British Columbia.

One of the most celebrated of early tows at sea was the scheme to get Cleopatra's Needle from Egypt to Britain in 1878. The tall stone monument was enclosed in an iron cylinder 90

CHAPTER 4

Ocean Towing

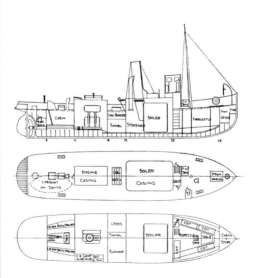

Typical British screw propeller steam harbour tug (Author's sketch)

Hardly suitable for the rough waters of the Bay of Biscay, the 219-ton Watkins tug *Victor* made the first major ocean tow in 1860, steaming from Gravesend to Cadiz with a dredge. A wheelhouse has been mounted atop the boiler casing. In sharp contrast, behind her is the first world war naval ocean tug *St.Bee's*. (National Maritime Museum, Greenwich P 30323)

Opposite top: "Three-Fingered Jack" was the nickname for the three-stacker *Anglia* of 1866. A paddler with auxiliary sails, vestigial bowsprit and steering wheel position between the paddle boxes, she was large for the day and made many ocean tows for Watkins of London. (National Maritime Museum, Greenwich)

Opposite bottom: Another *Conqueror*, of 1897, was sturdy and seaworthy for a paddler. She had boilers both ahead and aft of the engines, usual on a large sea-going tug. This tug carried out many rescues at sea in addition to carrying trippers as shown here. (National Maritime Museum, Greenwich P20040)

feet long and 16 feet in diameter with a watch crew on board. The floating cylinder was then taken in tow by the steamer *Olga*. The tow went well through the Mediterranean, but in the notorious Bay of Biscay rough seas broke the towline and forced *Olga* to lose the cylinder. Eventually another steamer found the missing needle and towed it into Vigo, Spain, to collect a salvage fee.

The expert services of the large Watkin's tug *Anglia* were needed to bring the errant cylinder the rest of the way into port. Even then, progress was very slow, the tow constantly sheering badly out of line. *Anglia* was built by Watkins in 1866 in order to handle the largest ships afloat. She was designed to have four boilers, each with its own smokestack, in two rows, two abreast. When one boiler was eliminated from the plans to allow more bunker capacity, it left the odd arrangement of three funnels, two abreast and one by itself. She became known as "Three Fingered Jack." *Anglia* performed various dredge deliveries from the Hook of Holland to Alexandria for construction of the Suez Canal. In 1875 she brought the crippled Union liner *Syria* home to Southampton from St. Helena, where she had taken refuge—a 4300-mile tow. Considered a big powerful tug, *Anglia* was 275 tons, 144 feet long and her paddle engines totalled 700 indicated horsepower(ihp). As with all tugs

of the time, she had a completely open bridge with no shelter whatsoever for the man at the wheel; but she was a fine seaboat.

Another of the British tugs was rather embarrassed by its tow a little later. The twin-screw *Knight of Saint John*, out of Liverpool, towed a dismasted barque all the way up the Atlantic from Rio only to run short of coal in the home stretch. The *Knight* dropped her tow and made for St. Vincent, 400 miles away. Returning, the tow was not to be found. After a long search the tug headed for home empty-handed. Meanwhile, the crew of the barque had set a jury rig to keep from drifting helplessly. The makeshift suit of canvas worked so well that they caught a favourable wind to Barbados where the barque was properly refitted and sailed home. In a similar case, another Liverpool tug, *Sarah Jolliffe*, lost a tow in bad weather in the Irish Sea, only to find it safely in port after a fruitless search had been given up.

The tug companies on the Mersey and at Liverpool had generally larger tugs in the mid 1800s than those on the Thames, but they were the specialists in ocean rescue and the recovery of disabled ships. They left the long distance delivery of dredgers and other awkward vessels to the Londoners. One of the earlier of these Liverpool tugs putting out to sea was *Resolute*, a vessel of 375

The Clyde Shipping Company's *Flying Cormorant* of 1868 was typical of the company's twin-screw seeking tugs that roamed the Clyde and the Irish Sea for long coastal tows. A hold forward carried extra bunker coal or, sometimes, a fish cargo. (National Maritime Museum, Greenwich G-1097)

tons, 161 feet long and having engines of 70ihp. She carried 200 tons of coal for a range of 1600 miles. In 1851 she went out to look for the derelict ship *Marianne* that had been reported 300 miles off the coast of Ireland by an incoming vessel. *Resolute* found the derelict and brought her into Queenstown in five days, despite very bad weather.

At about this time another Liverpool tug, *Stormcock* of the Gamecock fleet, steamed 4000 miles to Fernando Noronha off the coast of Brazil to bring back the 2000-ton ship *Ardencaple*. *Blazer*, also of Liverpool, carried out a contract to tow the badly damaged and partly flooded steamer *Moçambique* from Ceara, Brazil, to Rio for repairs. It is fascinating to realize that to get this job done the owners had *Blazer* sail 5000 miles down the Atlantic, coaling at St. Vincent and Las Palmas, to Ceara. Then she towed for 18 days, coaling at Bahia, to get her charge to Rio. Finally, there was the long trip home. Perhaps it was a case of British underwriters trusting only a British tug with a ticklish job rather than a lack of salvage tugs in Brazil. In this era, tug crews exhibited great courage, or great folly, in setting out across the stormy northern seas in their little paddlers, knowing little or no navigation, with no protection from the weather and little chance of help once in trouble.

Holland's Glory

One primitive British steamer paddled bravely across the North Sea to Rotterdam, demonstrating this marvellous invention to the Dutch. Taking the cue, Dutch interests built a little steamer called

Nederlander. Operated by Nederlandsche Stoomboot Maatschappij, it tried towing sailing ships on the coast during 1825, but was not successful. Small wonder—the British-built engine was only 20 horsepower. It was not until 1840 that the first real and successful Dutch tug was built, one of the many named *Hercules* to be found in tug history. This one towed sailing ships in and out between Rotterdam and the North Sea, or through the North Holland Canal. Two years later, at nearby Kinderdijk, a small shipbuilder and operator named Fop Smit secured a towing concession and built a wooden paddle tug of 160 horsepower which he named after the town. Such was the humble beginning of what was to become in modern times the world's largest towing and salvage organization. Today the Smit name is seen the world over, wherever work is done upon or under the sea.

The land of canals, shallow and tricky, coastal waterways and, above all, the entry to the great Rhine waterway, was a natural setting for tugs to thrive, as they still do. The Industrial Revolution had brought a strong demand for better transportation and the Rhine was a major focus. The seafaring Nederlanders became tugmen, expanding operations apace in their waterways, natural and artificial, and then like the British, venturing out on the sea.

The rise of the Netherlands to prominence in transoceanic towing came out of the growth of the country's harbour and waterway engineering industry. The land of dykes, sluices, pumps, dredgers and port facilities became purveyor to the world for these devices late in the 1880s. The market was particularly strong in the newly

Tug design and accommodations had improved significantly by 1924 when United Towing of Hull built *Seaman*, and she had the novelty of wireless radio. But she was still a small boat for trips from England to Brazil and Argentina, a 4000-mile ocean tow which her unusually large bunkers permitted. (National Maritime Museum, Greenwich P19932)

developing ports of countries and colonies that were not industrially advanced. The Dutch built dredgers, their hopper barges, lighters, floating cranes, sluice gates and other large installations for ports in South America, Africa and the East Indies. The biggest, most spectacular item was the floating drydock.

At first, many of these awkward devices were built, disassembled, and shipped for reassembly at their destinations. With skilled labour lacking on site and poor economics generally, this proved unsatisfactory, especially as the machinery grew bigger and more complex. Inevitably, someone reassessed the risks and gambled on the possibility that a tug could tow a completed floating crane from Holland to the Rio de la Plata, almost the length of both Atlantic Oceans away.

The British had been more advanced in tug development and had both bigger tugs and more experience. The Dutch must have been chagrined to have a British tug come over to the Hook of Holland to receive the hand-off of a big Dutch dredger from the local tugs and steam away overseas with it. However, the Dutch simply could not compete through the 1870s and 1880s. One attempt resulted in *Wodan*, a 500ihp double-engined paddle tug built in 1883 by Smit. She doubled as a local icebreaker, but was still too small to be a serious threat to the British.

Jan de Hartog, the celebrated author and sometime Dutch tugman himself, says that it fell to a certain Captain Bakker, master of a fragile coastal paddle tug, to be the first great Dutch ocean towing hero. He also suggests that Captain Bakker, while successful in

Top: In 1883 the Dutch Smit fleet built the paddler *Wodan* to compete with the British in ocean towing, but this vessel did not have sufficient power. Ice-breaking became her principal duty and she lasted 44 years. (Stichting Nationaal Sleepvaart Museum)

Bottom: The Dutch seized the lead in ocean towing and carried out epic tows like this one by *Roode Zee* and *Zwarte Zee*, seen departing the Tyne with a drydock for Callao, Peru, in 1908. Modest, economical power from two Scotch boilers and a single large, deep screw made these tugs very efficient. (Stichting Nationaal Sleepvaart Museum)

Having taken floating docks out of the Tyne River, Smit's tugmasters were apparently considered qualified for the big job of shepherding the new *Mauretania* to sea in 1907. Under the famous liner's bows is *Oceaan*, which became Watkin's *Racia* and made seven trips to the White Sea in the First World War. (Swan Hunter Shipbuilders Photo B128)

his tow, came back with tales of sea monsters, bats as big as windjammers in the Sargasso Sea and waves as tall as cathedrals. It must be surmised, he says, that the captain really saw the sea serpents, but only in an alcoholic coma as his cockleshell found its way to where the limitless ocean finally reached a limit in the vast bulk of South America. Absolute terror must have possessed him once he left the sight of land to embark on the deep ocean. There he lost the ability to find where he was by identifying a bit of bottom brought up on the end of a lead line.

De Hartog, in his novels of the earlier ocean tug crews of the Netherlands, is highly critical of both the primitive conditions under which they were sent to sea and the dangers and hardships they were obliged to undergo. In *Captain Jan* he portrays the hard times when the early coastal tugs set out on long, open sea journeys to pioneer Dutch transoceanic towing. Conditions were very competitive; there was no labour legislation to protect the seamen from abuse and the tugs were very frail. The steering position was more exposed to the weather than that of a sailing ship and the

engine power puny compared to the smallest harbour docking or berthing tug of today. As de Hartog says, the owners transformed their paddle boats into deep-sea tugs by mumbling over them some formula of seaworthiness.

Finally, the first proper seagoing tugs were designed and built for the pioneering Dutch fleet of L. Smit & Company in 1892. The two tugs *Noordzee* and *Oostzee* were competitive in horsepower, had large bunkers and a single-screw propeller. They established the shape of seagoing tugs, with their raised forecastles, well decks and tall twin funnels for the two Scotch boilers. This arrangement put the boilers in line ahead, with lots of bunker space along their sides. It contrasted with the common arrangement of two boilers set side-by-side in paddle tugs, with resultant bunker space limitations. The British copied the Dutch style and bought some tugs in Holland. Ironically, while 1892 saw the introduction of the first tugs suitable for transoceanic towing, it also saw thirty-six major tows carried out across the oceans, all by the older tugs.

The L. Smit fleet at rest in the port of Maassluis, Netherlands, about 1930. Smit grew to dominate long distance towing worldwide, and eventually was a big player in the servicing of modern ocean oil drilling. (Stichting Nationaal Sleepvaart Museum)

Smit's *Oceaan* (1894) was 424 tons, had the typical raised forecastle, well deck, open bridge and two funnels. The Watkins fleet of London acquired her for service in the First World War, renaming her *Racia*. In their service she went seven times on expeditions around the top of Norway to the White Sea and Russia. This very successful tug is believed to have been the model for the *Frisky* class of Admiralty tugs built toward the end of that war. The name ship of the class, *Frisky*, ultimately became *Foundation Franklin*, the celebrated Canadian salvage tug of the thirties and star of continuous adventures on the North Atlantic in the Second World War. She was a thoroughly durable iron vessel.

At the turn of the century the Dutch fleets were beginning to dominate long distance towing under the leadership of Sleepdienst L. Smit & Co, as the company was now called, and their new rivals, also Dutch, the International Tug Company. Smit had also accumulated considerable experience in salvaging ships that had come to grief along the Dutch coasts, establishing a partnership with an enterprising raiser of sunken ships named Willem Arnt van der Tak. The name Smit Tak is today famous in salvage worldwide.

It was in 1896 that Smit's *Oostzee* and *Oceaan* carried out the company's first long distance tow of a floating drydock, from Rotterdam to Brazil. Two years later, a giant dock measuring 510 by 110 feet, with a lifting capacity of 12,000 tons, was towed from the Tyne to Stettin on the Baltic. For this voyage there were now available two new tugs of 1500ihp, *Roode Zee* and *Zwarte Zee*. The Dutch now turned the tables on the British, picking up the British-built product for delivery.

Not only were the Dutch tugs now the commercial kings of ocean towing, but their crews were great heroes to their fellow citizens. Cards with pictures of great tugs and their captains were collected as are trading card pictures of sports heroes today. Inheritors of a tradition of great seafaring over the centuries, the tugs of this small nation and the men who manned them became "Holland's Glory" in this era.

The single stack *Witte Zee*, added to the Smit fleet in 1914, showed more enclosed space for ocean sailing comfort than her predecessors. Tall masts carried the primitive wireless antenna. She was stranded and lost in Wales in 1940. (Stichting Nationaal Sleepvaart Museum)

The Dutch specialization was trusted for reliability, to say nothing of experience, and brought them plenty of business. They gained all the big floating dock trade, a unique line of work due to the great above-water bulk of these structures, while declining for some time the towing-home trade in crippled vessels. Their specialized, transoceanic tug was designed for economy on long hauls. It featured a large single propeller, set deep to give both a steady pull at low speeds and a continuing bite without exposure of the screw by big wave troughs. The deep screw was also safer from fouling by towlines and wreckage. In these vessels there was no need for the high degree of manoeuverability and shallow draft often dictated in tug design. Nor did the Dutch go in for high power for this service after a reasonable level had been reached. Once a tow was under way, an economical, low power application could keep it going. A little over 1000 horsepower could handle all but the largest of tows at sea if there was no hurry and no lee shore to trap the tow if a gale should catch the high walls of a floating dock.

As an example, *Witte Zee* was only 700ihp, but was able to tow an 1100-ton dredge 9600 miles at an average 150 miles per day. Two 1300ihp tugs took a 17,000-ton floating dock from Rotterdam to New Zealand, a distance of 13,000 miles at a rate of 79 miles a day. Two Dutch coalburners of 1100 and 550ihp made a 13-month voyage covering 25,000 miles at 64 miles per day, including one stage of 13,000 miles, interrupted only by a stop in the Chagos Archipelago to refuel from the disabled steamer being towed. This feat may have inspired de Hartog's tale of Jan Wandelaar in *Captain Jan*, triumphantly performing a similar feat so as to evade typhoons in the Indian Ocean. It was common practice to use two tugs on long tows to both provide reliability and permit them to alternately leave the tow to refuel at ports along the way.

Until interrupted by the demands of the First World War, the British firm of Watkins competed bravely with the Dutch. They maintained both a London and a Thames fleet, and an ocean-going fleet that grew out of their early windjammer seeking activity in the

The third *Zwarte Zee*, of 1933, and *Thames*, 1938, both of Sleepdienst L. Smit and Company, ease part of the Singapore floating drydock through the Suez Canal in 1953. Both served the Allied war in exile from their homeland. (Stichting Nationaal Sleepvaart Museum)

English Channel. The longest ocean tow until then, in 1901, had been moving an oil hulk from Newcastle, England, to Sumatra. Watkins' tug *Oceana* accomplished the 8200-mile trip in 45 steaming days. One of the few long distance, floating drydock hauls to go to British tugs in those days was the delivery of the graving dock *Sir Alfred* 4500 miles to Nigeria by *Blazer* and *Cruizer*. The latter was built as a seeking tug for the Irish Sea, Mersey area, but spent most of her life working out of Sydney, Nova Scotia.

Oceana was a twin-screw vessel built in 1889. She looked a little like the Dutch tugs, with a well deck forward and exposed open bridge, but had a single funnel and the luxury of an enclosed charthouse. At 337 tons she produced 1000hp. Another great tow for her was bringing the Union Castle liner *Lismore Castle* home from the island of St. Helena in the same year as the Sumatra tow. When the war came, she was taken over by the Admiralty and helped on a number of salvage towing jobs, especially to assist smaller tugs of insufficient power.

In 1908, Watkins and Smit shared a job, each being given a paddle steamer to tow to the Persian Gulf. Watkins' *Hibernia* did

the job in 42 days; Smit's *Poolzee* took 53. However, in the same year, five British tugs brought a new floating drydock down to the mouth of the Tyne where they had to turn it over to a team of Dutchmen for the ocean tow. The Tyne tugs were generally built small to suit their river work, but this did not stop them from formidable ventures. The 1910 *George V* was fairly big for a Tyne tug, 100 feet long and 188 tons. She towed mud hoppers on the river with her 750ihp, but had no experience in ocean work. Nevertheless, in 1913, her owners sent her off to Vigo in Spain to help the Dutch *Poolzee* bring back the damaged ship *Glenmorven*, which was loaded with iron ore. *Poolzee* towed and *George V* steered from astern. Heavy weather came up, causing *Poolzee* to drop the tow, pick up her watchmen or "runners" on board the *Glenmorven* and head for shelter.

When the storm abated, *George V* found herself alone on the sea with the drifting tow. Undaunted and ignorant of her unsuitability for the job, she put a line aboard *Glenmorven* and towed her into Falmouth. The Tyne tug was certainly not suited for work at sea with her poor accommodation and small stores; she was a

The most famous ocean towing and salvage tug of the 1930s was Smit's *Zwarte Zee* of 1933, one of the first large diesel tugs. Her power was not so great, but following Smit policy, she had endurance and economy. She was scrapped in 1966. (Stichting Nationaal Sleepvaart Museum)

very wet vessel with little shear to deflect seas. Rebunkered, she took up the tow again to complete the delivery to the Tyne. Her owners got their contract price and a modest salvage claim. The Dutch were no doubt embarrassed.

In the twenties, the Dutch had a clear monopoly. Their overall excellent record for the delivery of tows gave them preferential insurance rates, and in 1927 these rates became the subject of complaints and official enquiries in Britain. An important point was the simple fact that the British owners had fewer of the very large tugs. Even more powerful than the Dutch tugs were those of the Bugsier Reederei firm of Hamburg. Their thirty-six tugs totalled 34,724 indicated horsepower; the largest one was 4000ihp. The insult to British pride was complete in this decade as big German and Dutch salvage tugs were put on station at the strategic ports of Falmouth, England, and Queenstown (Cobh), Ireland.

Although the spectacular drydocks moved behind the Dutch flag, the British companies were not altogether eclipsed in long distance towing. They did, after all, have important connections in the British Empire and the British shipbuilding industry was building for the world. In the twenties and thirties, the United Towing Company of Hull carried out 2064 major tows compared to Smit's 3554. The two companies lost at sea seventeen and nineteen of these tows respectively. And there were always the enterprising, even daring, cases like the little 100-foot *Hullman* of Hull which towed a trawler from Murmansk to Hull, a distance of 2000 miles through northern seas.

Another Hull tug, fairly small for the open sea, struck out upon incredible voyages as well. She was *Seaman*, also of United Towing. At 125 feet and 369 tons, she had a 150nhp triple expansion engine, a very modest tug, having a freeboard of only 18 inch-

While Smit International converted to diesel with *Zwarte Zee* and *Thames*, their great Dutch rivals Bureau Wijsmuller stayed with steam in their 1938 *Amsterdam*. (Stichting Nationaal Sleepvaart Museum)

es. There was no raised forecastle to meet the seas; she was really a coastal tug at most, but she had big coal bunkers. Burning 16 tons a day at 12.5 knots, *Seaman* could steam 4000 miles without refueling. Her enclosed wheelhouse and wireless were luxurious for the day in this type of tug.

Seaman's crew sailed her blithely off to Buenos Aires at the bottom of the world in 1926 with three river minesweepers in train. One was lost in the normally rough Bay of Biscay, but the other two were delivered. Ten years later, down in the South Atlantic again, *Seaman* started off from Bahia Blanca, Brazil, with an old naval cruiser in tow for Copenhagen to be scrapped. During the long voyage the tow was resold and the port of delivery changed to the UK. Little *Seaman* did from 69 to 129 miles a day on this run.

Long distance towing was less a part of the American scene in the earlier days, there not being any significant share in overseas shipping and shipbuilding. A few hardy east coast tugs and crews negotiated the long trip around South America to the burgeoning west coast after the beginning of the California gold rush and development of ports such as San Francisco. But it was deep water coastal towing of barges that became highly developed by American tug operators. The salient characteristic of their deep water tugs was their low freeboard and essential similarity to their smaller inshore sisters. Instead of using a high forecastle to break the seas, they pushed through them, trusting to their well battened-down decks and deckhouse.

Smit remained dominant through the second half of the twentieth century, but there would be both competition and co-operation on large projects with British, German, French, Canadian and American towing and salvage interests. Internationalization and consolidation of the industry under fewer owners occurred at the end of the century, much as was the case in other areas of commerce.

Top: A raft of timber on the St. Lawrence River under tow by a tug, partly assisted by sails. A plume of smoke comes from the paddle tug behind a sail. Most of the timbers are hewn, some sawn. The wood wythes tying the raft together may be seen on the right hand edge. (A.A. Calvin Collection, Queen's University Library, PAC-C3747)

Bottom: Booth Company tugs on the Ottawa River below the Chaudière Falls in 1873 include the small propeller *Barger* and the large walking beam paddler *Aid*. Woodburners, they have screens on their stacks against sparks. (NAC PA 12533)

Rafting on the Ottawa and St. Lawrence Rivers

THROUGHOUT MOST OF THE NINETEETH CENTURY, the economy of Canada was driven in large part by a waterborne boom in the market for timber. Tugs and towing soon became a vital part of the system that delivered the huge, roughly squared logs from the inland forests to coastal ports.

The Industrial Revolution and the Royal Navy created a great demand for wood to be used in construction in Britain. New England supplies had been cut off by the American Revolution and, in 1806, Napoleon's Berlin Decree cut off the traditional Baltic sources. In this same year, a farmer-cum-lumberman named Philemone Wright, of Hull, Quebec, sold for export at Quebec City, a raft of timber from the Ottawa Valley. There were no roads or railways; he had floated it 260 miles on the currents and rapids of the Ottawa and St. Lawrence Rivers. It was the first time such a feat was accomplished with only the aid of steering sweeps and sails.

This demonstration opened up the huge timber forests of the Ottawa Valley for exploitation. And exploited they were. Hundreds of square miles of virgin pine forests were laid waste by the timber barons before changing markets and declining accessibility of fresh timber sources ended the age in 1900.

In the early years when the rafts were moved in Wright's method, only by currents, favourable winds, rowing sweeps and sometimes kedging with a capstan, they were formed entirely with wood. The great pines were felled in the winter, squared off with hand axes to about two feet on a side, then twitched by horses to a stream or river bank. In the high waters of the spring runoff, they were driven downriver to an assembly point where the 60-foot timbers were tied together in cribs with wood pins and wythes. Numbers of cribs were coupled together into groups called "drams." Big rafts consisting of up to a hundred cribs, or 80 to 100,000 cubic feet of white pine timber, were put together to navigate the open stretches of rivers and lakes. These would be about 1500 feet long, one and a half times the length of a modern supertanker. At major rapids, the rafts were taken apart and the individual cribs shot through on the current, to be reassembled at the foot.

Slides were constructed at major rapids such as the Chaudière at Ottawa to smooth the passage of the cribs. Shooting a slide on a crib was a thrill and even visiting royalty, including Edward VII and George V and their wives, tried it. The great rafts carried a sizeable crew to handle the sweeps. There was a cooking shanty and a fireplace, doghouse-like sleeping shelters and various lots of added revenue-producing freight. Sawn lumber, especially heavy wood like oak which floated poorly, was often carried aboard, along with the pioneer settlers' main cash crop, barrels of wood ash for potash.

The crew of about fifty men were under a captain or pilot, and might have the company of a hundred casual passengers. In some situations, rafting was dangerous. Many lives were lost as rafts were smashed in rapids or in storms on the larger lakes like St. Pierre, where they were helpless without power. The art of rafting was brought from France, the French-Canadian pilots becoming the highly skilled experts. Their crews were Iroquois Indians and Irishmen. The "Raf'smen" were a proud, tough and brawling crowd who gave Bytown (Ottawa) very much a frontier atmosphere, like a goldrush town.

Sailing ships crowded the port of Quebec every spring to load timber. By 1840, the summer raft traffic on the St. Lawrence was heavy, some 400 enroute at a time. They arrived in the port

CHAPTER 5

The Great Canadian Waterway

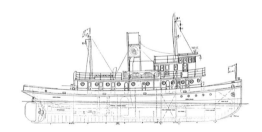

William Price (German & Milne)

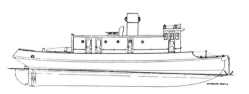

Coosie (German & Milne)

Ottawa river screw propeller tugs and barges for sawn lumber are winterbound in the ice, probably late in the nineteenth century. Meanwhile, the lumbermen are in the woods cutting the next spring's logs. (Archives of Ontario S9023)

of Quebec's loading areas at Wolfe's Cove in a steady stream, having spent months afloat.

Enter the Tugs

The arrival of steam-powered vessels, and particularly the purpose-built tug, soon proved of great significance on the Canadian commercial scene. The rivers, lakes and sheltered waterways were especially important to the transport of all the bulk resource products of a pioneer economy. In the absence of roads and railways, the steamboat, as the Molsons demonstrated on the St. Lawrence, made possible rapid, relatively reliable and continuous travel on these waterways. This was also demonstrated on the sheltered passages and inlets of the west coast after the first steamer, *Beaver*, arrived there. Because the most important commercial product needing transportation throughout most of the nineteenth century was raw unprocessed timber, the towing of rafts and barges was key. After bringing timber down to the seaports these steamboats found a complementary return trade in supplies and people.

Very early, the burgeoning market for Canadian timber in Britain stimulated large-scale cutting operations far up the St. Lawrence

and Ottawa River system, on the Saint John and Miramichi in New Brunswick and, later, on the British Columbia coast. The first rafts of logs were floated down the rivers on the current, helped by sails when winds were favourable. Man-powered sweeps steered and sometimes supplied a little locomotion. But steam power was seized upon where the timber trade flourished. Steam navigation was fairly advanced when west coast timber began to be moved to market. This was just as well, because there were not the river currents required to consistently propel rafts along.

In the East general purpose steamers began by towing rafts and lumber barges as opportunities arose. Then, fully-fledged tugs took up a full-time role, operating from about mid-century on the Saint John, Ottawa and St. Lawrence Rivers. The Saint John River's general purpose steamers were sometimes towing rafts in the 1820s. The pioneering Ottawa River lumber baron Philemone Wright put a steamer into operation in 1822. Similarly, below the border, the older passenger packets on the Hudson River found second careers as tugs in the twenties.

While the wave-swept expanses of Lake Ontario were not suitable for rafting logs because of storm damage and the lack of a suit-

The steam alligator *Bonne Chere* demonstrates the reason for the type's name, winching itself overland. This enabled it to get around rapids, over log booms or from one lake to another. (Archives of Ontario 34860)

able current, barge tows soon became an adjunct to the timber boom. A considerable trade for schooner loads of lumber and logs developed, and tugs found work helping them through the canals and rapids on the St. Lawrence.

Steam power came to Lake Ontario in 1816 with the packet *Frontenac*, running between Prescott and York (Toronto). On the Upper St. Lawrence there was *Queenston* in 1824.

The connection of towing steamers and rafts seems to have started with some help in places where there were narrow waterways, no current or too much current. The first use of tugs on any regular basis to tow rafts on the St. Lawrence appears to have started near Quebec City and on Lac St. Pierre, working its way up to Montreal. The St. Lawrence, above the Ottawa and through to

Kingston, had both several series of rapids *and* slow stretches to be passed. The Calvin interests at Kingston thrived on the timber trade running from Lake Ontario down through this part of the river. They supplied tugs to assist others' vessels and rafts in addition to assembling and moving their own rafts. The Calvins commanded the key point where the current draw of the St. Lawrence made the start of a raft run practicable.

Philemone Wright built *Union of the Ottawa* in Hawkesbury, Ontario in 1822, using a British engine. This boat plied a run between Grenville and Hull. By 1830, Wright had added two more steamers, *St. Andrews* and *William King*, for service between the rapids on the Upper Ottawa and those at Lachine. There is no indication whether they were involved in the towing of rafts, but it

Top: Many lakes and rivers had locally built rough and ready tugs to provide barge transport where roads and railways were few. *Ajax* barged firewood on the Trent River to the town of Peterborough. (Archives of Ontario S6631)

Bottom: *Dokis* of 1927 was not a true alligator tug, having winching capability only from the stern. This vessel served on Lake Abitibi. (Abitibi-Price Ltd.)

A typical small rafting paddle tug brings a raft of logs to the sawmill. Both raw logs and finished lumber were exported to Britain and the United States on a large scale. (National Library of Canada C19259)

seems likely they were, at least occasionally. The increase of timber movements led to greater use of towing to expedite the delivery of rafts to Quebec in the 1840s. Schooners and brigantines maintained a substantial freight traffic between Quebec and Lake Ontario when the early canal system was completed, but rafting was the most economical method for transporting big timber.

Between Montreal and Quebec City, once the Lachine and other rapids had been passed, towing rafts all the way became common by about mid-century. In 1872, *A.G. Nish* had recorded towing fifty-five sailing vessels and seventeen steamboats. Earlier, from the 1830s on, there were steamers out looking for raft pilots who might be persuaded to accept some help. By the 1860s, rafts could count on help from a tug anywhere assistance was likely to be needed. Tugs permitted the reduction of rafts' crews in the stretches of river between rapids and carried the crews back up river. In the 1870s, tugs were pulling a few rafts in Lake Ontario, although there were some disasters when storms came up. Poor visibility in a squall made it hard to see what was happening to the raft astern. Big logs

driving down on the tug from a raft that was breaking up were a nightmare to the crew and meant the raftsmen were in even greater danger.

Rafting on the St. Lawrence-Ottawa system peaked in the 1860s. Markets changed, and so did transportation. It became faster to carry sawn timber, especially for the growing demand for finished lumber from the United States that began to replace the British market. As the end of the century approached, there were numerous tugs and barges in the trade up the St. Lawrence into Lake Ontario and beyond, as well as through the Erie and Chambly Canals. It was the beginning of a new era of tugs and barges. Self-propelled canal steamers would later cut into this trade. The railways were now also bleeding off some of the traffic from the river and canal systems. But water transport would always remain competitive for bulk freight such as lumber and coal. The era of squared timber rafts was finished by 1900, although there was one last ceremonial raft passage from the Ottawa River to Quebec City in 1908, carried out by the timber baron J.R. Booth of Ottawa.

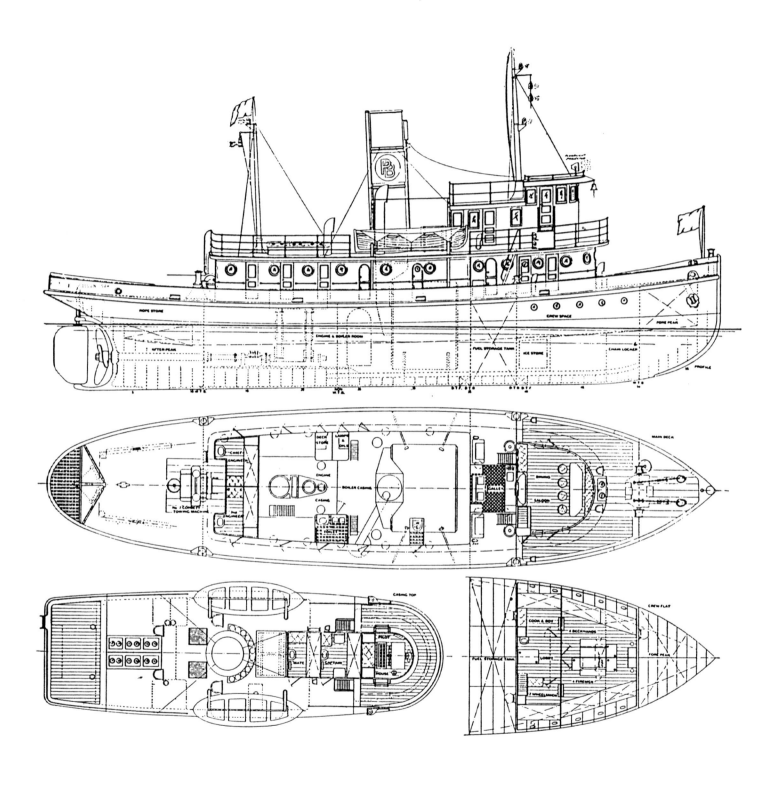

A later and more sophisticated steam tug built for Price Brothers lumbering interests was *William Price*, a 100-foot vessel with 500 horsepower, triple expansion engine. She accommodated a crew of 16. This tug was fabricated at the Davie yard in Lévis on the St. Lawrence River, transported in pieces to Lake Abitibi, Quebec, and assembled there. (German & Milne, Naval Architects, and Maritime Museum of the Great Lakes)

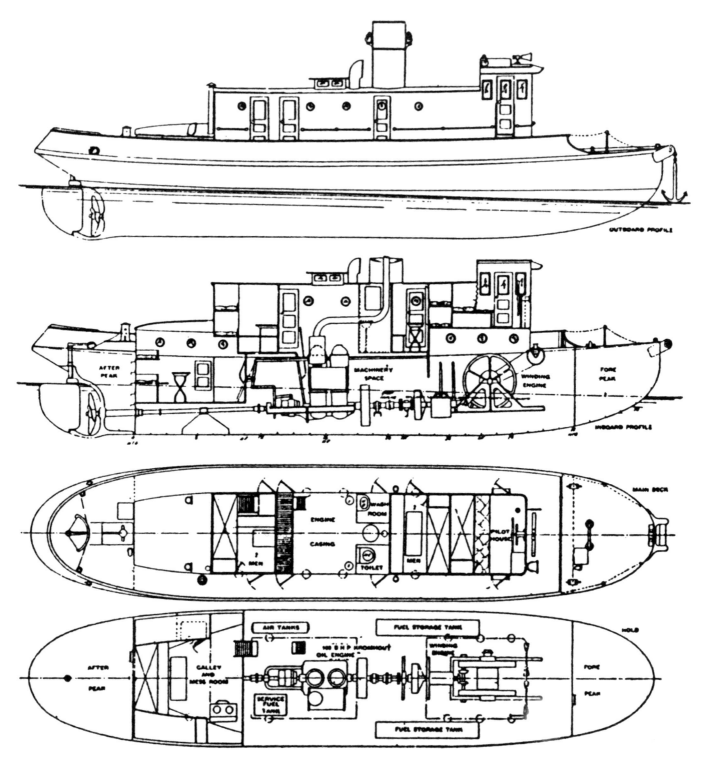

A "Winding tug," used for hauling logs on lakes and rivers with an anchor, a long towline and winch below deck. (German & Milne, Naval Architects, and Maritime Museum of the Great Lakes)

The faster moving Upper Ottawa River was suited to spring drives of loose logs and, with numerous entrepreneurs involved, co-operation was necessary. The Upper Ottawa Improvement Company was set up in 1868 to handle log drives and the delivery of logs to the owners' mills at the Chaudière Falls between Ottawa and Hull. The company operated various works along the river that were connected with log handling, notably the slides for passing rapids. Its domain extended from Ottawa to the far end of Lake Temiskaming.

With the coming of steam-powered vessels, the company hired the towing services of the Union Forwarding Company and other towing and navigation operators. In 1900, they took over the Union firm and operated their own tugs. Generally, as on the St. Lawrence, logs were driven on the current in fast stretches and towed in rafts or booms where it was slow. With its periodic rapids, the Ottawa River was not well suited to continuous navigation. However, logs could be passed down by varied means with reasonable efficiency. The timber entrepreneurs seem to have been reconciled to this situation. They built their mills at the foot of the Chaudière Falls, receiving the logs from flumes at this point, and canal locks were never built to bypass this cataract.

Above the Chaudière Falls, on Lac Deschênes and beyond, the Upper Ottawa Improvement Company operated numerous tugs, conveying logs through the sections where power was needed. In the modern era, a dozen diesel tugs replaced the steamers and the mills moved above the falls. Log holding booms were still in evidence in recent times at the mouth of the Gatineau River below Hull.

In the waning nineteenth century, as the production of finished lumber for export gained ascendancy over squared timber, a number of forwarding or transportation companies built up tug and barge fleets to carry it. There were around 250 barges and 50 tugs working on the Lower Ottawa and the St. Lawrence by the 1890s. There were larger barges for the locks of the Ottawa and Rideau Canals and smaller ones to fit the Erie Canal. From the great production centre of Ottawa-Hull, the product fanned out via the Rideau Canal to Lake Ontario and New York State's Erie Canal system, as well as through the Ottawa River, Ste. Anne's and Lachine Canals to the St. Lawrence and Richelieu Rivers, and Lake Champlain.

The integrated Booth company operated its own tugs. A major independent transport operator was Moss Kent Dickinson, who owned as many as sixteen tugs and eighty-four barges. The Ottawa Transportation Company had eight tugs and sixty-seven barges in the nineties. Hull was the location of yards where many of the tugs

and barges were built. Railway expansion rapidly eroded this waterborne trade early in the new century. Old-timers recalled the barges on the Lower Ottawa, pulled by tugs with puffing, noncondensing engines; the older boats were accompanied by the slap of their paddles announcing their approach. As late as the 1920s there were more than fifty tugs hauling pulp and lumber on the Ottawa in boom trains of up to 20,000 logs, travelling at a speed of about one mile per hour.

A variation on the river tug for handling logs was the alligator boat, devised by John West and built in Simcoe, Ontario. It was used extensively in the Ottawa Valley and spread across North America. The alligator was a small scow with paddles or a screw propeller and a large winch on deck, both powered by the one steam engine. It was capable of paddling through deep water, then kedging or winching itself over shallows, even up on shore and overland so as to portage from one lake to another. The principal builder became the firm of Russel Brothers in Fort Frances, Ontario, who pioneered the use of the Campbell internal combustion engines in these vessels. Russel Brothers became major builders of conventional tugs in the Second World War at Owen Sound on Lake Huron.

Timber was still pursued actively and recovered from remote stands in Northern Ontario and Quebec throughout the first half of the twentieth century. It then had to be carried out to large mills across lakes and down usable stretches of river. Alligator boats and a later refinement, the diesel winding boat, winched rafts along a lengthy cable from ground tackle to cross lakes and transit rivers. On large lakes, such as Nipigon and St. Jean, fairly large conventional tugs were required. These were usually fabricated in major shipyards and carried inland by rail for assembly on site. *William Price* was a 500hp steam tug operated on Lac St. Jean for Price Brothers; the later diesel boats *Nipigon* and *Orient Bay* operated on Lake Nipigon.

Calvin's River

In the early days, the City of Kingston held a strategic location where Lake Ontario ends in the St. Lawrence River. This was true not only militarily, but commercially, especially for squared timber and the succeeding lumber trades. A Vermonter, Delano Dexter Calvin, saw the potential early. He moved his embryonic rafting operation from Clayton, New York, to Garden Island, on the Canadian side, off Kingston. He began first with a branch in 1836, then moved completely in 1844. Calvin had started out with a suc-

Hodgeville, one of fifteen small Ville class day boats, the first tugs built for the Canadian Navy in the Second World War, charges out of Oakville Harbour into Lake Ontario in 1998. Many of them performed light duties for government for many years. (Author's Collection)

Two former steam tugs, since converted to diesel and in private use, moor in Oakville Harbour. The first, *Glen G.* is a traditional low profile Upper Lakes harbour tug. The second is *Wendy B.*, built for Great Lakes service in 1940, but requisitioned by the navy to function as an antisubmarine gate tender in Halifax Harbour. (Author's Collection)

Left:
Six of the many TANAC class small tugs built in Canada for war service overseas lie up for the winter in the Lachine Canal near Montreal in the nineteen-fifties. They towed sand barges through the canal. A new wheelhouse is mounted atop the original main deck-level house, the original wheelhouse windows still in place. (Author's Collection)

Below:
TANACs of J.D. Irving Ltd. towed logs and chip barges on the St. John River system in New Brunswick for more than 30 years. Seen is *Irving Poplar (I)* proceeding through the short Jemseg River from Grand Lake to the Saint John and a paper mill at Saint John. J.D. Irving operated a number of such tugs on the St. John through the nineteen-sixties. (David Baird)

An enlarged series of "short house" Glen tugs in 1944 was quite successful for the Canadian Navy and continued in use for many years. McKeil Marine of Hamilton rebuilt several, raising the power to as much as 1450bhp, changing from single to twin and even triple screw drive. They were very useful in seaway service. *Glenside* is seen here guiding the freighter *Wheat King* out of a Welland Canal lock. (McKeil Marine Ltd.)

One of the 144 Empire class British-built steam tugs to go into civilian service around the world was *Irving Oak* (ex-*Empire Spruce*) here about to pass under the Reversing Falls bridges during slack tide at Saint John. She was converted to diesel and is still in service as a harbour tug. (John Weeks Collection)

Canadian inland builders produced twelve Rock class British style steam tugs for the British Ministry of Transport, all delivered in 1945 after the war ended. Fine docking tugs of 1000bhp, they became scattered around the world in peacetime service. *Rockswift* became *Ocean Rockswift* with Saint John Tugboat Company. (Author's Collection)

Rivtow Marine was active in log towing and barging with boats like *Rivtow Viking*, a former British built wartime Assurance class tug. She handled company self-loading log barges along the coast. (Pacific Coast Tug Society)

Maintained for special events as a company yacht at North Vancouver, *Seaspan Chinook* is a United States Ocean class tug. Built in New York in 1943, she has a wooden hull and diesel electric drive. (Seaspan, Washington Group)

The specialist in ship berthing on Burrard Inlet, Vancouver has long been the C.H. Cates company, which depended for many years on its large fleet of small wooden "day boat" tugs in their distinctive yellow livery. (Author's Collection)

Among the oldest tugs still in service in the 1990s was *James Battle*, built as a steam powered fireboat for Detroit in 1900, revived for similar service at Halifax in the Second World War and then, converted to diesel, used primarily for towing with McAllister Towing and Salvage on the St. Lawrence River and Seaway system. She is seen here at the opening of the 1967 Montreal World Exposition. (Author's Collection)

An unidentified former steam tug under diesel power plies the Richelieu River with barges in the 1950s, once a busy route from the St. Lawrence to Lake Champlain and the Hudson River to New York. (Author's Collection)

Long the oldest active tug in Canada and now working in the Caribbean, *Argue Martin* is seen here in the regular tug races at Detroit-Windsor(the larger boat in the centre). She was built as *Ethel* for Sincennes McNaughton Line at Sorel in 1895 and was operated until recently by McKeil Marine at Hamilton, Ontario. (McKeil Marine)

cessful rafting of some oak timbers to Quebec in 1825 for a profit of $610. Buying up Garden Island and making it his base for rafting, towing, salvage and freighter operations, he established a commanding position astride a burgeoning commercial boom.

With no formal education to speak of, Calvin became a perpetual local reeve and magistrate, eventually a member of the Legislature. When he died at age 86, Prime Minister John A. MacDonald and other dignitaries attended his funeral, held on two of his steamers on the river. Colourful as well as successful, he was a devout Baptist, an abstainer and strong in his opinions. His pet hates were dogs and short men. Like many others of his time, he was an unlicensed steamboat captain and performed as his own salvage master, learning these arts as he went.

Starting by making up rafts of timber collected from the vicinity or brought in his own and other vessels from the Great Lakes, Calvin took advantage of the improved Welland Canal to operate barges and freight steamers up and down the lakes. Timber and lumber came down and manufactured goods went up. His own large, freight-tug steamers towed barges across Lake Ontario, turned them over to smaller Welland Canal tugs, then preceded them through the waterway to Lake Erie to resume the tow. It was a trip of three or four weeks from Garden Island to the North Shore of Lake Michigan, a major source of cargo. Upbound, barges were dropped off at various loading points and were later picked up loaded on the downbound trip. The towing steamer also carried finished lumber aboard. Some runs to gather timber went as far as Fort William (Thunder Bay) at the head of Lake Superior.

In the early eighties, the tug *Chieftain* made these runs with many adventures en route, as she was a side wheeler, not built for the rough seas encountered on Lake Superior. She was soon succeeded by bigger lake vessels such as the "propeller" *D.D. Calvin*, a vessel of greater power, with engines aft and timber-loading ports in her bows. Bigger barges were also supplied.

Calvin's first vessels were schooners that brought timber across Lake Ontario. Most of his vessels were built in his own Garden Island yard; some were secondhand. "Make do" was the motto.

Traditional log towing tugs like *Superior,* 1903, on the Great Lakes were large, with accommodation for supplies and woods crews. (Archives of Ontario 10337-12)

Passenger boats were cut down to be tugs and home-built engines were used several times over in different boats. Almost all of his steamboats were side paddlers and used the American-style, overhead, walking-beam engine with usually one huge cylinder, sometimes two. Boilers were wood-fired until local, convenient sources began to run out and coal had become competitive. The stokers of the wood burners were allowed to keep their ashes to sell for making potash.

The first Calvin steamer was *Prince Edward*, built at Garden Island in 1838. Next was long the pride of the fleet, *Raftsman*, built in 1841 for towing Calvin rafts between Montreal and Quebec City. This was the slower moving part of the St. Lawrence where the use of tugs on a regular basis first became common. *Raftsman* was built before the canal system was complete and could not then be engined at Garden Island, so she went down the river like the timber rafts, under sail and running on the currents and rapids with fore and aft sweeps. Boilered at Montreal and engined at Lévis, she was obliged to stay on the lower river towing rafts until the canals were built a few years later. This early tug served for many years, being remodelled as the screw-tug *William Johnston* in 1876 and later lengthened. Some parts of her, at least, were still afloat after 90 years.

Another famous Garden Island-built, Calvin tug was *John A. Macdonald* of 1866, used for towing timber rafts from Rivière des Prairies at Montreal to the Quebec City timber coves.

In the 1870s she was towing seven drams of logs at a time. Captain Alex Gignac was highly skilled in handling the tow, perhaps a quarter of a mile in length, in the tides and currents of the lower river, equal to the modern Mississippi barge tows, but with a fraction of the power. Timing of the passage to suit the tide was critical. Otherwise, the flood tide would push them back upriver. At night, small drifting rafters would edge alongside and hitch a ride with the tow. Other problems were log thieves and overzealous "salvors" of wood that broke loose from the rafts.

Tugs were used on a regular basis to handle the rafts on Lake Ontario and the St. Lawrence above the Lachine Rapids from about 1860 onward. The earlier completion of the canal systems was useful in permitting easy return of the tugs upriver, but they went down the various rapids as did the rafts, the fast and exciting way. A tow would start from Garden Island and head through the Thousand Islands into the St. Lawrence. A paddle-tug such as one of the three successive ones named *Chieftain* pulled a dram of rafts tied snugly together on a 600-foot towline. Each raft had its crew of men, sweeps and sails. Before each set of rapids, the tug let go the rafts one at a time to space them apart for the run, then steamed furiously on ahead of them through the rapids. In the slow water below the rapids the rafts were collected and the tow resumed.

It was good going to make Montreal from Kingston in three days. The tug captains achieved their responsible positions from the lower deck the hard way. For 34 years the head raftsman for Calvin's was a tough, smart old hand called "Le Vieux Aimé" Guerin who knew every standing wave in each series of rapids. The historic Victoria Bridge at the foot of the Lachine Rapids at Montreal has a long central span in it, placed there for the benefit of the passenger-carrying *Rapids Prince* and for Calvin's rafts. The tug picked up the rough, roistering raftsmen and their gear at Quebec, returning them to Montreal where they were carried home to Garden Island in railway cars with barred windows, still wildly celebrating their safe arrival at Quebec.

Calvin—known as "Gov" to the men who worked for him, as many as one thousand at one time—was strictly religious, but was not above tying down the safety valve on the boiler of his main rapids tug *Chieftain*. This dangerous practice made extra steam pressure that helped the tug fight its way upriver against the rapids before canals were available. In 1858, however, his tug *Hercules* blew up while towing a disabled steamer up Rapide Plat, killing several men including D.D. Calvin, Jr. This was a severe blow to the father, who was over 60 and had planned to turn over his empire to his 22-year-old son. As was so often the case when boats sank in the shallow waters of the river, *Hercules* was raised, towed home and rebuilt. Succession in the business, however, fell upon a second son, H.A. Calvin, a mere boy.

Every resource used in the far-flung Calvin timber moving operations that centred upon Garden Island seems to have been built for the moment, all of wood. Vessels, wharves and buildings all disappeared quickly when the business foundered. The homemade boats and their engines appear to have been poorly built and expendable. The engines, though, lasted through two or three flimsy hulls. The squared-timber market disappeared and the railways took away the finished lumber trade around the turn of the century. At this point, The Calvin Company was the only major rafting business left. The last Calvin raft was floated to the City of Quebec in 1911 and the company was wound up in 1914. Some detail on Calvin's tug operations and salvage business is covered in a later chapter.

The British Royal Navy Adopts Steam Towing

VERY SOON AFTER THE FIRST STEAM-POWERED VESSELS had demonstrated their ability to do useful work and were spreading throughout the waters of Britain, Europe and North America, additional possibilities were being explored. The famous British engineer, Brunel the elder, whose son built the *Great Eastern*, discussed the uses of steam power with the Admiralty. Lord Melville issued the judgement that he considered steam power unnecessary for general navigation but, "it would be attended with material advantages to His Majesty's service if it could be used for towing ships out of harbour in the Thames or Medway and at Plymouth and Portsmouth."

A towing trial was carried out, but the sadly underpowered steam packet *Eclipse* had difficulty attempting to tow the big 64-gun *Hastings* against the tide from Woolwich. Nevertheless, the Royal Navy acquired a small steamboat called *Monkey* of 212 tons with an 80-horsepower paddle engine and the next year had built a similarly powered vessel called *Comet*. Through the 1820s additional small steamers were acquired. All seem to have been used for towing, carrying dispatches and a variety of miscellaneous duties.

For a long time to come, the Royal Navy still would plan to go into battle with full-rigged sailing ships-of-the-line. The use of steam power for towing warships into advantageous positions for doing battle by gaining the wind gauge would be appreciated, but some important disadvantages held back the installation of steam engines in major fighting ships. In these earliest days, side-wheel paddles were the tested method of propulsion. The RN saw the paddle wheels as vulnerable to battle damage as well as taking up space along the ship's side that should be used to mount guns. Insufficient coal capacity for extended trips was another liability. There was also an underlying fear at the Admiralty that steam power, if encouraged, could rapidly make the entire battle fleet obsolete. This was the same fear the naval reformer and First Sea Lord, Jackie Fisher met head on in 1906 with the building of *Dreadnought*, thereby making his own battle fleet obsolete, along with everyone else's.

Inevitably, larger steam-powered, paddle-equipped naval vessels were built. By 1830, there were about thirty such vessels, many of them rigged as brigs or barkentines, serving as dispatch vessels and carrying out towing as needed. One of the better known was *Lightning*, built at Deptford in 1823. She was 296 tons, 123 feet long and was powered by a Maudsley engine of 100 net horsepower with a boiler pressure of two to three pounds per square inch. *Lightning* was described both as a paddle gunboat and as a tug. As early as 1824, she towed bomb vessels to Algiers and two years later went on the RN's expedition to Kronstadt, Russia, probably towing major ships when needed. On the return she put in at Copenhagen and Egersund on the way to Sheerness. Her engineer, John Chapender, reported that she performed well, that Mr. William Maudsley was pleased at how well his engine stood up and that he, Chapender, had been careful to blow the salt accumulations out of the boiler periodically.

Lightning performed a variety of towing jobs, moving the big "74s" between naval bases and helping the major sailing ships to sea, like a seeking tug. Edward Cree, a contemporary naval surgeon who kept a detailed diary of his service in these times, sailed in a naval transport to the Far East in 1839. He notes, "The *Lightning* steamer took us in tow, at 9 a.m., as far as Gravesend, where we anchored to take in troops for Ceylon." Several days later after wait-

CHAPTER 6

Towing and Naval Strategy

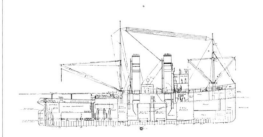

Foundation Franklin (ECTUG)

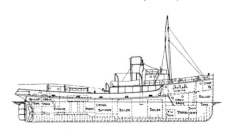

Saint class tug (Author's collection)

The relative merits of paddle and screw propellor propulsion were settled for the Royal Navy in 1843 by a contest between *Alecto* and *Rattler*. The screw equipped *Rattler* proved faster and could pull *Alecto* astern though they were of equal horsepower. The Admiralty then plunged ahead with screw steam power. (National Maritime Museum, Greenwich B1783)

ing out a fog, he writes, "The *Lightning* steamer towed us from the river to the Downs where we anchored for the night."

Cree shows that the navy's own sloops and gunboats did much towing. The British fleet at Baltsch in the Baltic consisted of one hundred sailing transports towed by fifty steam vessels, each filled with troops.

Even C.S. Forester's celebrated, fictional naval hero, Horatio Hornblower, came to realize toward the end of his career, the importance of steam power in naval matters. In *Hornblower in the West Indies,* set during 1822, he suddenly had an urgent need to pursue his enemy the French Count Cambronne out of New Orleans. However, he was left to chafe impatiently in port, as Cambronne had cleverly stolen a vital lead by hiring not one but both of the available steam tugs in New Orleans to tow him the 100-mile distance down the Mississippi. Hornblower was forced to await the arrival of another tug from downriver before he could transit the confined river channel. The great admiral of the popular fiction series, no doubt true to the feelings of his real contemporaries, found it a strange experience to be under tow, plowing steadily through the water on a completely even keel with no sail set.

The Honourable East India Company had equipped itself with a number of armed paddle vessels and some of these joined the Royal Navy's expeditions against China in the Opium Wars in 1841 and 1842. The expeditions involved forays up the devious channels of the Pearl River to Canton and up the great Yangtse 250 miles to Nanking, forcing the infamous treaty that ended the war. Troopships were towed efficiently and the guns on the paddlers proved very useful, as their platforms were not subject to the vagaries of wind and current. These campaigns in difficult and narrow waters, beset with tides, currents and poor navigational aids, clearly showed the value of steam power, vulnerable paddle wheels or not. Frequently, major warships ran aground and had to be pulled off by the steamers. The Admiralty commenced building steam sloops and frigates with full sail rig as well. On this type of vessel, a large, swivelling gun was mounted fore and aft in addition to broadside guns, adding to the flexibility and choice of targets that came with steam.

When the Board of Admiralty was sent a model of a screw propeller by Berthon in 1835, they replied that it was "a pretty toy that never would and never could propel a ship." Two years later, John

Stormcock of 1881 was a tug of the prominent Liverpool Screw Towing Company that sailed over long distances despite the lack of shelter. She was chartered by the Royal Navy and went to Egypt for the military campaigns there in the 1880s. (National Maritime Museum, Greenwich G1651)

Ericsson, acknowledged as the inventor of the successful propeller, demonstrated his version by towing the Admiralty barge on the Thames. But the Lords were very cautious. Many people believed that propulsion at the stern would lack manoeuverability. Ericsson went off with his propeller to the United States where the U.S. Navy (USN) installed one in the frigate *Princeton*.

All around them the screw propeller was being adopted and accepted, so the Admiralty took another look. After all, the paddle wheel had weaknesses from a warship point of view. A competition was arranged in 1843. The paddle sloop *Alecto* had a sistership, *Rattler*, under construction. Both had 200nhp engines. It was decided to install a screw propeller on *Rattler*. Seemingly convinced the propeller would lose in the comparison, no gunports were installed in the hull space liberated by the omission of paddle boxes. On speed trials, the screw-driven *Rattler* proved the faster vessel; then, in April of 1845, a towing tug-of-war was staged in which *Rattler* pulled *Alecto* astern at a speed of 2.8 knots.

Well convinced at last, the Royal Navy immediately plunged into screw propulsion with twenty new vessels. For the Baltic expedition against Russia in 1854, there were numerous steam gunboats, sloops and frigates, some sixteen screw-driven and eight with paddles. Again, towing was an important part of the operations. Steam vessels often towed sail frigates and troopships in the confined waters, moving them into position for bombardments and occasionally pulling them off shoals. During the attack on Bomatsund Fort, HMS *Penelope* was driven ashore and came under fire. She was floated by jettisoning her guns and towed to safety by *Hecla*, *Valorous* and *Lightning*. Steam towing was now a significant element in the RN's tactical operations, not by regular tugs, but by gunboats that could perform as tugs as needed.

Towing was also important in the Crimean War, fought at the end of a long supply line that ran through the Mediterranean Sea and the Bosporus. The heavy traffic in supply ships from the arsenals on the Thames greatly encouraged the local tug business. Watkins and others built thirty more tugs for this bonanza. Bigger, more powerful ones were needed to keep the transports on schedule despite winds and tides. The tugs were all paddlers; many had two engines and two boilers, and ran from 100 to 200nhp. A few were now being built with iron hulls. Civilian tugs were also pressed into service for work at the Crimean front.

The Royal Navy did some long distance towing themselves. The frigate *Odin*, of 1846, towed three mortar boats for bombarding Sevastopol through the Mediterranean and Bosporus to the Black Sea from the Isle of Wight. She lost them twice in storms, finding them the following day in each case, arriving at Balaclava in one month. *Odin* was a paddler, 208 feet long with 560 horsepower engines. She served in the Baltic, Black Sea and at the Pieho Forts in China.

The RN made good use of steam in the 1840s and 1850s. The great, heavily gunned ships-of-the-line were still sail powered, but increasingly given an assist by the steamers at critical points. Towing vessels thus aided in the continuation of the sail battle fleet, much as they helped sustain the commercial sailing ships. The first

steam powered ship of the line was *Agamemnon*, built about 1850. Sail declined steadily from then and steam fighting ships were no longer called upon to include towing among their duties.

Numbers of tugs for harbour service were maintained at the naval bases and, in wartime, the best civilian tugs were conscripted and new ones built. At war's end the surplus tugs were sold off to the civilian operators.

Monitor and *Merrimack* and Their Tugs

In the American War Between the States, the Union side was short of warships and very early lost its main naval base at Norfolk, Virginia. Wanting to establish an effective sea blockade of the Confederacy, all possible vessels were armed and pressed into

Taken over by the navy during the First World War, *Hibernia* of 1884 became HMS *Carcass*. This open bridge, 219-ton tug helped escort naval monitors to East Africa to rout the German cruiser *Koenigsberg* from the Rufiji Delta, and served in the Gallipoli campaign. (National Maritime Museum, Greenwich 19857)

Numerous very basic steam tugs were built for the heavy barge traffic of war materiel from Britain to France in the First World War. *Dartmothian*, built in 1915 is an example. (National Maritime Museum, Greenwich G12057)

service, including ferries and tugs. Small vessels like tugs were adequate for intercepting merchant ships and could operate in the shelter of the sounds that abound on the southeastern coast.

Lacking many things, especially manufactured goods, the Confederacy tried desperately to break the blockade. Their main plan in 1862 involved building an ironclad warship. They did this using the salvaged hull of the U.S. Navy frigate USS *Merrimack*, which they renamed CSS *Virginia*. With a heavy, iron-clad fortress instead of only the traditional timbered sides above the waterline, she promised to be a serious threat to the Union's polyglot fleet. The North rushed to build a worthy opponent, coming up with the famous benchmark in warship construction, USS *Monitor*. Another creation of the brilliant Swedish engineer, John Ericsson, *Monitor* lay mainly below the water surface, leaving only a big, armoured turret and a small pilot house for enemy gunners to aim at.

On her first trials, *Monitor's* engines failed due to improper engine-valve adjustment and she had to be towed home by a tug. On the second trip, she performed well and soon left Brooklyn for Hampton Roads to meet *Virginia/Merrimack*. The great flaw in *Monitor* now appeared when she hit rough weather on the open sea. Her ventilation failed and her fires were doused by water coming in via the smoke outlets, there being no funnel. She took on water that the failing engines could not pump out. Fortunately, the authorities had been nervous enough to send along a tug, *Seth Low*, as escort on this sea voyage. *Monitor* was towed into shallow water for easy raising if she should sink, saved by an unsung tug whose name is seldom mentioned in history.

With calmer seas, Ericsson's marvel was put in order and continued on until rough waters caused a repeat of the former problems, plus a steering failure. The crew of *Monitor* had a desperate and

The tug-tender *John Green* loads troops in St. John's, Newfoundland, to be ferried to the troop ship *Calgarian*, too big for the local piers. (Public Archives of Newfoundland and Labrador, S.M&I Collection)

frightening night, so dark that they could not signal for help from the tug or other steamers. She managed to pull through on her own, making Hampton Roads the next day, much to the relief of her crew and those of the Union vessels then being devastated by *Virginia*.

The Confederate ironclad had boldly sallied forth into Hampton Roads to do battle with the blockaders, escorted by the armed tugs *Beauford* and *Raleigh*. The Union broadsides bounced off the Confederate ship while she demolished them, sinking two. *Monitor* arrived at the river in time to frustrate *Virginia's* attempt to destroy the grounded *Minnesota*. The Confederate ship then retired upriver after the two ironclads had inconclusively bounced a few cannon balls off each other.

A month later the two sides came forth to do battle again, armed with new multi-ship tactics in mind rather than a two-ship duel. Unable to harm *Monitor* with her guns, *Virginia* was to distract the Union vessel while tugs put boarding parties on the enemy's low deck. But *Monitor* would not enter the river because there was no room for her support ships to carry out ramming plans against *Virginia*. The Confederate ironclad, on the other hand, declined to go out into the wide waters of the bay where her tugs would have difficulty carrying out the boarding plan. Twice battle was declined and the great *Monitor-Merrimack* contest fizzled out. The Union was the winner, though, since its blockade was preserved.

At the end of December, *Monitor* left Fortress Monroe to help in the blockade of Charleston. Expecting storms off Hatteras, she was towed by the powerful side wheeler *Rhode Island* in addition to using her own engines. A great wind did come up, causing water to enter the smoke and ventilation ports. Despite a new, larger pump, the water gained the upper hand and the powerful warship that had captured the attention of the world ignominiously sank, coming to rest upside down on the bottom.

Tugs To The Rescue

The British Admiralty appears to have acquired a variety of towing vessels for use around its bases, even after the fighting fleet had converted to steam power. Perhaps they were low in power as befits harbour tugs and not as up to date as the commercial tugs. As an indication of the probable superiority of the privately owned vessels, the Admiralty felt it necessary to charter the 1000ihp *Stormcock* from the Liverpool Screw Towing and Lighterage Company for use in the war in Egypt during 1881. They liked the 325-ton tug and kept her. The Liverpool company built a replace-

ment in 1883, but the Admiralty bought it as well two years later, so the owners had to build a third that year. The Admiralty must have been pleased with the judgement of the Liverpudlians, because they promptly purchased even this tug. Possibly the RN was developing a need for powerful tugs that could handle the big ironclad warships now joining the fleet and were not swift enough in planning for themselves.

By the First World War the Royal Navy had acquired a small fleet of tugs of over 1000hp and capable of manoeuvering the new dreadnought battleships that were approaching 20,000 tons displacement. The RN, like many others who operated tugs for ship berthing in British ports, liked paddlers. The advantage was strong steering power when working alongside a big ship. The RN even had paddle-tugs built for handling aircraft carriers after the Second World War. Naval tugs gleamed with regularly polished brass and were always clean and tidy compared to the civilian tugs. The crews were three or four times the size as well.

For the increased shipping activity of the First World War, especially the run across the English Channel to supply the armies, the British government requisitioned many civilian tugs. In fact, John Watkins was forced to complain that there were too few left on the Thames for other essential work. At that stage, 426 had been requisitioned.

Tugs were handy for a variety of wartime jobs. Some were used as boarding vessels to inspect incoming ships at ports. Some forty-nine tugs were chartered or purchased during this war from Canadian and American sources, even from Australia. These included *Julie Moran* of the famous New York Moran fleet and *J.O. Gravel* from the Montreal based Sincennes McNaughton Line. The latter served out her postwar days on the Manchester Ship Canal as *Clarendon*.

Some of the bigger tugs made major expeditions during this war. In 1914, the German light cruiser SMS *Koenigsberg* had holed up in the delta of the East African Rufiji River and the Royal Navy was striving vainly to get at her. Regular warships could not venture up the silted channels without charts so they used two captured German East African tugs, *Adjutant* and *Helmuth,* to reconnoitre. Both were armed. *Adjutant* was sent up one of the many branches of the Rufiji to spy on the supposedly trapped cruiser, but was fired upon by a land party using portable guns from *Koenigsberg*. Later, when she tried again, her steering gear was hit and she ran aground. Her crew abandoned her, so the Germans were able to reclaim and salvage their tug.

Above: The Dutch
world-ranging ocean tug
Oceaan of 1894 was
bought by the London
firm of Watkins for
service in the First
World War and renamed
Racia. In this role she
made several trips to
Northern Russia.
(Nationaal Sleepvaart
Museum, Maassluis)

Left: For rescue of
crippled ships in
wartime the British
Admiralty built
numerous salvage tugs.
Said to be based on
Racia, the Frisky class
of 1919 was very
successful. This is the
name ship of the class
seen before fitting a
raised forecastle and
becoming the celebrated
Canadian salvage tug
*Foundation Frankli*n.
(John Weeks Collection)

A large and successful class of naval rescue tugs were the Admiralty Saints. They performed in two world wars and in peaceful trades worldwide in between. This is *St. Arvans* which became *Ocean Eagle* under Canadian government and Canadian Pacific colours, having a varied career from the Maritimes to Port Churchill and Newfoundland. (CP Rail Corporate Archives 13777)

In this long drawn-out affair, which tied up British warships now needed to mount guard on the Indian Ocean shipping lanes, the RN was stymied by its inability to take heavily gunned cruisers up the river. The mere existence of the German cruiser in that part of the world caused the same disruption of British and Allied shipping as *Emden* had a little earlier. Only shallower draft monitors could do the job and these were eventually ordered up from home bases in Britain. Three monitors eventually arrived on the scene, having been towed via the Mediterranean by the Liverpool tugs *Blackcock, Sarah Jolliffe* and *Revenger.* There followed a successful battering of the helpless cruiser hidden in the jungle using the monitors' big guns. In this task they were aided by a spotting aircraft. The three tugs then hauled their charges back to the

Mediterranean. Returning home, *Blackcock* and *Sarah Jolliffe* nonchalantly took up tows of barges of supplies for Russia which they eventually delivered in Archangel at the top of the world. In 1918 *Blackcock* was crushed by ice in the White Sea.

As in the Second World War, an important need developed for tugs to put to sea and bring in casualties among shipping on the sea tracks that converged on Britain from the far-flung Empire. These vessels had been torpedoed, mined or shot up by gunfire. Tugs were in extensive use towing barge traffic along the coasts and assisting the many sailing ships that had been pressed into service. During the war, the British tugs rescued or salvaged 140 vessels, while assisting about 500 others around Britain. Naval and civilian tugs under government control steamed off on some

Seen in barging service well after the Second World War with Canadian Pacific on the British Columbia Coast is *Kyuquot*, British built as *Saint Florence* for the First World War. These tugs produced 1250 horsepower, very respectable for their day. (CP Rail Corporate Archives 22227)

long expeditions, vulnerable to enemy attack. A U-boat would not often waste a torpedo on a tug, preferring to surface and shell it. One German submarine met its match in the captain of the tug *Homer*. When the U-boat surfaced and fired warning shots, *Homer's* master dropped his tow and repeatedly charged the submarine. After several hair-raising close shaves for both sides, the German captain retired from the scene.

In addition to the expedition to the Rufiji, the 219-ton *Hibernia*, built in 1884, operated at Gallipoli, while *Marsden* was wrecked there at Suvla Bay. *Racia* was another tug that sailed to Northern Russia, making the trip several times.

As the Great War progressed and the need for large seagoing rescue tugs became clear, the Admiralty ordered a number built. Three of the Frisky class were built on traditional lines and looked like the

Dutch ocean type, having a well deck forward and two tall funnels. These are thought to have been patterned after Watkins' *Racia*, originally the Dutch *Oceaan*. They were 155 feet with a 31-foot beam, 612 tons and powered by a 1200ihp triple-expansion engine. Several more of an enlarged version were called the Stoic class.

The class-name ship, HMS *Frisky*, was rusting in Hamburg with many other vessels in the Depression, when found and bought by the Foundation Company of Canada in 1930. Foundation built a famous dynasty of deepsea salvage tugs around her as *Foundation Franklin* during the Second World War. Another of the Friskys to survive went to Shanghai as a salvage tug. These vessels were the last of an era in design, very good sea boats, and durable. *Foundation Franklin* finally went to the shipbreakers 30 years later with her hull and machinery hard used by an arduous career in the Second World War.

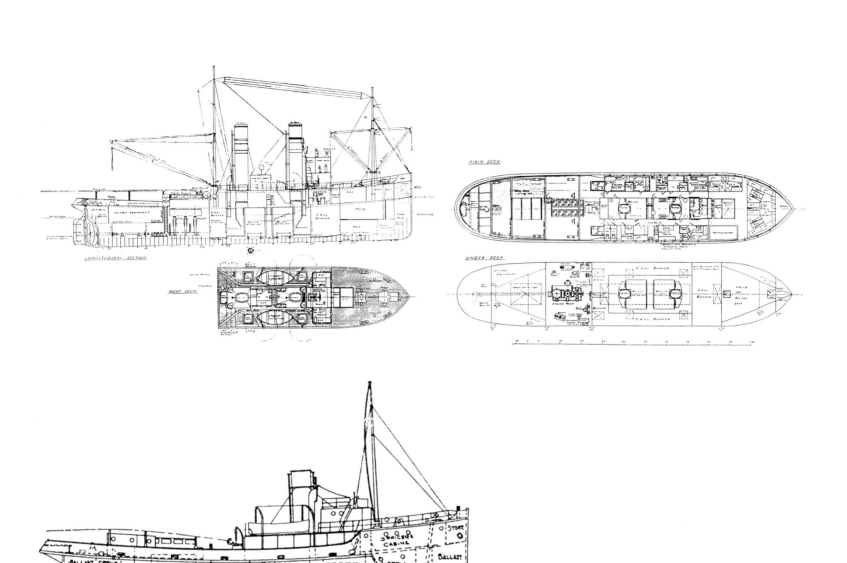

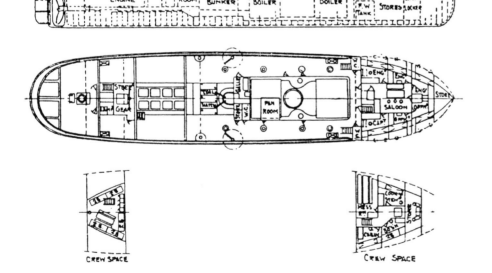

Top: *Foundation Franklin*, a First World War rescue tug that performed heroically in the second war as Canada's only East Coast deep sea salvage tug. She had two boilers and holds for pumps, compressors and other salvage gear. (ECTUG)

Left: Plan of the British Saint class rescue tugs, of which forty-six were built for first world war service. (Author's Collection)

Leader of the numerous tugs that played a vital role in the evacuation of Dunkirk was the Dover Harbour Board's tug-tender *Lady Brassey*, popularly known as the Dover Rescue Tug for her activity in that busy sea traffic area. She was twin screw compound, 362 tons, built in 1913. (National Maritime Museum, Greenwich P918)

A much larger group of Admiralty tugs was the highly successful Saint class, forty-six in number. These rescue tugs were the first of a new design type, having a raised forecastle with a break under the bridge and the shorter funnel that goes with forced draft on the boilers. These coal-burners were 440 tons and had a 1250ihp triple-expansion engine. Many carried a 12-pounder gun forward.

Eight of the *Saints* served the RN for many years after the war; others were sold into civilian service worldwide. They went as far as New Zealand, China, Australia, Iraq, Brazil and Spain, with seven to Canada in the early 1920s. *St. Arvans* and *St. Faith* went to the Canadian Department of Marine and Railways, one for each coast. They worked for various government agencies and private companies, lasting into the Second World War. The former was renamed *Ocean Eagle* and the latter *Haida Monarch* and then *Polaris*. *St. Catherines* went to Canadian National Railways on the West Coast as *Canadian National No. 2*. Extensive long distance tows were chalked up by the *Saints*, including a 6879-mile haul to the United Kingdom from Argentina by *St. Florence*.

The largest of the wartime built tugs were the six in the Rollicker class. They were twin-screw, with two funnels and reminiscent of the Friskys with the Dutch well deck, but much larger at 1400 tons and 4500 horsepower. One, *Rollcall*, was sold later and converted into the passenger-tender tug *Romsey* for Cunard at Southampton. She became a familiar part of most pictures and posters of great liners entering or leaving that port between the wars.

Small tugs were built, too, notably in 1916 and 1917, to handle 1000-ton barge traffic to France. One of these was still operable at Toronto in the 1980s. They included a single-screw type for the channel crossing and a shallower twin-screw class for the rivers and canals of France and Belgium. Both types were 400ihp and had army crews. To save steel, a dozen concrete tugs and attendant barges were built, with completion only in 1919 and 1920. Some of them subsequently operated successfully in the coal trade from the United Kingdom to Northern Europe and the Baltic. The war program tugs were widely dispersed in commercial service after the war.

Giant liners like *Queen Elizabeth* frequented Halifax as troopers in the Second World War, straining the berthing resources of a hard-pressed tug fleet. Here are two navy Glen class boats assisting *Bansun* and *Banstar*, (former *Sandusky* and *Milwaukie*) and *Bansurf* (ex-*Coalopolis*), 1923. (NAC PA 177252)

The Second World War: A Scarcity of Tugs

When the Second World War broke out, Canada's puny navy had neither tugs nor much need for them. The fighting fleet of six destroyers disappeared on missions in foreign waters, leaving the entire East Coast to be defended briefly by a squadron of two little coal-burning minesweepers. But all manner of non-naval, government owned vessels were pressed into service as auxiliaries while defense strategy was developed and an incredible expansion of the Royal Canadian Navy began to take shape.

Shipping traffic increased and was focussed on the key ports of the Maritimes as the Canada-Britain supply lifeline was organized. Halifax was the major naval base and trooping port. Saint John, New Brunswick flowed with freight. Sydney, Nova Scotia became the slow convoy marshalling point, while St. John's, Newfoundland became the mid-Atlantic antisubmarine base and a haven for stricken vessels. Canadian West Coast and American ports geared up for their roles later.

Halifax was the most hard pressed by naval and merchant service demands. Tugs were an especially valued item. Aside from their ship handling purpose, their tough, abuse-taking hulls and manoeuverability suited them to jobs as boarding vessels, for firefighting, salvage and general errand-running in a busy harbour. There was a rush by the various authorities to snatch up any available tugs. Of course, wherever tugs were normally used as part of the transportation system, the war now demanded their increased use.

Tugs old and new were mustered to Canada's East Coast ports from points spread from Philadelphia to Lake Superior. Modest little boats from the Great Lakes found themselves pushing around great battleships and glamourous liners like the *Queen Mary, Queen Elizabeth*, *Aquitania* and *Ile de France*. Some of the individual tugs are mentioned in a later chapter.

It was in the first frantic months of the war, when there were virtually no resources and little experience in dealing with war situations that the Battle of St. Jean d'Orleans was fought. It seems that two long, low Royal Canadian Mounted Police patrol boats

Some civilian tugs like *Foremost 43* were under obligatory recall by the British government because of construction subsidies. This fine Aberdeen-built vessel disappeared from Saint John for overseas war service, ending up in British civilian service after the war as *Battleaxe* then *Loyal Celt*. (John Weeks Collection)

were mistaken for German U-boats by the newly organized coast watch and reported as heading upriver towards Quebec City. Local naval control in Quebec realized that some action had to be taken and sent out the best task force they could muster. In the lead was the government tug *Lanoraie*, armed with fire pumps and water cannons. Following up was the buoy tender *Druid*, on whose deck was a light field gun set behind sandbags and manned by soldiers of the famous *"Van Doos"* (Royal 22nd Regiment). In the early morning mists some shots were fired, but all ended well as the supposed enemy was recognized before *Lanoraie* opened fire with *her* cannon. This strange episode has been reported by reliable but unofficial naval sources.

On the other side of the Atlantic there was also a marshalling of all available tugs, principally upon the port of Liverpool and the Mersey and Clyde Estuaries, where the other end of the transoceanic lifeline was located. Production of new tugs at a wartime pace would come in Canada, the United States and the United Kingdom only after rushed programs to build convoy escorts. In the meantime, the British government called in its loans in the form of

British-built and subsidized tugs. These included *Banshee* of Halifax and *Foremost 43* of Saint John, state of the art, Aberdeen built vessels, as well as the big *Salvage King* from Victoria.

Operations Dynamo and Sealion

The name Dunkirk conjures up pictures of the little pleasure yachts and lifeboats that streamed across the English Channel to rescue the better part of two armies. Most of them were towed across, of course, by tugs. The bulk of the British and French troops lifted out of the trap at Dunkirk in 1940 were carried by destroyers and ex-channel steamers, among which there were heavy casualties. The cockleshell fleet of small boats provided staging from the beaches to larger vessels offshore.

Much of the activity that was urgently required in the melee in and around the evacuation ports and the English receiving ports was tugs' work. Handling ships, manoeuvering in close quarters, edging close to shore to tow out crippled vessels and all the while dodging bombs was their special talent. They responded in the form of more than forty British and five Belgian tugs. As in the case of

The 1929 Toronto harbour tug *Rouille* (214 tons, 1000hp) had a distinguished career during the war fighting dangerous fires involving ammunition as the Halifax Fire Department's fireboat. She then went on to less exciting private sector dredging operations. (Public Archives of Nova Scotia)

the destroyers, channel ferries and small pleasure craft, not all of them made it home again.

Some of Britain's big rescue and salvage tugs were already stationed at Dover and other English Channel ports for wartime duty under government control. Well-known tugs like *Simla*, *Cervia*, *Gondia* and *Roman* responded under the leadership of *Lady Brassey*, famous as the peacetime Dover Rescue Tug, whose territory included the notorious Goodwin Sands. She was a large tug-tender with two stacks. The tugs were trying to get bargeloads of food and supplies to the troops on the beach as well as help move the evacuation

ships in and out of the ports. All the while, they dodged bombs, magnetic mines and shelling from artillery. Sometimes, on the way over, they might have a single Lewis gun for protection. On the way home it was usually augmented by several more of these machine guns in the hands of the returning soldiers.

The great company names in the towing business on the Thames—Alexander, Watkins, Gamecock, Elliot and Gaselee—sent all their tugs around to Dover. There was only one docking tug left in the huge port of London. A little procession of five Belgian tugs, fleeing their abandoned ports, came down to help in Dunkirk

Seagoing rescue tugs were in demand to help in the Normandy invasion. *Empire John* towed Mulberry pierheads and pontoons across the channel, then went to Sydney, Nova Scotia. Firefighting capability was provided in these largest ocean rescue boats of the Empire class. (John Weeks Collection)

Harbour. They continued through shot and shell all through Operation Dynamo, until, on the last day, all had been sunk except *Goliath*, which finally departed for Dover carrying the surviving crew members.

A little later, Adolph Hitler was peering through binoculars at the clearly visible cliffs of Dover. He faced the same problem as had Napoleon and Philip of Spain. All three were prevented from marching on England by a few miles of currents, tides, winds and waves, augmented by the Royal Navy. The problem was to get 100,000 invading soldiers across the Channel very quickly, then resupply and reinforce them.

A plan by Grand Admiral Raeder of the Kriegsmarine compromised on a need for 115 transport vessels, 1161 motorboats, 1722 barges and 471 tugs. On the last item, the best he could do was 386 tugs, and it caused serious worries about the German war production system. Tug and barge traffic on the canals and rivers of Europe was vital to their war effort. While the British kept wondering when they would come, William L. Shirer, the American correspondent, visited the scene from the German side. He concluded that there were simply too few tugs and barges for an ambitious attempt to invade Britain. Soon, Hitler turned his attention eastward and the tugs and barges filtered back into the continental supply system.

The British Build Tugs

THE FORCED PACE OF GREATLY EXPANDING NAVIES and merchant shipping fleets, in addition to many new war-related jobs and plans for huge seaborne invasion operations, created heavy demands for the services of tugs. A thorough beating of the bushes in the beginning for idle vessels helped only a little. As in the First World War, tugs were found useful for more than their designed service. The sturdy, manoeuverable vessels were pressed into use as patrol and inspection vessels at port entrances, for coastal minelaying, as barrage balloon platforms and a variety of odd jobs.

The war at sea developed into a desperate struggle to keep open the critical sea lanes for supply convoys moving across the Atlantic and south around Africa. The losses of shipping to German U-boats and bombers rose to alarming levels and the necessity of recovering damaged vessels became an important part of the battle. Large ocean and coastal rescue tugs were soon at a premium.

The convoy system was set up without delay at the beginning of the Second World War. The British concentrated harbour tugs on the Clyde to handle this activity and moved requisitioned ocean-going tugs to strategic ports for the rescue of damaged ships off the coasts.

Many of the numerous tugs built by the British government in the Great War had been disposed of, serving in lieu of new private sector construction in the intervening years. Some tugs had found their way to South America, the Far East and Australasia. For the new war, about 150 requisitioned tugs were marshalled, some purchased from overseas, including from Canada. In addition there were German prizes and boats that escaped from occupied Europe.

At the time of Dunkirk, when the Low Countries were over-run, most of the famed Dutch towing fleet and some Belgian tugs escaped to join the British war effort. Some Dutch salvage tugs had, in fact, been on station in various foreign ports. Their services became very welcome as the sea war produced heavy shipping casualties, bringing a need to recover and repair those that could be saved from the bottom. The Smit tug *Thames*, for instance, sailed from her station at Gibraltar to the aid of the stricken aircraft carrier HMS *Ark Royal* when the enemy finally did torpedo her in November 1941.

Thames took the heavily listing carrier in tow, while the Admiralty tug *Saint Day* and the destroyer *Laforey* helped on the vain but almost successful salvage operation. *Thames* continued to tow even after the increasing list caused pumping attempts to be abandoned and the remaining personnel of the 1600-man crew were removed. Thirty miles short of Gibraltar, *Ark Royal* rolled over and went down in 1000 fathoms.

Of the numerous tugs built during the First World War, the RN still retained five of the big two stack Rollicker class, very powerful for the day at 4500 horsepower. There were also eight of the numerous Saints left, although *Saint Abbs* was lost at Dunkirk. New in the late 1930s were six 840-ton, twin screw steam tugs of the Brigand class. For ocean rescue duties, they produced 3000ihp. For work around ports and naval bases there were sixteen old paddle-tugs.

Major construction programs for tugs got underway after the building of large numbers of corvettes was well in hand. A number of steam tugs of conventional British design were built for the Ministry of War Transport by sixteen builders. These tugs all had names with the prefix "Empire" as did large numbers of freighters built under similar programs. The tugs were all

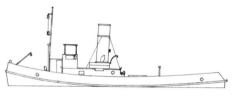

TID Class tug (Author's sketch)

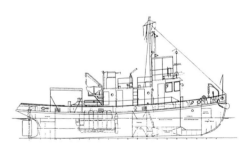

TANAC tug (German & Milne)

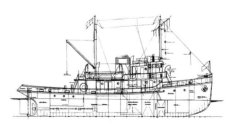

Norton (German & Milne and Maritime Museum of Great Lakes)

single-screw driven by triple expansion steam engines and in sizes classed as: "Deep Sea," 135 feet long, "Coastwise" at 105 to 115 feet and "Estuary," 90 feet. Most were coal-fired, some by oil, and their power ranged from 600 to 1200ihp. The larger Empires were equipped for firefighting and salvage; however, all were intended primarily for ship handling. Many were involved in the placing of the Arromanches spud pierheads and pontoons for the Normandy landings as later described.

The Empire tugs, large and small, were a broad class based on established designs to save time and were eminently successful. At war's end, they formed a replacement fleet for the now worn-out, prewar civilian tugs, until the arrival of the more powerful and economical postwar breed of diesel-powered tugs. Some went to Canada, including *Empire John* to Sydney, Nova Scotia, and, third-hand, *Empires Spruce* (renamed *Irving Oak*), *Jenny* (*Irving Teak*) and *Darby* (*Irving Beach*) to Saint John. Dieselized Empires still ply their trade in many parts of the world. *Empire Sandy*, a Deep Sea Type brought to Lake Superior for log towing, is unrecognizable in her present incarnation as a three-masted, excursion sailing vessel based at Toronto on Lake Ontario. The Empires were produced between 1942 and 1945, ranging from 143 to 274 tons.

Mass production of smaller harbour tugs was carried out in the type known as TID tugs (possibly meaning "Tug Invasion Duty"). Inland contractors prefabricated them in eight sections of a maximum length of 10 feet and weight of 10 tons. The components were transported to the coast, then assembled on temporary ways. There were 182 produced, between 1943 and 1946. At the peak, one was completed every four and a half days.

The TIDs were simple hard chine hulls for easy fabrication, half of them oil and half coal fired, with 220ihp compound steam engines, most having the open bridge typical of British harbour tugs. They were 54 tons and 65 feet long, easily recognizable by their squared-off sterns. Small jobs like harbour lighterage were their assignment. For all their small size and quick construction, the TIDs ranged far, wide and for a long time. Three served for years on the Saint John River in Canada as *Irving Pine*, *Irving Fir* and *Irving Elm*, refitted with 500hp diesel engines and enclosed wheelhouses. The *Pine* remained in service until 1992. One is preserved in Britain and runs under steam occasionally.

Powerful new rescue tugs were acquired for the Royal Navy. Eight, twin-diesel, 1100-ton, Bustler class vessels of 3020 bhp, having a range of 5000 miles and capable of 16 knots were produced between 1942 and 1944 to accompany the North Atlantic

The first war-program tugs to ease the strain in Canadian naval ports were little yard tugs like *Beamsville* of the Ville class built by Russel Brothers in Owen Sound, Ontario. Some were still operating in civilian and government service in the late 1980s. (Author's Collection)

convoys. The 205-foot tugs were very effective in this role, picking up crippled ships and often bulging with survivors of torpedoed vessels. One was lost in the war. *Hesperia* tried to hold a floating dock off a lee shore onto which it was being blown in a storm. She failed and was swept onshore by the dock. These fine tugs were in demand by the private sector after the war. *Samsonia* of this class served for a time after the war at Halifax as the salvage tug *Foundation Josephine*.

Numerous steam tugs were operated by the Admiralty in the Assurance class, built between 1940 and 1943. They had a triple-expansion steam engine of 1350ihp. Five out of twenty-one of these boats were lost on war service. There were also six Envoy class steam tugs of 1700ihp built in 1944. Four more tugs of the Nimble class, completed only in 1945, were 3500ihp, steam-powered, twin-screw tugs capable of 16 knots. American production capabilities were capitalized on by the British in the acquisition of eighteen ocean-going tugs of 1875bhp, with diesel-electric drive, designated by the USN as BAT type, and four wooden hulled, Director class steam tugs of the same power.

Canadian Tug Production

The Royal Canadian Navy had no tugs at the beginning of the Second World War. The Canadian government operated a few tugs in the Department of Transport and the Department of Marine. A naval building program was set up by the Department of Munitions and Supply using inland contractors on the St. Lawrence and Great Lakes. The first small tugs came into service in 1943, after first priority in shipbuilding had gone to the corvette and minesweeper programs.

As in the case of the fighting ships, an astonishing number of tugs were turned out by inexperienced shipyards and steel bridge fabricators of Canada. In 1943, forty-five tugs were built. In 1944 the number was 137 and in 1945 there were 72 produced. The Department of Munitions and Supply records show that 254 tugs were built in the war program, but this figure certainly includes some other auxiliary vessels. Almost all were steel hulled and diesel propelled with a single screw. Towards the end of the war, Munitions and Supply also completed a contract with the British government to produce eighteen Warrior class steam tugs. It is noteworthy that no large, ocean-going tugs for salvage or rescue were built or acquired during the war for naval or government use. Such work was left to the RN and one private Canadian salvage firm, Foundation Maritime, Ltd.

The first new tugs to come to the aid of the Navy, whose ship handling problems were becoming exacerbated by the presence of dozens of new warships, were the fifteen little, 40-foot, 150bhp, steel yard tugs of the Ville class (e.g. *Otterville, Marysville, Merrickville* and *Beamsville*). These were built in the tug specialist Russel Brothers shipyard, now in Owen Sound, Ontario, to work mainly at Halifax and Esquimalt. They arrived on the scene in 1943 and 1944 and were fine for handling corvettes, but too small to handle berthing of larger ships. Three, even smaller, wooden tugs of 135hp were also built. It was a relief for the naval authorities, in Halifax particularly, when boats of a little larger type appeared on the scene. These were the 102-ton, 80-foot, Glens of 300hp, (e.g. *Glenmont, Glenvalley, Glenada, Glenside*) built by Russel Brothers and Canadian Dredge and Dock Company of Kingston. Eventually, there were sixteen of these diesel harbour tugs built of steel and four of wood, three of which were built on the West Coast, including *Glenshiel* and *Glendevon*.

The Glen class tugs proved very useful, doing nine knots on their single Vivian or Enterprise engine. Although they did venture out on coastal trips at times, they were really only suited for harbour work, having very low freeboard and not being noted for stability. In war, and later peacetime service, several were capsized. The first built were known as "long-house Glens," because of their long deckhouse. The design was then modified for greater stability, resulting in the "short-house" or "revised" Glens. Some of this tug class went to private companies after the war and some were used by government agencies. Three, renamed *Bansturdy, Banswift* and *Bansaga*, became berthing tugs for Foundation Maritime at Halifax and Port Alfred. A few were still operating in the private sector in the late 1990s, notably five in service with McKeil Marine Limited of Hamilton, Ont.

These tugs were still too small for large ship handling under strenuous conditions. Battleships, cruisers and aircraft carriers were more and more on the scene in Canadian East Coast ports. There was also a need for tugs that could venture to sea with some confidence, at least for some coastal trips.

For this purpose, the RCN was provided eventually with six 1000bhp diesel tugs of the Norton class (*Riverton, Alberton, Beaverton, Heatherton,* and *Clifton*). They were 104 feet long and 462 tons, capable of 11 knots. They arrived on the scene in 1944 from the builders, Canadian Bridge Company. One was in the McKeil Marine fleet after some years as *Techno-St.Laurent* at Quebec and Remorqueurs de Trois Rivières has *Heatherton*, now *Robert H*.

The Glen class were bigger tugs built for the Royal Canadian Navy (102 tons, 300 hp), but these were still low powered for handling large ships. This "long house" Glen is seen in peacetime service at Halifax as *Banswift* of Foundation Maritime Ltd. (Maritime Museum of the Atlantic, Wetmore Photo MP23.16.1)

A sturdier RCN tug was the "short house," or revised, Glen type. This is *Glenevis*, little changed in appearance from her navy days, one of several still in operation with McKeil Marine of Hamilton, Ontario. (McKeil Marine, Wayne Farrar Photo)

In 1944, the Canadian shipbuilding program shifted emphasis to large scale production of landing craft and tugs in anticipation of the major amphibious operations that were in the offing. The bulk of the 137 vessels classed as tugs and auxiliaries that Canada built in this year appear to have been mass produced, nameless little 50-to 60-ton tugs. They were turned out for the British government, mainly by Canadian Bridge Company and Central Bridge Company in Ontario, although some were built by Russel Brothers. Twenty-two were built of wood by small east coast boat yards. The

total number built in this tug class, called Tanacs, is elusive, possibly in excess of 100. They had 240 to 270bhp diesel engines, usually Vivian, and were shipped out of the country, ultimately, in war and peace finding their way around the world. (One was commissioned in Australia as HMS *Wooloomooloo* to serve in Hong Kong.)

They went as deckloads to Britain and the Mediterranean, as well as sailing through the Erie and Chicago Canals to American government destinations. A few were retrieved for civilian service in Canada after the war. Much modified, usually with a new wheel-

Last of the wartime tug types built for the Canadian navy were the six 1944 Norton Class of 1000bhp, capable of coastal operations. They were 462 tons, ice-strengthened and equipped for salvage, serving the navy well long after the war ended. This is *Birchton* on trials. (German & Milne Ltd, Naval Architects)

house atop the old, they were still operating well into the 1990s, half a dozen hauling logs in the sixties on the Saint John River in New Brunswick. These tugs had been given the names of Canadian cities, but changed to the usual Irving tree names. *Irving Spruce* (ex-*Quebec*), the longest surviving, had been to France for war work before retiring to a long career on the pastoral Saint John, her power boosted to 450bhp. Five other Tanacs hauled sand barges from Lake of Two Mountains to Montreal before entering long service with McKeil out of Hamilton on Lake Ontario (*Lac Como, Lac Erie, Lac Manitoba* and *Lac Vancouver*).

Concern for fire risks on ships and in the dock areas prompted the modification of three Tanacs as naval fireboats. They were fitted with sponsons for greater stability, 3000gpm in pumping capacity and two large monitor nozzles. They were stationed at Halifax, Esquimault and St. John's, remaining in service into the 1960s.

In a contract with the British Ministry of War Transport, eighteen harbour-coastal steam tugs were built by Midland Shipyards and Canadian Shipbuilding Company of Kingston, Ontario. They were ordered in May 1944; delivery was between April 1945 and October of 1946. They were too late for any war service and the British government took over thirteen only, the others being put up for disposal. Called the Warrior class after the 1935 British prototype, but with the name prefix "Rock," these were fine harbour and berthing tugs of typical British pre-war design.

The Rocks were 233-ton coal burners with a triple-expansion engine producing 1000ihp. These tugs were sold overseas for the most part, travelling under their own power. Three went to Russia, at least two to South Africa, several to Hong Kong and Sydney. Two saw long service in Eastern Canada. *Rockswift* became *Ocean Rockswift*, a berthing tug at Saint John until about 1960. Another became *Maritime Guardian*, then *Foundation Vera*, used for ship berthing and salvage operations out of Halifax.

American Tugs Join the Fray

Although the Americans came into the European and North Atlantic war officially only after it had been underway for over two years, they quickly developed the same urgent need for tugs. The tough little ship handlers were required in the maintenance of the "arsenal of democracy's" supply lines to its Allies and war campaigns across the Atlantic. The incredible American war production machine also managed to turn out a procession of large tugs for the use of the hard pressed UK under Lend-Lease. These consisted of the eighteen BAT type, 1800hp diesel-electric powered tugs and four wooden, 1360-ton, Director class steam tugs of 1875ihp in 1943. In turn, the US government received numerous Tanac yard tugs from Canada.

However, the United States was also fighting another war in the Pacific Ocean, one that involved sea transport over distances of grand proportions. In much of this ocean, harbour facilities were

Large numbers of originally nameless Tanac type tugs like *Irving Spruce* were produced in Canada and exported to the European theatre and the U.S. Some had long peacetime use in Canada, even into the 1990s with Atlantic Towing on the Saint John River system and McKeil Marine on the Great Lakes. (John Weeks Collection)

noncxistent. Air bases, docks, fuelling and supply centres had to be built from scratch on isolated islands all around the Pacific rim.

Even before the war with Japan, efforts to bolster their Pacific defences found the U.S. military looking to the tug for assistance in transportation and building of facilities. The prominent Foss Launch and Tug Company of Tacoma, Washington, experienced in long distance barge hauling, had contracts on USN projects as early as 1939. Several small tugs of this company were towed by freighter to Pacific islands to work on naval facilities.

One was *Justine Foss*, a wooden boat built in 1930, only 57 feet long, with a 200bhp diesel engine. But, like many of the Pacific Coast tugs, she often undertook lengthy coastal trips with barges, despite her large glass windows and low freeboard. The range of Southern California to Alaska was accepted as being in her operating territory. In 1940 she sailed as far as Kodiak.

Not long before Pearl Harbor, *Justine Foss* underwent tow by freighter, not carrying enough fuel herself, to join three other Foss tugs in the Central Pacific. On the leg from San Francisco to Honolulu, the tow parted in bad weather and she pushed on to Hawaii on her own power. Taken under tow again for Wake Island, her destination, the towline parted once more. Again, little *Justine* forged ahead on her own.

At Wake, the Foss tug was employed lightering materials from large vessels located outside the lagoon during the build-up of the naval base. But the project was overtaken by the attack on Pearl Harbor. There were air attacks on Wake Island and the Japanese came ashore on 23 December, capturing the 500-man force of marines and 500 civilian workers.

The Americans were sent away to prison camps, except for a few workmen and the *Justine's* crew, kept to lighter Japanese ships.

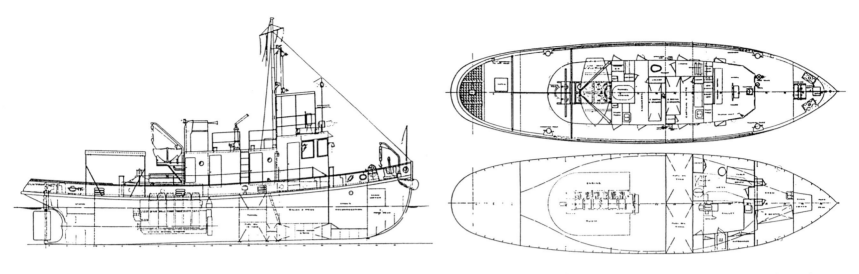

Tanac tug - A Canadian mass produced wartime harbour tug for invasion duty, with 6-cylinder diesel engine and five-man crew accommodation. (German & Milne and Maritime Museum of Great Lakes)

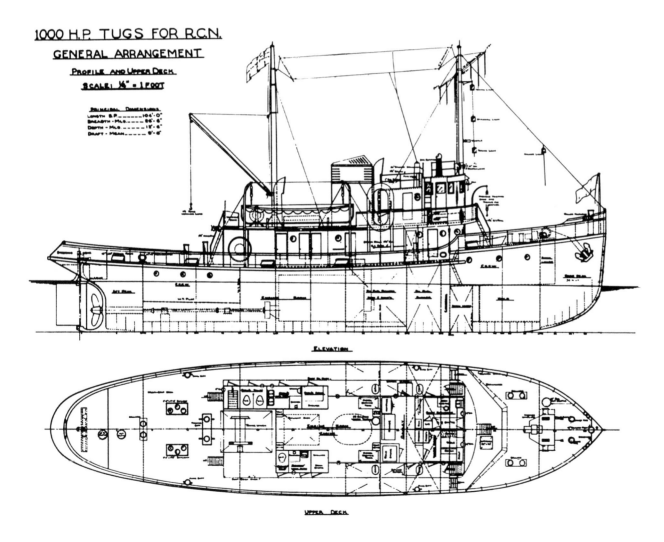

Norton - A Class of RCN diesel tug 1000hp produced late in the second world war. (German & Milne and Maritime Museum of Great Lakes)

Prominent among the many wartime program tugs in Britain were the steam powered Empire types. Here is the medium sized *Empire Jenny* placed in service as *Irving Teak*, a harbour tug for Atlantic Towing Limited in Saint John in 1961. (Atlantic Towing Ltd., Wilson Studio)

When the job was finished, *Justine Foss* was sunk and her crew shot. Two other Foss tugs on assignment there had managed to escape earlier.

In the build-up of Pacific rim defences before Pearl Harbor and after, the United States Army launched a large-scale defensive effort against the Japanese in Alaska and out along the Aleutian Islands chain. The Pacific Northwest encouraged coastal marine traffic because of the coexisting rugged mountain chains and the sheltered Inside Passage along the British Columbia and Alaska Panhandle coast. There was a well developed tug and barge trade, carrying supplies northward and raw materials south. Companies like Foss, from Puget Sound to San Francisco, knew the territory and were prepared to carry the construction and war materials.

Because of this resource and in the interest of saving scarce shipping, the U.S. Army Transport Service (ATS) had numbers of tugs and barges built for the Alaskan route to counter the scarcity of available freighters. Many of these tugs were operated for the ATS by the established tug firms.

One class of ATS tug became famous for dependability, seaworthiness and pulling power during the Second World War, in commercial service after the war and even in the Vietnam War. This was the Miki, or Hawaiian type. These, large for the day, were wooden diesel tugs built in 1943 and 1944 in a style compatible with Pacific Northwest traditions. They were built not only for the Alaskan route, but also to meet Gulf of Mexico and Atlantic Coast service requirements.

As in the British war models, a successful existing prototype was sought. The result was a modified version of a 1929 tug that had been designed in Seattle for a Honolulu firm, named *Mikimi*. Authorized in 1942, 61 tugs of the class were built by ten shipyards on both coasts. On the East Coast, ten were built of oak and pine. On the West, it was fir and Alaska cedar for the other fifty-one.

Some Miki class tugs were twin screw and called "Mikimiki's," but all the later ones were single screw. Their power, at 1500bhp, was considered ample then, and many heavy ocean tows were undertaken during and after the war, even in the Korean and

MEETING WARTIME DEMANDS

The largest Canadian war-built tugs were the 12 Warrior class steam tugs built on the Great Lakes for the British Ministry of War Transport. Some were delivered to the United Kingdom, but none saw war service. *Rockswift* is seen in the livery of Saint John Tugboat Company, her last peacetime owners, as *Ocean Rockswift*. (John Weeks Collection)

Vietnamese theatres. They became obsolete by the early 1960s in the face of competition from much higher powered tugs of a new generation. While a crew of eighteen was customary in army service, postwar commercial service saw this cut to ten, partly due to such mechanical refinements as wheelhouse engine control and an automatic dishwasher in the galley. Two Mikimikis went to the Canadian Tugboat Company and one to Young & Gore, both Vancouver operators.

The Alaskan defence work eased off early in the war, but the Mikis became a fixture in West Coast commercial runs for many years under both American and Canadian owners. They went to sea in all kinds of weather and, in the tradition of that coast, had no raised forecastle. They just battened down and let the seas run over them.

Some of the smallest tugs produced for the U.S. Army were not so successful, being hurried designs for hurried construction. They suffered faults such as a lack of baffling in their fuel tanks that made them jerky rollers in a sea. But another very successful class of U.S. Army tugs were 88-footers of 600hp. Looking like good-sized harbour tugs, they nevertheless sailed to Alaska and even braved the Bering Sea on their vital military support operation.

There was also another, bigger class of army tug, a steam-powered 149-footer, an ocean-going boat that travelled all over the Pacific rim and along the coasts of continental USA, Alaska and Japan.

The Pacific War

The US Navy, building great new battle fleets for waging war in both the Atlantic and Pacific, required many tugs, from large fleet and rescue types to small harbour "yard" tugs. In the former category there was the 1943-44 Abnaki class of 69 vessels. They were intended to accompany the fleet on its long expeditions in the Pacific, providing towing and salvage service. Four diesel engines coupled to an electric drive provided a speed of 16 knots and 3000 horsepower. This power proved rather light, however, on jobs like handling a disabled aircraft carrier. A three-inch gun was mounted on the Abnakis. In spite of their weakness in power, these 1280-ton, 205-foot tugs have remained in service for many years in a number of navies all over the world, as well as a few remaining on the USN lists.

A second large USN class was the wooden ATR Type steam tug of 850 tons of which 75 were built in 1942-43. With 1500hp triple-expansion engines, they were designed for quick construction to fill

Island Tug and Barge's *La Brise*, formerly *Sea Giant*, a long-lasting British Columbia coastal tug was one of the many wooden wartime tugs built by the U.S. for defence of the Alaskan coast. Built in Texas in 1944, these 182-tonners had an eight-cylinder oil engine. (Bob Martin, Pacific Coast Tug Society)

the urgent needs of the early years. They were similar in size and power to an existing sixteen Cormorant class steam tugs built at the end of the First World War.

A heavy convoy assistance class of ocean-going tugs was the ATA Type of 1943, powered by two 900bhp diesel-electric sets driving two motors and screws. They were 135 feet long and had a raised forecastle in the North Atlantic style. These tugs were noted for problems with their complicated engine electrical systems, but they got around. One served on loan as HMS *Mindful*, was returned to the USN as ATR 48, became *Gay Moran* in 1947, then served as *Margaret Foss* in Vietnam and on the Alaska Run. Another ATR was

for a time engaged out of Halifax on many tough salvage and rescue jobs as *Foundation Lillian*.

Some fine-performance harbour tugs of 500hp, the YTL 360s, saw widely scattered service, as did a class of 1270hp twin-screw tugs equipped with fire pumps and monitors. Both became popular as good ship-berthing tugs after the war.

The stupendous naval forces, including a large British carrier and battleship squadron, that launched the final Okinawa campaign was provided with the ultimate in rescue and salvage support. It was needed: the Japanese kamikaze planes caused heavy damage. The logistics support group of the American Fifth Fleet in

Seaspan Chinook, preserved as the "company yacht" by Seaspan International of Vancouver, was built in New York in 1943, one of a series of diesel powered, wooden hulled ocean going tugs for the U.S. Navy. (Bob Martin, Pacific Coast Tug Society)

the South Pacific included twelve fleet tugs, four ocean tugs and three ocean rescue tugs. They operated from Base Kerama Retto, near Okinawa. A logistics support screen for escort duty consisted of ten fleet, five ocean and eight ATR tugs along with two salvage vessels. Their base was at Ulithi Island Base, south of Guam. The Royal Navy brought along two rescue tugs of their own. Damaged and powerless vessels, thousands of miles from regular repair bases, were picked up and taken to floating docks and repair ships at these forward bases. In the large roadstead at Kerama, an out-island of Okinawa, there were fourteen different kinds of help vessels, from escort carriers to floating docks. Emergency responses were made with a tug escorted by a destroyer.

The European Theatre

As the tide of war turned, the western Allies went on the offensive with large amphibious forces, well equipped armadas roaming the seas in each theatre of operation. They sailed forth with hitherto undreamed-of numbers of aircraft carriers, battleships and cruisers, along with attack transports, landing craft and support auxiliaries of every conceivable type.

In September 1943, during the fierce battle off the Salerno landings, a German aircraft put a 3000-pound guided bomb into the British battleship *Warspite's* vital innards. One boiler room was demolished and four of the other five flooded. All power was out, steam pressure gone, there was no steering and flooding increased the hitherto lucky ship's draft by five feet. She was only a few miles from Salerno and could be attacked again at any time.

The U.S. Navy rescue tug *Hopi* picked up the tow and *Warspite* moved slowly out of Salerno Bay towards the Strait of Messina. Soon two more American tugs arrived, *Moreno* and *Narragansett*. The three could only keep their sluggish tow moving at four knots. She was a dead and silent ship except when there was an air attack and her anti-aircraft batteries opened up. The normal 33,000-ton displacement of the battleship was now equivalent to almost 40,000 tons.

An attempt to tow *Warspite* with the light cruiser HMS *Euryalis* failed because the towing wire parted, a common result of such tactics. Two British tugs, *Nimble* and *Oriana* then joined, accompanied by the salvage vessel *Salveda*. The tidal current through the Strait was so strong that all towlines broke and *Warspite* was carried

Another series of large ocean tugs for the American war effort was propelled by twin, 12-cylinder diesel-electric sets. They were 136 feet long and 514 tons. They were a little temperamental. One became *Noord Holland* of Bureau Wijsmuller after the war. (Nationaal Sleepvaart Museum, Maassluis)

through broadside. Finally she was brought under control and headed for Malta, three tugs towing, two lashed on her quarters and *Salveda* on a stern line to steer.

The climax of the colossal shipbuilding effort, after which all seemed anticlimactic, was the invasion of Normandy in June 1944. For the tugs it was their hour in the sun. They followed up the naval, army and air force assault on the shores of France with the building of two complete seaports. These instant harbours received the enormous flow of war materiel required to keep the Allied armies in the field. They were the key to a bold scheme to avoid critical dependence upon capturing and making usable one or more French seaports. The Allies decided that they should build their own ports at a point of landing where they would not be expected, towing over the necessary parts for two unloading ports. These would be capable of accommodating numbers of full-sized

freighters. There would be a port at St. Laurent for the American Omaha Beach (Mulberry A), and for the British Gold and Sword and Canadian Juno Beaches at Arromanches (Mulberry B).

Assembled and ready two weeks before D-Day were sixty old ships that were to steam to the Normandy beachhead immediately after the first landings and be sunk in lines, forming breakwaters offshore. After them would come 146 Phoenix caissons, enormous concrete boxes of 1500 to 6000 tons. Their seacocks were to be opened and in their sunken positions five and a half miles of breakwaters were to be formed. To do this, 1.5 million tons of caissons and pontoons had to be delivered. It was, of course, a job for tugs— many, many tugs.

Inside the breakwaters a variety of unloading pontoons and floating roadways would be installed to carry the millions of tons of supplies and vehicles ashore. Under the code name "Pluto," a 1650-

Johnstone Straits of Straits Towing in British Columbia was one of the highly successful and far ranging 117-foot, Miki type of wooden war-production tugs. They did just as well in the Korean and Vietnam operations and West Coast commercial service. (Bob Martin, Pacific Coast Tug Society)

For the logistical maintenance of large numbers of ships scattered across the Pacific Ocean the variety of salvage tugs included several very large vessels like this one (seen later as *Sudbury II* ex-*Cambrian Salvor*), salvage vessel of Island Tug and Barge Ltd., Victoria. (Pacific Coast Tug Society)

Seagoing rescue tugs were in demand to help in the Normandy invasion. *Empire John* towed Mulberry pierheads and pontoons across the channel, then went to Sydney, Nova Scotia. Firefighting capability was provided in these largest ocean rescue boats of the Empire class. (John Weeks Collection)

tonne drum holding 60 miles of 3-inch gasoline pipeline was ready for towing across the water, paying out the pipe as it went. The drum was in the charge of the 4000hp British tugs *Bustler* and *Marauder*. They could tow it singly or together at five to seven knots.

In the months leading up to the invasion, hordes of tugs were busy in numerous British ports, helping with the construction and assembly of the Mulberry port components. Among them were the newest of the war program tugs, together with all sorts going back to the 1867-built wooden paddler *Troon*, still on the job. To move the many parts across 90 miles of water to their destination it was first estimated that 130 tugs of at least 450hp, would be required. Eventually, it was decided that 200 were needed, but there were only 420 tugs in the UK and only 132 of them available for the invasion. To tow the Mulberry components across 108 tugs were assigned and

ten, helped by six corvettes, assisted in positioning the blockships. In charge of organizing the Mulberry tows was Admiral Edmond J. Moran, of the famous Moran Towboat Company in New York.

D-Day came and the amphibious forces stormed the beaches, consolidating their beachhead. On D+1, Operation Gooseberry was carried out. This was the arrival of the old blockships. They wheezed in under their own power, shepherded by their escort of ten tugs and six corvettes. Included among the ships that sacrificed themselves by sinking in a line to protect the landing areas were two old battleships, the French *Courbet* and British *Centurion*. The powerful Admiralty Bustler class tugs *Samsonia* (later *Foundation Josephine*) and *Growler* struggled to control the ponderous *Courbet* and get her in line, but all ships finally dropped into their assigned places in spite of the boisterous seas.

One of many large ex-American war
vessels to become salvage tugs in
postwar commercial service, *Foundation
Josephine* was built in 1944 and
changed hands several times in her
career. This type was wooden, 861 tons,
with a 12-cylinder oil engine coupled to
an electric motor. (Maritime Museum of
the Atlantic Wetmore N13,536)

A fine modern Dutch diesel salvage tug built in 1938 was *Thames*, stationed at Gibraltar. This Smit tug remained in Allied war service and was trying to get the torpedoed *Ark Royal* into port when the British aircraft carrier finally rolled over and sank. (Stichting Nationaal Sleepvaart Museum)

Meantime, the world's greatest towing operation was underway. The 1.5 million tons of Mulberry parts, a giant "Lego" set, were arriving from the Sussex coast and the Solent in England. On D+2, as the last blockships sank into position, the big Phoenix caissons were coming into their places to be held precisely there while the seacocks were opened. The weather was deteriorating so the giant concrete boxes were hard to control, but all of Phase One was complete by D+5 at St. Laurent and D+6 at Arromanches. There were now solid piers in lines parallel to the shore.

Another million and a half tonnes were yet to come. Floating roadways, designated "Whales," were to be pulled in by 150 tugs starting on D+12 (June 18). Watching the stormy weather with concern, Admiral Tennant, in charge of the job, decided to dispatch twenty-two tows on D+13 as the seas had abated somewhat. Unfortunately, a powerful Nor'easter gale swept down the Channel, striking the tugs and their tows when they were too far out to turn back. The tug masters fought hard to control and hold onto their awkward charges, but one by one the towlines snapped and the floating pontoon structures were carried away, to sink or be dashed ashore on the Normandy coast. Only one of these tows got through intact.

The storm raged, turning into the worst in 40 years. Small craft in the harbours were thrown ashore, 800 landing craft being stranded high and dry. Amazingly, 600 of them were rapidly refloated and sent on their way for the essential additional trips. The salvage job in the wake of the storm was a greater trial for the tugs than the storm itself. The remaining vessels were recovered in another two weeks.

The violent seas had smashed into the two artificial harbours. Some of the blockships forming the outer barrier broke their backs,

From war to a relatively peaceful existence; that was the lot of the Empire type ocean-going tug *Justice*, waiting for a call as government tug at Hamilton, Bermuda. (Author's Collection)

the seas sweeping over their decks. At Mulberry A, the American port, there was devastation. The US caissons had been put together with gaps between them, allowing the storm to break up the wall, causing greater damage. The British Mulberry had the advantage of some protection from the Calvados Reef. Mulberry A was smashed and had to be abandoned, its surviving equipment being moved to Mulberry B. In any case, the Americans overran the Cotentin Peninsula and, by June 27, captured the Port of Cherbourg, much earlier than expected and relatively intact.

The demand for tugs appears to have remained high after the initial invasion and construction of the Mulberry harbours, doubtless for maintaining supply lines and rehabilitating liberated ports. The Americans brought over more of their vast war production of these so highly useful craft, now sliding down the ways in a stream. Likely these included some of the little Canadian tugs from Ontario. Two convoys serve as examples.

On 23 July, eleven of the highly successful U.S. Army Transport Service Miki Class wooden tugs left New York for Falmouth, a journey of 3000 miles. They were towing ten small tugs and several railcar floats, while accompanied by a refuelling tanker. The weather and trip were easy. Not so for another tug convoy that left the U.S. for Falmouth on 19 September. In the convoy were an ATS 141-foot steam tug and nine other large tugs. The tows included sixteen car floats, twelve deck cargo barges, sixteen small tugs and sixteen self-propelled yard oilers. The convoy was six miles across. Beset by storm after storm, towlines parted or fouled propellers, the small tugs plunged badly under tow and the runners aboard the tows were tossed about severely. There was no enemy action other than that of the sea itself, but three small tugs, eight car floats and five barges were lost along the way.

When the fighting stopped in 1945, the tugs disappeared into the massive projects of rehabilitation and supply for the devastated European continent. Some made their way back across the Atlantic, in fact spreading around the world in naval and commercial service. Some are still at work.

Point Viking in the traditional livery of Eastern Canada Coastal ploughs into a headwind passing George's Island at Halifax. As *Foundation Viking*, she was launched at Lauzon, Quebec, on the same day in 1963 with three sister ships of the V class. (Mac Mackay)

Point Vim and *Point Vigour* together pit 3000 horsepower against the side of a cruise ship. Newer tugs of the ECTUG fleet individually put out much more power. (Mac Mackay)

A large container ship is pulled away from the terminal in Halifax in a cold misty sunrise. In the foreground is *Point Halifax*, pulling backward in modern ASD tug style; behind her, the older *Point Vibert* pulls ahead on a traditional stern towing hook. (Keith Vaughan)

A pioneer in navigation through heavy ice in the eastern Arctic and Gulf of St. Lawrence was the ice-rated *Irving (now Atlantic) Birch* of Atlantic Towing. A single variable pitch, Kort nozzle screw with a 3750bhp Nohab diesel drive got her through some risky ice situations. She was built at Saint John Shipbuilding in 1967. (John Weeks Collection)

Irving Teak is a 265-ton, 2250bhp docking tug at Saint John for Atlantic Towing Limited. She was acquired from Jurong Shipyard of Singapore in 1979, and is powered by two Deutz diesels. (John Weeks Collection)

The Canadian Coast Guard ice breaker *Louis St. Laurent* is started on a dead tow from Saint John by *Irving Maple* and *Irving Birch*. The common system of connecting towlines to the anchor cables is shown. Once in open waters, the towing wires will be lengthened out on the tugs' towing winches. Both ice-rated tugs have carried out lengthy tows to the far north. (John Weeks Collection)

An aerial view of a very large tanker moored at the Canaport Buoy near Saint John, which provides a deepwater terminal using an underwater pipeline for moving the cargo on and off shore. A tug holds the tanker in position and tenders service the vessel. (Wilson Studios)

A cable layer prepares to lay a power cable to Campobello Island on Passamaquoddy Bay with the assistance of tugs *Irving Beech* and *Irving Oak* from the Atlantic Towing harbour fleet. (New Brunswick Power)

Stormont, a busy tug with McKeil Marine, is caught in one of the heavy sea conditions that can occur on the Great Lakes. With their broad beam and low centre of gravity, tugs can weather such conditions if well battened down. (Dan Conway)

A small harbour tug at Victoria, 465bhp *Seaspan Rocket*, demonstrates her firefighting capabilities in 1987. Tug companies often collaborate with local port fire departments providing a valuable adjunct on the seaward side of a ship or pier fire. (Gilles Proulx)

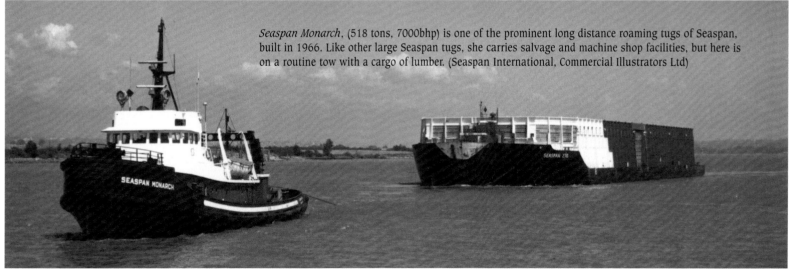

Seaspan Monarch, (518 tons, 7000bhp) is one of the prominent long distance roaming tugs of Seaspan, built in 1966. Like other large Seaspan tugs, she carries salvage and machine shop facilities, but here is on a routine tow with a cargo of lumber. (Seaspan International, Commercial Illustrators Ltd)

Tending the world's largest self loading and dumping log barge on the coast of Vancouver Island in 1988 is *Seaspan Commodore* (1974, 657 tons, 5750bhp from twin 16-cylinder GM diesels), an oceangoing tug that has circumnavigated the world pursuing varied jobs. (Author's Collection)

One of the traditionally difficult tows, a big floating drydock arrives in Vancouver Harbour under tow of *Dahlia,* a very large Japanese tug, while local tugs gather to assist in its positioning. (Author's Collection)

Tugs do get around and the typical little west-coaster *Gulf Diane* is no exception as she is seen here hauling aggregate from the Nova Scotia mainland to Prince Edward Island. (Author's Collection)

Norton Class tug *Hugh Jones*, 1949. (A.J. Foster)

Model of *Hugh Jones* (ex Maxwellton) built by A.J. Foster. The following pages present plans and drawings, suitable for modellers, of a Norton Class tug, a type used by the RCN during the Second World War.

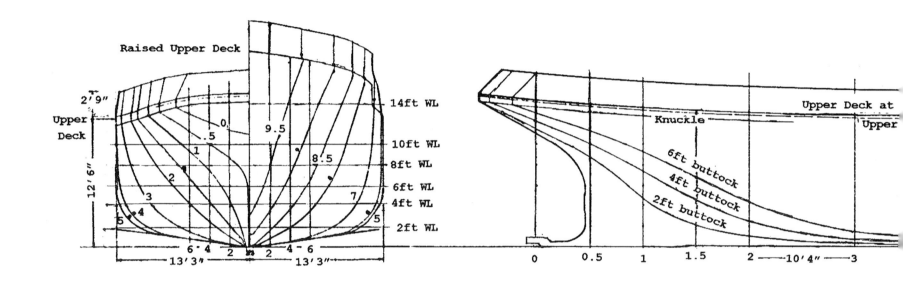

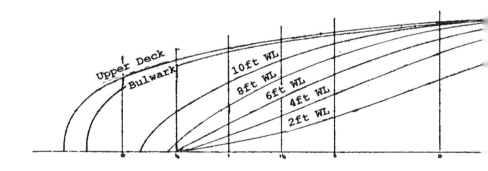

1,000 H.P. Tugs for R.C.N.

Lines

Principal Dimensions:

Length Overall	110'-6"
Length B.P.	104'-0"
Breadth MLD	26'-6"
Depth MLD	12'-6"
Draft Mean	9'-6"

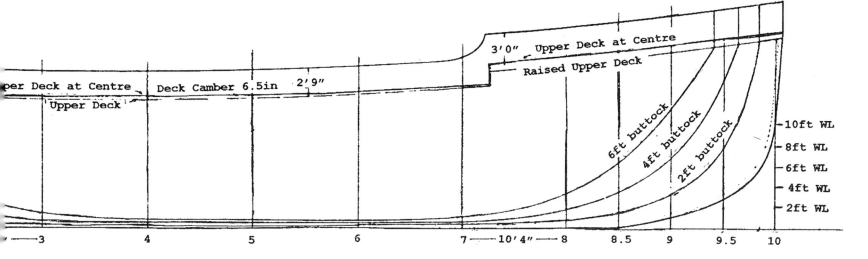

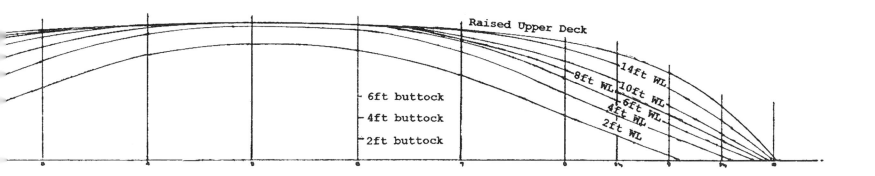

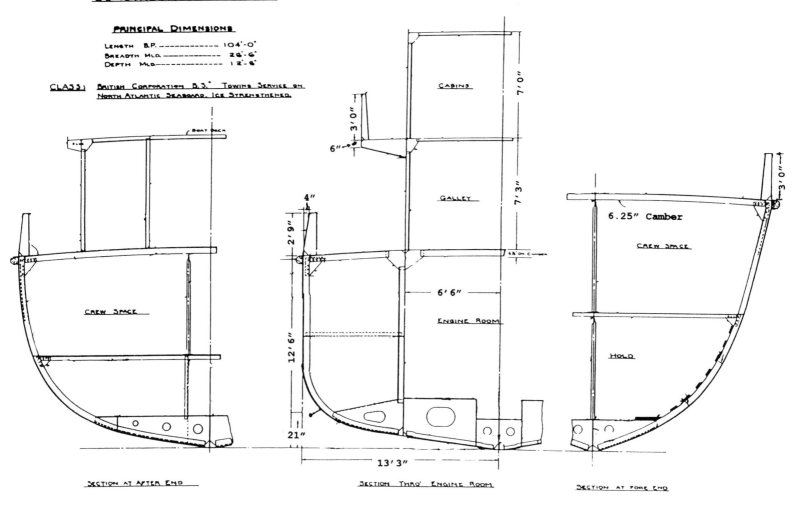

1000 H.P. TUGS FOR R.C.N.

CONSTRUCTION SECTIONS

PRINCIPAL DIMENSIONS

LENGTH B.P. ------------ 104'-0"
BREADTH MLD. ------------ 26'-6"
DEPTH MLD. ------------ 12'-6"

CLASS: British Corporation B.S. Towing Service on North Atlantic Seaboard. Ice Strengthened.

BOAT DECK

CREW SPACE

SECTION AT AFTER END

CABINS

7'0"

3'0"

6"

GALLEY

7'3"

4"

2'9"

6'6"

ENGINE ROOM

12'6"

21"

13'3"

SECTION THRO' ENGINE ROOM

3'0"

6.25" Camber

CREW SPACE

HOLD

SECTION AT FORE END

With the Lumber Barons

THE FIRST IMPETUS FOR THE USE OF TUGS in the old Loyalist port of Saint John in New Brunswick came from the demands of the long navigable river running inland from its harbour. Considering its great potential for timber and other commercial traffic throughout the nineteenth century, much of the Saint John River lacked sufficient current, and sailing room was too cramped for moving awkward rafts of logs effectively. The answer came with steam power. As elsewhere, steamboats built to carry passengers and freight on board were soon pressed into use for towing. A number of the steam passenger packets on the St John served time as tugs and then reverted to their original use. Little difficulty was involved in this as there was little difference between tugs and general carriers until the middle of the century.

Virtually all of the early steamers were side wheelers. Some of the early engines were Scottish-built, others built locally in foundries at Saint John and neighboring Portland in New Brunswick. A number were imported from centres like Portland, Maine, Boston and New York. The American style of overhead walking-beam, vertical engine became the norm on the Saint John. This type was slow turning and reliable, based on the early British mine pumping engines, and lasted throughout the paddle wheel era. Right up to the Second World War the tugs of the Atlantic Coast were built of wood. The few exceptions on the scene were iron, then steel hull vessels brought from Britain.

Squared timber and logs had been rafted on the river utilizing sweeps, sails and the slow current of the pastoral Saint John and its various tributaries. In the spring, when they ran briskly with snow runoff, there were great log drives on the upper reaches. Logs were driven by the woodsmen over the Grand Falls and down to Springhill or Fredericton. Here they went into local sawmills or were made up into rafts to travel the remaining 90 miles to Saint John. Squared pine logs and birch lumber went to Britain, while pine and black spruce were in demand for the local shipyards. Much of the wood was absorbed by the extensive shipbuilding industry around Saint John, but for the first three-quarters of the century, there was a heavy export of squared logs and sawn timber deals to Britain. Around 1900 there were thirteen sawmills at Saint John, above and below the Reversing Falls, finished lumber having replaced the squared timber and deal market.

A famous lumberman and timber baron of the nineteenth century was "Main John" Glasier who, from his base at Fredericton, produced logs in the woods, drove them on the rivers and sawed them into lumber. When steamboats arrived on the scene, Glasier soon had his own fleet of towing vessels.

On the broad, slower ninety miles of the lower river, and on Grand Lake and major tributaries, the towing of timber rafts and lumber in scows or barges took over from the more primitive forms of locomotion. Large rafts with sweeps had previously used as many as 100 men to scull them on the weak current. By 1860, numerous specialized towing vessels were in use, including some with screw propellers. An example was *Sunbury*, a side wheeler built in 1863 to carry passengers and freight. She was 122 feet long and had two boilers. The engine was of the unusual oscillating cylinder type, built by Fleming Foundry of Saint John. *Sunbury* soon took up towing for Glasier, but blew up and sank after two years of service. She was raised and rebuilt, becoming a full-time tug for the Glasier operations. Later the hull was scrapped and the engine installed in a new tug named *Lily Glasier*.

CHAPTER 8

Saint John and its River

A tug eases a log raft down through the Reversing Falls Gorge into Saint John Harbour at slack tide on the way to a sawmill or ocean-going ship. This passage could be tricky even when ocean and river were in balance like this. (National Archives Canada PA 20646)

A small unidentified tug steaming up Saint John Harbour about 1910 is representative of half a dozen independently owned vessels that made a living handling a variety of tows in and around the harbour and through the Reversing Falls. Numerous sailing ships are still around. (John Weeks Collection)

The Tapley Bros side wheeler *Hope*, based at Indiantown above the Reversing Falls at Saint John, was considered a tug, but certainly could accommodate freight when opportune. The towing bitt was on the upper deck where there is no railing. (Provincial Archives New Brunswick P21-11)

Operators of *Frances Huntley (ex-James Gregory*, 1911, 140hp*)* take advantage of the low tide at Parrsboro, Nova Scotia for a quick drydocking. Paint and caulking mallets will do the job. This kind of tidal drydocking has always been an advantage on the Bay of Fundy. (Maritime Museum of the Atlantic N-7151)

Opposite top: Long a fixture in Saint John Harbour, *Gregory* was one of several tugs operated by Gregory lumbering interests. The patent towing hook suggests she also shared in the harbour ship docking activity. (John Weeks Collection)

Opposite bottom: Canadian Pacific's passenger liner *Duchess of York* is turned into Pier 2 at West Saint John in the thirties by *Foremost 43* and *Neptune*, on the weekly winter schedule from Liverpool via Halifax. (Author's Collection)

SAINT JOHN AND ITS RIVER

Ocean Hawk II in her steam-powered days pulls *Beaverdell* into her berth in West Saint John, *Ocean Hawk I* holding the stern. The little line boat stands by to pull mooring lines to the pier. (CP Rail Corporate Archives 7109)

For a large part of the nineteenth century Saint John was the hub of a golden age in the building and owning of oceangoing ships. About a dozen shipyards were busy turning out square-rigged vessels for local and British owners at any time. Many more were being produced in the little ports and creeks around the Bay of Fundy and up the Saint John River system. As long as there was a plentiful supply of timber nearby, a vessel could be built on just about any beach and launched on a high tide. Often there was little in the way of a wharf or sheltered anchorage. Ships were launched and immediately picked up by a tug to be towed off for fitting out elsewhere. As time went on, a considerable degree of specialization arose. The fitting of accommodation, spars and rigging became centred upon Saint John. Tugs did a fair business

bringing in unfinished vessels from shipyards around the Bay of Fundy, from Tynemouth Creek and the Petitcodiac River to the Minas and Annapolis Basins, as well as from yards up the Saint John River. The first of these tugs was probably *Maid of the Mist*, built sometime before 1850. *Hercules, G.D Hunter* (1885), *Dirigo* and *Storm King* (73 tons, 1885) were well-known names in this trade during the latter 1800s. The tiny but prolific shipbuilding and owning port of St. Martins, just up the bay from Saint John, had its own "towing steamer," *Gazelle*, to serve its needs as early as 1836.

More specialized tugs, including many in the 1880s with screw propellers, came into common use as the century wore on, although some of the big old side wheelers continued in use well beyond 1900. At this time, prominent side wheelers still active included Tapley Brothers' *Hope and Champion*, based at Indiantown above the Reversing Falls at Saint John, and *Lily Glasier. Tarantine* was said to be the first "real tug" on the river, short, fat and manoeuverable. One of the best known was the 158-ton side wheeler *Admiral* of 1876, built in Portland, New Brunswick for Parker Glasier. She was fitted with the compound engines designed by Benjamin Tibbetts and installed in his earlier *Reindeer. Admiral* was active as a tug on the river for many years, and still registered in the name of Parker Glasier in 1913, her engines almost seventy years old.

Another famous tug name here was *Conqueror*. For a time she had a contract to carry the mails across the Bay of Fundy to Nova Scotia in the winter. She was also chartered to carry press dispatches on this route, linking the arrival of Cunard's transatlantic ships at Halifax and pony express through the Annapolis Valley to New York newspapers via the telegraph system, at that time terminating at Saint John.

The Glasier family had eight to ten tugs working on the Saint John River system late in the 1800s. Failing lumber markets at this time, however, started the long decline of lumber and freight traffic on the river. The Glasier family carried on after "Main John," from his brother Parker Glasier to Henry Mitchell and his son Parker. The once dominant Glasier river empire dwindled to the St. John River Log Driving Company in 1910, and as the Lancaster Tugboat Company, owned the last of the old line of log towing steam tugs on the Saint John. These included the New York built *Flushing* (1882), a single-cylinder tug of 61 horsepower, still operating in 1924. The last tugs of this line and era were the little wooden steeple-compounds *Joseph* (1899, 54 tons, 170hp) and *Eldred* (1907, 38 tons, 130hp), used by Parker Mitchell to tow large booms of four-foot pulpwood logs from Fredericton to a Saint John pulp mill in the 1930s. They were aided in 1936 by the only prewar diesel tug on the river, the little, 11-ton *Padumi*, the last commercial vessel built in West Saint John.

After this era, the pulp mill operated its own log towing tugs, the slightly larger diesel vessels *Allagash* and *Madawaska*. The towing booms, or bags, of pulpwood varied from 1000 to 2000 cords and were sometimes split into two booms at Acamac on South Bay before going through the narrow Pokiok Gorge to the mill above the Reversing Falls. This operation was all that was left of a great age of river traffic on the Saint John, leaving its beautiful reaches empty but for pleasure craft—until the 1960s.

After the Second World War the Irving interests of New Brunswick acquired one, then two, pulp and paper mills at Saint John and developed large lumber mill operations, including a sawmill on the river at nearby South Bay. About 1960, they assembled a fleet of small, war program diesel-powered tugs on the river to supply these industries, towing booms of pulpwood and rafts of lumber logs in a vigorous renewal of the former river traffic. At its peak, this traffic reached a boom a day.

There were six to eight Irving river tugs on the go in the 1960s between Fredericton and Grand Lake on the one hand, and their pulp and paper and sawmills above the Reversing Falls at Saint John on the other. A spring log drive brought many logs down the upper river to Fredericton. Pulpwood was also dumped by trucks into the river, gathered in a chain-log boom comprising a thousand cord bag to be towed at a snail's pace down the river. With the steam tugs of the thirties, young boys, spotting the approaching tow from their summer colony beaches, could row out to the tug, have a visit with the crew, cadge something from the cook and row back to shore before the tug had gone another mile. The pulp towing booms were parked at Acamac on South Bay until the right moment to go through the Pokiok Gorge and cross the head of the Reversing Falls to the Fairville mill at a prudent phase of tide.

The Irving river tug fleet was set up primarily between 1958 and 1960, drawing from the plentiful supply of small tugs built during the war. When the Irving interests spread to harbour and coastal towing, this fleet became part of their Atlantic Towing Limited operation. Most of these war production vessels had been sent overseas during the war and now some were brought back. The fleet included the ex-RCN *Glenfield*, Irvings' first tug, which later capsized and was lost. Then came three of the little 165-hp Wood class target-towing tugs, six of the large number of Tanac tugs built by Central Bridge of Trenton, Ontario, and three TIDs from England. All were diesels of 250-to 500hp, the TIDs having been repowered from steam, and all were steel boats except the Woods. The Tanacs (previously numbered) were now named appropriately for trees, *Irvings Spruce, Poplar, Willow, Alder, Cedar* and *Juniper*; The TIDs became *Irvings Pine, Elm* and *Fir*. When all these boats were retired, the names were re-used for the next generation of new larger tugs, now concentrated on salt water.

This new log towing era was shortlived. The completion of the Mactaquac power dam above Fredericton stopped the driving of logs on the upper river. By the 1960s, the pulpwood supply industry was being revolutionized by the conversion from four-foot logs to the more easily handled wood chips. The huge booms of logs were abandoned in favour of truck, railcar and barge loads of chips

Pumping out the salvaged *Ocean Hawk II* after she was trapped under the bows of a freighter and rolled over in Saint John Harbour. Tug masters had to be constantly wary of this peril. This was the first of two sinkings for this tug. After this accident she was converted from steam to diesel power. (Maritime Museum of the Atlantic MP23.58.1)

amply handled by a couple of tugs. Then, in 1987, the towed barge operation also stopped for a time. Highway transport, increasingly competitive and not subject to shutdown each winter while the river was frozen, took over.

This development seemed to end entirely about a century and a half of wood transport on this river system. The last traditional tugs in regular service were the TID *Irving Pine* and the Tanac *Irving Spruce*. But then, fighting back, the tug men of Atlantic Towing recaptured the trade. They brought in a more powerful, Mississippi-style push towboat, *Grandpa Shorty*. Renamed *Irving Pine (II)*, this 900bhp boat could make a faster and more economical trip from

Chipman, in the heart of the province, down the Salmon River, across Grand Lake and down the Saint John, made fast to the stern of its 1000-ton barge-load of pulpwood chips. This added for a time one more water route to the many waterways of the world adopting the successful American system of pushing towboats.

Below the Falls

Many tugs worked the dual role of river and harbour tug in years gone by, as do some of today's tugs. Enterprising tug operators handled tows of woodboats, schooners and scows through the Reversing Falls Gorge and its right-angle turn at the bottom, sometimes with a raft of timber destined for an ocean ship in the harbour. They would go up from the main harbour on one slack water, returning immediately or staying to work above the gorge until another slack water period when they came back down, perhaps to seek tows at the harbour mouth. The strong tides of the Bay of Fundy controlled the timing of all vessel movements and helped provide the tugs with a living. They still do, although commerce up the river has become negligible.

For many years there had been both independent tug operators and tugs owned by the major lumbering operators for their own use. The Tapley Company operated its tugs out of Indiantown from about 1850 onward, notably the paddlers *Tiger* (1855) and the later *Hope and Champion*, then the screw tug *Wee Laddie*. Gregory was a well-known lumber-milling name in Saint John with several tugs named after family members, the last one simply called *Gregory*.

One famous tug name, everywhere popular for any kind of vessel, was *Neptune*. This one was built in 1870 at Portland, New Brunswick, a 64-foot, wooden boat that her owner, Peter Lynch, advertised "Will tow in the harbour, through and above the Falls." Her single-cylinder, noncondensing engine, also built in Portland, drove a single screw. She puffed about the harbour for about 40 years, then the engine (190ihp) was "rehulled" as was so common in those times. The new *Neptune* was built in Port Greville, Nova Scotia in 1911 and was a little larger at 120 tons. Having no condenser either, the second tug also puffed about like a railway locomotive, unable to stray far outside the harbour beyond a fresh water supply for her boiler. Through the thirties and forties *Neptune*, personification of the saucy, self-important little tug, was a familiar part of shipberthing operations for the Saint John Tugboat Company.

Numerous small wooden screw tugs served on the river and in the harbour of Saint John and its adjoining arm of the Bay of Fundy, Courtenay Bay, from the 1880s until the depression. They were mostly screws with a single-cylinder or a steeple-compound engine of about 100 horsepower and vertical firetube boilers, changing hands from time to time. Built locally anywhere from Saint John to Fredericton, they bore names such as *Waring*, *Lord Kitchener*, *Mikado*, *Joseph*, *Daniel*, *Eldred*, *Kingsville* and *Martello*. Their size, about 50 feet long and 50 tons, was suited to handling the sailing vessels and lumber scows that made up the local traffic, not the ocean steamship berthing and coastal work that grew up after 1900. A crew of five or six, including a cook, was usual. A large owner in this era of small tugs was the J.F. Brydges Tugboat Company, with at least five boats.

These tugs also engaged in short range seeking, helping sailing vessels in and out of the harbour entrance channel which was S-shaped in those days, hurrying them along before the tide turned against them. *Bessie B.* was one of these seekers in 1871. With her five-man crew, she worked in the harbour at high tide when there was lots of depth for vessel and scow movements. On the slack water on the ebbing tide, she took a tow up through the Reversing Falls gorge and another down again on the flood tide slack water, if she was lucky.

One day when business was poor, *Bessie B.* was off Partridge Island at the harbour entrance, vainly seeking for an incoming vessel. Finally, a schooner came by. The tug master proposed a tow in for $2.00. Even $1.00 was declined. Giving up gracefully the tug captain offered the schooner a tow if a preacher who was aboard the schooner would give his crew a sermon on the way. This was agreed to and the schooner was towed, on a short line presumably, all the way to Market Slip at the head of the harbour on the theme "They That Go Down to the Sea in Ships." *Bessie* later met her end off Partridge Island, capsizing when, as a contemporary account put it, "her machinery got disarranged."

In the early 1920s, tug operations underwent a drastic change. The small tugs were not up to berthing the large steamers now coming to Saint John. The job was taken on and the scene rapidly dominated by the Wilson enterprises under Charles "Tugboat" Wilson, who operated the large new drydock just built on Courtenay Bay. Wilson began assembling a fleet of larger steam tugs in 1923, eventually under the name of Saint John Tugboat Company. These boats started with the former Hackett barge tugs of Quebec, *Margaret Hackett* (1912) and *J.H. Hackett* (1901), renamed *Ocean Hawk* and *Ocean Osprey*. The Quebec-built wooden boats were large compared to the contemporary Saint John screw tugs and had compound engines. *Ocean Hawk* was 94 feet long and 192 tons.

To these were added a variegated collection. *Ocean Eagle* was formerly *St. Arvans*, a 420-ton, steel sea-going tug of the British First World War Saint class; *Ocean Gull* was a smaller Admiralty tug with compound engine, originally named *West Hope*. Smallest was the oil-fired *Ocean Teal,* the largest, *Ocean King* (ex-*Gopher* of Canadian Pacific). The last was powered by a triple expansion engine. The company's plans were evidently too ambitious for the times, so these latter tugs were disposed of within a few years, except *Ocean Teal*, which burned off the harbour mouth during the Second World War.

Ocean Osprey joined the Saint John Tugboat Company fleet after the Second World War. She was previously the Empire type tug *Thunderer* and had a 1000ihp, triple expansion engine. (Maritime Museum of the Atlantic, J.R.Stevens Photo, MP23.3.1a)

Ocean Eagle belonged to the Canadian government's Department of Railways and Canals, but seems to have been on charter to Wilson. She was stationed at Canso, Nova Scotia, for a few years, apparently in line with the accepted theory that a strategically located salvage tug could steer ship repair business to the drydock of its choice. Possibly there was a government subsidy involved. Two other tugs acquired later were the old, wooden *Neptune* and *Foremost 43*, a fine Scottish-built steel coastal and harbour tug, brought down from Quebec after several years' service there.

Wilson's Saint John Tugboat Company took over all the berthing of ships, dredging and miscellaneous work around the harbour, as well as barging pulpwood from small ports around the Bay of

Fundy and Minas Basin, leaving no other resident tug in this harbour by the 1930s. Pulpwood barging included runs down the coast to paper mills in Maine. The barging operations started with old sailing ship hulks and ended following the Second World War after some use of ex-landing craft. A strange tug was used in this work during the 1940s. *Ocean Kiwi* was a long, lean, un-tuglike diesel vessel of 108 tons that looked as though she were designed for speed. Her 14 knots speed was quite respectable for the day. It was hinted she might originally have been a rum-runner. This has not been clearly established, but, though built in Nova Scotia in 1932, her original name was *Golmaccan* with Bridgetown, Barbados, as port of registry. Nevertheless, *Kiwi* worked out her days towing, even helping at ship berthing during the war. Tiny ports around the Bay of Fundy, Annapolis and Minas Basins produced prodigious numbers of home built vessels and timber for export. Other than Saint John, tugs were based only at Hantsport on Minas Basin and at Yarmouth. For many years there was a regular export of gypsum through Hantsport for the American seaboard. Original sailing ships were converted to barges and hauled by American seagoing barge tugs, large wooden vessels typical of the well established American seaboard barge trade. Long familiar on the Basin was the unusual two-stacker, *Springhill*. A later tug here was the second to be named *Otis Wack*, a motor tug used latterly as a docking tug at Hantsport for freighters loading gypsum.

Until shipping patterns changed around the time of the opening of the St. Lawrence Seaway and the building of the ice barrage at Montreal, activity in the port and river of Saint John was very much seasonal. In summer, ocean shipping largely deserted both Saint John and Halifax for Montreal and Quebec City. The former were known as the "winter ports." In midsummer during the thirties, the Saint John fleet was often down to one working tug, the old *Neptune*. During the Second World War ocean shipping activity at Saint John became a year-round affair, keeping the tugs busy. In the middle of the war, *Foremost 43*, apparently built under a British government subsidy like the great liners, was recalled to the UK. She simply disappeared from the scene to steam off across the Atlantic, a drab grey coat of paint covering the bright red of her superstructure.

This splendid tug was one of many built by Alexander Hall of Aberdeen. The James Dredging, Towage and Transport Company in Southampton was in the habit of ordering new tugs from Hall frequently in the 1920s, selling them off after very short use. They were given numbered names with the prefix *Foremost*. There were at least 104 *Foremosts* in all, including some self-propelled hopper barges, and many tugs. *Foremost 43* represented an improved design in 1928, having a triple expansion engine of 900ihp and generous coal bunker capacity at ninety tons. Rated a fine coastal and harbour tug, she was 105 feet in length, measured 221 tons and steamed at 12.5 knots. She stayed in Britain with the Ministry of Transport until 1949, then served Steel and Bennie of Glasgow as *Battleaxe*, and finally Bristol Channel Towage Company under her original name, *Loyal Celt*, from 1957 until towed to the breakers in 1964 by the Dutch *Tasman Zee*.

The Wilsons ordered, in 1940, a new 178-ton wooden steam tug, built at Port Greville, Nova Scotia to replace the ageing *Ocean Hawk*. Named *Ocean Hawk II*, she was powered by a triple expansion engine from an older tug, the engine having been built at Portland in 1918. The loss of *Foremost 43* required the retention of *Ocean Hawk* (I), however, and she sailed on until 1960, a career of half a century and a tribute to her Quebec builders. The second *Hawk* was a large wooden tug with a storied career. She sank twice, once when run down and capsized in the harbour by a freighter in the classic trap alongside the larger vessel's bows. Raised and repowered with a diesel engine she sank again after striking a ledge in the Reversing Falls. Restored once more, *Ocean Hawk II* worked in the harbour and as far afield as Montreal before her retirement when the company closed down its towing operations around 1960. This tug was mounted on land as a focal attraction in the downtown Market Square commercial centre at Saint John but, without the preserving action of salt water, soon rotted away and had to be scrapped.

The old *Neptune* and *Ocean Hawk* were replaced after the war by two typically British harbour-coastal tugs. The first was *Ocean Rockswift*, built at Midland, Ontario, one of the 1000-horsepower steam tugs of the Canadian wartime Warrior class. The other was the very similar second *Ocean Osprey*, formerly *Thunderer* of the Empire class. Both served as berthing tugs at Saint John until the company closed down the operation. Other tugs employed by Saint John Tugboat Company latterly, for barge towing around the bay, were the motor tugs *Ocean Weka* and *Spruce Lake*.

The wide ranging Irving industrial empire in oil refining and marketing, pulp and paper, transportation and lumber required shipping. More and more their products were carried in their own bottoms. Very compatible with their operations was the acquisition from Wilson of the Saint John Drydock and Shipbuilding Company. This provided a base for their own fleets' shipbuilding and repair, as well as the creation of a strong entry in the shipbuilding indus-

Before entering the Narrows above the Reversing Falls, pulpwood towing booms awaited the right tide at Acamac Cove. Here are three parked while the TID tug *Irving Pine* heads out with another in the Saint John River traffic renaissance of the 1960s. (Atlantic Towing Limited, Wilson Photo)

The newly established Atlantic Towing Ltd. harbour fleet circles in Saint John Harbour in November 1961 to show it is ready for business. Shown left to right are *Irving Teak*, originally *Empire Jenny*; *Irving Oak*, formerly *Empire Spruce*, and *Irving Beech*, former *Empire Darby*. *Oak* has been converted to diesel. (Atlantic Towing Limited, Wilson Photo)

try at large. It was inevitable that these entrepreneurs would extend their own tug operations from the river to the harbour of Saint John and beyond, rather than hire the services of the now staid and apparently unambitious Saint John Tugboat Company.

In 1959 the river operation, called J.D. Irving Marine Division, became Atlantic Towing Limited. Four large harbour tugs were bought in 1959-60 in Britain, where there was a glut of war-built steam vessels and the British companies were actively changing to new diesel-powered tugs. They were all originally steam tugs, Empires or similar Admiralty types built between 1942 and 1945. *Irving Teak* and *Irving Tamarack* continued for a time with steam power; *Irving Beech* and *Irving Birch* were dieselized. Other British imports over the next twenty years were *Irving Oak*, a steam tug built in 1942 as *Empire Spruce*; *Irving Hemlock* (ex-*Atherfield*), a 1956 twin diesel vessel and *Irving Willow*, ex-*Dunnose*, a 1958 diesel. The first was bought from the Admiralty, the other two from

Red Funnel Tugs of Southampton. By the nineties all these tugs would be replaced by new tugs with the same tree names, but having the prefix changed from *Irving* to *Atlantic*.

The larger tugs were put to work in the harbour, performing various duties for the Irving companies, then entering into competition with the Saint John Tugboat Company. In addition, the fleet expanded into coastal and river barging of pulpwood and chips, and petroleum products from the Irving refinery. Specialized barges for these purposes and then several large ocean-going tugs were built in their shipyard at Courtenay Bay in the late sixties and early seventies. The tugs included the ice-strengthened *Irving Birch* (827 tons, Ice I+ rated, 3200bhp), *Irving Elm* and *Irving Maple* (827 tons, 3750bhp, Ice II). *Birch* and *Maple* carried out pioneering long tows to the eastern Arctic.

Irving Miami, the flagship in this generation later renamed *Atlantic Hickory*, was built in the Saint John yard in 1973, a spe-

The Atlantic Towing's *Irving Poplar* (former *Amherstburg*) and *Irving Elm* come to the rescue of a bargeload of pulpwood chips aground in Saint John Harbour below the Reversing Falls. (Atlantic Towing Limited)

cialized 912-ton barge hauler of 7200bhp. She has been occupied primarily in hauling newsprint and some containers in covered notch barges from Saint John to American eastern seaboard ports as far as Miami. Another vessel identifiable as a notch tug by her auxiliary, high-level wheelhouse was *Irving Cedar*. This was the 1974, Norwegian-built tug *Sinni* of 5600hp, with twin engines and single screw. She was used for a variety of coastal and overseas tows, but was recently sold for service in the Great Lakes. Several smaller and older tugs have handled ship berthing at Saint John, a service somewhat reduced over the years of containerization and

the advent of bow thrusters on large vessels. However, activity has picked up with an end-of-century development of regular calls by numbers of large cruise ships in summer and autumn.

The Atlantic Towing fleet grew very rapidly, based substantially on business generated by the diverse Irving interests. It also carved out a niche for itself in competition with the other major towing companies plying the eastern seaboard, the Gulf of St. Lawrence, transatlantic and to the far north. By the 1990s, however, recession and increasing obsolescence of the sixties fleet in the face of new propulsion systems and docking methods resulted in lay-ups of

In the recent era of Notch barging large seagoing tugs with auxiliary wheelhouse for seeing over the barge ahead are common. *Irving Cedar (ex-Sinni,* Norwegian-built), is of this type, with many long tows to her credit. (John Weeks Collection)

some tugs. With a business upturn came the ordering of new vessels in the mid-nineties from Irving-owned shipyards, including Azimuth steering drive (ASD) docking types (*Atlantic Spruce, Atlantic Willow* and *Atlantic Hemlock*, 1997 and 1998). They were powered through twin Rolls Royce-Aquamaster ASD, 4000 to 6000bhp, and were built in the Irving-owned East Isle Shipyard small-vessel yard at Georgetown Prince Edward Island. The yard has produced this successful class design by Robert Allan Ltd. serially, including some sold overseas.

A broadening of the Irving group's operations brought the 1999 and 2000 introduction from their Halifax Shipyards of the 2950-ton anchor handling tugs, *Atlantic Eagle* and *Atlantic Hawk*. Twin-screw with bow and stern thrusters, they put out 14,400bhp. With the acquisition of the big Halifax Shipyards and Dartmouth Marine

Slips, a presence in that port was consolidated. Recently the fleet's name prefix "Irving" for all the company's tugs was changed to "Atlantic," more closely identifying the vessels with Atlantic Towing Limited, their operating company. With sixteen tugs of up to 7200 horsepower, barges and heavy engineering capabilities, the company has worked on the construction of the Hibernia oil-drilling platform and the Confederation Bridge project as well as maintaining a winter station on Cabot Strait. Deckload barging remains a major service.

Early tugs seldom had nonessential frills. *Iona* of Liverpool operated in the North Sydney area in Nova Scotia about the turn of the century, had a vertical boiler, no masts or davits. Her lines were lean and she probably handled sailing ships and barges from alongside. (Maritime Museum of the Atlantic N-6120)

CHAPTER 9

Halifax and East

The Navy's Port

HALIFAX HAS A SPLENDID HARBOUR IN A STRATEGIC LOCATION, but no river system to provide inland waterborne traffic to meet with ocean commerce in the port. The city has, however, prospered as the easternmost major port of mainland Canada, a position of both commercial and naval importance. Without the river traffic the development of towing was slow, but military history has made the towing art here and in its ocean approaches an exciting business at times.

An attempt was made to establish a waterborne traffic route inland with the Shubenacadie Canal. This ran from the Dartmouth shore of the harbour up through the Dartmouth Lakes and on to Grand Lake. Although short-lived, this canal system had small tugs built to handle barges. *Avery*, of 1857, was a 64-foot side wheeler of 60 tons. She had a draft of 3 feet, 9 inches. Rafts were towed on Grand Lake by a sternwheeler, *Mayflower*. At different stretches along the canal and lakes, barges were moved by tugs, horses on a towpath, or sails.

The early history of tugs at Halifax is sketchy, with indications of a number of individual, independently owned tugs in operation before and after 1900. Until the 1930s a number of tugs were registered individually to companies bearing the tugs' own names. This is a practice that has been sometimes resorted to elsewhere to reduce liability risks. There are indications that a number of these tugs were actually part of the G.S. Campbell towing organization, the first multi-tug operator in the records.

Some of the earliest tugs were brought from American sources. *Goliah*, built in Philadelphia in 1863, was in operation in the late 1880s. She did not look much like a typical tug and might have been converted from another use. *F.W. Roebling* was another secondhand American and the earliest to appear as registered by G.S. Campbell. Among the individually registered tugs in the early part of the twentieth century were the locally built 97-ton *Togo* (1904, 330ihp), owned by the Togo Company; the Saint John-built *G.S. Mayes* (110 tons), of the G.S. Mayes Tug Company; and the steel-hulled *Scotsman*, from Britain, of Campbell's Scotsman Company. The latter two tugs were first registered about 1910.

During the late 1920s the records show some of these tugs coming together under the name of the Halifax Towboat Company, owned in turn by Campbell. With large passenger ships of lines such as Cunard, White Star, Allan and Canadian Pacific calling at Halifax, it was certainly necessary to assemble four or more tugs for berthing on a regular basis.

Halifax was considered a strategic location for the operation of salvage tugs and also had a drydock and repair facilities that needed business. Concerned for the safety of their ships off this coast, Canadian Pacific Steamships turned over their Liverpool tug *Cruizer* to C. Bristler Company in Halifax in 1913, after considering and rejecting Saint John and its very large drydock, and sent *Musquash* to the Atlantic Salvage Company in 1920, after her return from the war in Europe. However, CPS evidently maintained control and changed their minds, using the two big tugs elsewhere very soon afterward. Halifax Shipyards, in any event, acquired their own inshore salvage vessel, *Reindeer*, from Britain in 1922.

By 1934 Campbell's had increased their berthing and coastal capabilities with the acquisition of two new tugs from Alexander Hall in Aberdeen. These twins were *Bonscot* (renamed *Banscot*) and *Banshee* of 215 tons and 900ihp, capable of coastal towing. In 1931 the upstart salvage firm of Foundation Maritime Limited, a new marine arm of the construction firm Foundation Company of Canada, arrived in Halifax with their *Foundation Franklin*, an oldish tug, but one designed for ocean operations. With her came the tough and uncompromising Captain Robert Featherstone, taking charge as the company's salvage master. His ruthless drive would be the power behind the success of Foundation Maritime in the dicey business of ocean salvage. The busy years of the Second World War on the Western Atlantic added to this success.

In 1935 Foundation Maritime bought Campbell's best tugs, including the British-built steel vessels *Banshee* and *Banscot* and an ex-seeker, *Coalopolis* (1923, 175 tons) renamed *Bansurf*, which left a sistership, *Steelopolis*, back in Avonmouth. Also included were *G.S. Mayes* (1913, 110 tons), which became *Bansaga*, and later *Banspray* (1915, 70 tons), another older wooden tug. The Campbell pier was also acquired. This gave Foundation a ship-berthing fleet and coastal tugs to back up their salvage tug

One of the earliest tugs in Halifax was *A.C. Whitney*, built in 1873, seen under way in the harbour in 1907. (Maritime Museum of the Atlantic, Gauvin & Gentzel Photo, MP 23.63.1)

Foundation Franklin. A company called Maritime Towing and Salvage was set up for this purpose. The two companies continued throughout the war to the mid-1950s, by which time the fleet was all under the Foundation Maritime name except two ancient American wartime acquisitions, *D.F. McAllister* and *J.W. Martin*, still registered under Maritime Towing.

Even this fleet, all steam-powered and adequate perhaps for the work of the port of Halifax in 1939, became woefully inadequate overnight when Halifax prepared for its role as Canada's principal wartime naval base and convoy assembly point. There was a scramble to buy up available tugs. Maritime Towing added the two little Great Lakes non-condensing steam tugs (*Milwaukie* and *Sandusky*, sisterships of 85 tons) that became *Bansun* and *Banstar*, and were later converted to diesel at 400hp. They served faithfully for the duration of the war and on through the 1950s for ship berthing, throwing themselves against the flanks of such monsters as *Queen Elizabeth*, *Queen Mary*, *Ile de France* and *Aquitania*. The two old American steam boats, *Joseph H. Martin* (162 tons, 1910) and *D.F. McAllister* (207 tons, 1919) were also pressed into service. Foundation Maritime also found a big old American coastal barge-haul tug, *Security* (1907, 397 tons), and converted the ancient, iron-hulled coaster *Aranmore* into a salvage vessel. Eventually the Department of Marine's seagoing tug *Ocean Eagle* (ex-*St. Arvans*) was put under Foundation control.

The Canadian Navy assembled several tugs for a variety of non-towing duties, such as the splendid twin-screw, Lake Superior log-ging tug *Kam* for use as the boarding vessel, and a new unnamed tug as an anti-submarine net gate vessel. This gate at the harbour entrance was, incidentally, dutifully opened and closed for ships to pass for some time before the actual underwater net could be installed. The German navy was successfully fooled by this ruse. Eventually the RCN took delivery of wartime production tugs, eliminating their shortages, but this was late in the war, after the corvette and frigate programs had crowded the port with new vessels.

Essential harbour firefighting capability in the port was supplied by the fire-pump equipped, former City of Toronto tug *Rouille*, manned by the Halifax Fire Department, and the one-time Detroit Fire Department steam-powered fireboat *James Battle* (1900, 226 tons, 6000 gpm pumping capacity), manned by National Harbours Board personnel. Later dieselized, the *Battle* would still be standing guard against fire until the early 1990s in the Port of Montreal.

Any production or provision of ocean salvage and convoy rescue tugs by the Canadian government was conspicuously absent.

J.A. Mumford (1903, 115 tons) and *Otis Wack I* (1921, 226 tons) were typical well developed tug models of Nova Scotia early in the twentieth century. Seen at Spencer's Island, they operated in the Minas Basin area handling barges and ships for the Gypsum Packet Company. (Maritime Museum of the Atlantic MP23.4.1a)

The British and American governments took control of their civilian salvage tugs and produced flotillas of new ones for operation under naval and government agency operation. The Canadian government was apparently happy to accept the blandishments of the Foundation Company that salvage operations off the East Coast should be left in its professional hands. The result was the heroic performance of the overworked *Foundation Franklin* and a few other makeshift salvage vessels. Contemporary naval sources have suggested, however, that the Foundation vessels tended to be unavailable for salvage jobs that did not promise a good financial return to the company.

Some of the exploits of the Foundation salvors working out of Halifax are described in Farley Mowat's book *Grey Seas Under*, which helped make *Foundation Franklin* famous. However, doubt has been cast upon the accuracy of some of the accounts. When the freighter *Pontiac* was approaching Halifax in a foundering condition, for example, Mowat's book has *Foundation Franklin* dashing out in heavy seas to bring her in through the submarine net and safely beach her just in the nick of time.

According to the late Commodore O.C.S. Robertson (GM), who was King's Harbourmaster at the time, *Pontiac* was brought in by two of the small RCN Glen class tugs because *Franklin* apparently did not have steam up. The seas could not have been very rough either, the Commodore points out, because the little Glens would not have been able to go outside the harbour. They did not quite make it on time to the Meagher's Beach grounding point for satisfactory beaching in any case. *Pontiac* sank with the water just over her main deck, necessitating a major salvage job. *Franklin* arrived later, eager to participate in the salvage.

When the burning American troopship *Wakefield*, the former liner *Manhattan*, was towed into Halifax by *Foundation Franklin*, assisted by American tugs, *Franklin's* skipper refused Navy instructions to bring her to a pier. He said the Halifax Fire Department might flood and sink her, thereby blocking the berth. This gratuitous insult did not square with the record, in which various ship fires had been effectively handled through RCN and city fire department cooperation. *Wakefield* was, instead, kept at anchor, ensuring continued involvement in the salvage by *Foundation Franklin*.

Top: One of many tugs operated by the Canadian Department of Public Works for maintenance of harbours and canals was *Canso* (1910, 460hp, 225 tons). An early steel tug in Canada, she and her triple expansion engine were built by Burrill Johnson Ironworks of Yarmouth, Nova Scotia. (Maritime Museum of the Atlantic, J.R.Stevens Photo, MP23.5.3a)

Bottom: The major tug operator in Halifax was long the G.S. Campbell Company. When the huge White Star liner *Majestic* (ex-*Bismarck*) called in 1931, they were hard put to muster enough horsepower to handle her using their low powered steam tugs. (Public Archives of Nova Scotia)

The G.S. Campbell Company bolstered their harbour fleet in Halifax in the latter thirties with the two 900hp tugs *Bon Scot* and *Banshee*, built by Alexander Hall of Aberdeen in 1934. The former is seen here in livery of Foundation Maritime Limited, her name changed to *Banscot* and an auxiliary wheelhouse added. (Maritime Museum of the Atlantic, Wetmore Photo MP23.25.2)

In his book, Mowat seems to have taken up with enthusiasm the Foundation people's prejudices against the Navy as a bunch of amateurs. On the other hand, in the view of Commodore Robertson, a lot of financially unpromising salvage jobs were performed by the RCN when Foundation vessels were inexplicably too busy. He had many qualified Naval and civilian salvage people among his crews, some of them former Foundation men, but they were stretched too thin, with too much to do. As Mowat states, Foundation wielded considerable influence in Ottawa.

Halifax was a busy place during the war and the harbour was the principal reason for it. Hundreds of ships entered and left the Bedford Basin anchorage without berthing, but there were myriad problems and accidents requiring tugs. A number of the great transatlantic liners called regularly as troopships and had to be berthed. These included the *Queens, Aquitania, Ile de France, Nieuw Amsterdam, Pasteur* and others. Ships entered the safety of the anti-submarine net in various states of calamity to be drydocked or even beached to prevent sinking. Burning ammunition ships had to be moved away from other ships and the city.

The most hair-raising case was that of the burning American ammunition ship *Volunteer*. When she caught fire in Bedford Basin one night, firefighting efforts by the Naval firefighters and Halifax Fire Department's fireboat *Rouille* were progressing poorly. The available tugs were rounded up, consisting of the three oldtime steamers, *Bansaga, Joseph Martin,* and *Security*, and the anchor cable cut through. With the constant threat of a repetition of the cataclysmic Halifax disaster of 1917 before them, the courageous naval and civilian crews steamed down through the Narrows and past the

The Foundation Maritime Company became a power in towing and deep-sea salvage after acquiring and stationing *Foundation Franklin* at Halifax shortly before the Second World War. A rugged vessel that suffered much punishment in her 30-year salvage role, the former HMS *Frisky* was 612 tons, with a 1200hp triple expansion engine. (Eastern Canada Towing Limited)

city to the beaching ground on McNab's Island. Here, *Volunteer* was scuttled and sunk at a depth sufficient to extinguish the fires.

Rouille and her Halifax Fire Department crew under Captain Donald Preston deserved a collective medal for courage for the risks they took. The climax to their service came at the end of the war with the massive series of explosions at the naval magazines on Bedford Basin. *Rouille* went in to the remaining north ammunition jetty and pumped water into the broken hydrant system so the fires could be fought, while missiles and pyrotechnics whizzed about.

After the war, borrowed tugs went home and others were laid up. The Royal Canadian Navy was left with plenty of reserves and good tugs were available at reasonable prices. Some of the larger civilian tugs were busy for a time towing decommissioned warships from the coast to St. Lawrence River ports for storage and eventual scrapping.

With the return of shipping to peacetime routines, Foundation Maritime was in a good position, developing a well-rounded business in ship berthing, coastal towing and ocean salvage. The fleet was rationalized and modernized. Salvage tugs were maintained on station according to season at Halifax, Quebec, St. John's and Bermuda. These included a series of American and British war program vessels. Names like *Foundation Josephine I* and *II, Frances, Lillian* and *Vigilant* (the last 3000 bhp, 718 tons), became well known for their salvage and rescue adventures through newspaper publicity. The Canadian-built Rock (Warrior) class steamer *Foundation Vera* (1000ihp, 254 tons) assisted the bigger salvage vessels. Harbour berthing duties were taken up as well at the newly developing ports on the north shore of the Gulf of St. Lawrence.

Old steam harbour tugs were soon disposed of, and three of the 400-and 600-bhp RCN Glen class diesel vessels, renamed *Bansaga,*

Bansaga of the Foundation harbour fleet shows evidence of the rigours of winter on the Atlantic coast. The spare bow fender shows how these were made from rope before old automobile tires became plentiful. (Maritime Museum of the Atlantic, Wetmore Photo MP23.17.1)

Halifax has always been a naval port. Here, in 1952, the aircraft carrier HMCS *Magnificent* is moved into a floating drydock by a combination of RCN Glen class and Foundation Company tugs. (National Archives Canada PA 138351, Thomas C. Galley, DND)

Bansturdy and *Banswift*, joined the fleet. *Foundation Vera* was finally scuttled in 1968. The last of the steam powered harbour tugs was *Banscot*, sunk at sea by the Navy after many hard years' usage, including frequent ventures to sea with the bigger salvage vessels.

In the late 1950s and early 1960s a major fleet replacement program was undertaken and the name prefix "Ban" was dropped. With the prefix "Foundation," the new tugs were named *Victor, Valour, Vibert* (all 244 tons, 1280 bhp), and *Viscount, Viceroy, Vim, Vigour, Viking, Vanguard* (all identical at 207 tons, and 1200bhp).

These new ice-strengthened diesel tugs for coastal and harbour work were single-screw vessels except *Valiant* and *Vibert*, with twin screws. The smaller six were built by Davie Shipbuilding at Lauzon, Quebec, with jigs, and all launched on the same day. *Valiant* was somewhat larger at 317 tons and 2100bhp, intended for salvage and ocean towing.

The Foundation Company sold its Foundation Maritime towing fleet in the 1960s, with the reduction in demand for towing, both in berthing and salvage. The buyer was Marine Industries Limited (MILTUG) of Sorel, Quebec, long established in these areas on the

Sydney, Cape Breton, was a strategic location and various salvage tugs were put on station there, but it was never a great success except during the Second World War. The 1921 *Ascupart*, a former Southampton Red Funnel tug, was operated there for a time by Dominion Coal Company. (National Maritime Museum, Greenwich P27896)

St. Lawrence. MILTUG soon resold the business to Smit and Cory International Port Towage Limited, in turn owned by Cory Towage of Britain and the worldwide L. Smit towing and salvage empire of the Netherlands. A new name, Eastern Canada Towing Limited (ECTUG), was adopted and the "Foundation" prefix on the vessel names changed to "Point." Full control of the company was soon assumed by Cory.

ECTUG continues much the same operations in ship berthing, coastal and Gulf of St. Lawrence towing, with occasional salvage. New tugs have been added to the fleet, including *Pointe Comeau*, a Voith-Schneider water-tractor of 4500bhp and others ranging to 5400bhp for handling large tankers. Flagship of the fleet is the twin-screw, Z-drive and azimuthal steering (ASD) docking tug *Point Halifax* of 4200bhp and 417 tons. ECTUG operated under the Cory houseflag and added *Point Chebucto*, another large berthing tug similar to *Point Halifax*. Pilots and ship masters everywhere were showing a marked preference for the versatility of ASD propulsion and "tractor" towing methods on their appearance in the 1980s.

In 1999 the very large British Cory firm was bought by the smaller Dutch Wijsmuller group. More recently a second *Point Valiant* replaced her namesake (sold to Three Rivers Boatmen on the St. Lawrence), introducing to the port of Halifax the latest design in Azimuth Steering Drive tractor tugs specialized for ship berthing. Built by Ocean Industries at Isle aux Coudres in 1998, she produces 4000bhp with two Mitsubishi diesels. As in other ports the numerous old break-bulk freighters and the express passenger liners are gone, replaced by a few very large container vessels. Along with the increasing numbers of large cruise ships in summer, these may or may not require berthing tugs, often relying on their own bow thrusters alone when wind and tide permit. Nevertheless, a demand for the services of docking tugs remains.

Similarly, modern navigational aids have reduced the frequency of salvage work. Other opportunities have opened up, however, and sometimes just as quickly petered out. On-and-off oil refinery operations at Port Hawkesbury on the Strait of Canso and at Come-by-Chance, Newfoundland, have been examples of abrupt change in demand for powerful tugs contracted to berth very large crude car-

The port of St. John's, Newfoundland has been a fine haven for vessels in trouble, but the entrance used to be a problem for large ships. The liner *Metagama* found refuge here after a collision. On departure she ran aground. *Ocean Eagle* and a local tug are trying to pull her off without success. (Public Archives, Newfoundland and Labrador)

riers. Tugs with firefoam capabilities, *Point Tupper* and *Point Melford* (both 300 tons, 4250 bhp) were brought from Britain for work at Port Hawkesbury. Berthing at the Come-by-Chance oil refinery in Newfoundland was handled by firefighting and oil spill control tugs from the Cory fleet, *Points Gilbert* and *James*. Others joining the fleet were *Point Carroll* and *Point Spencer* (366 tons, 3300 bhp). All of these were owned by Cory and operated under the ECTUG name.

Since gaining control of Halifax Shipyards and the Dartmouth Marine Slips, the Irvings' Atlantic Towing Limited has maintained a token tug presence in Halifax harbour and taken on ship handling at Point Tupper. Anchor handling tugs (AHT) of Secunda

Marine work out of this company's facility at Dartmouth. The company is heavily involved in the construction and maintenance of oil exploration and development drill rigs and platforms off the East Coast and overseas. Major endeavours such as the tow-out and placing of the giant Hibernia ocean oil platform have been multinational operations, marshalling a dozen high powered ocean towing and anchor-handling tugs. This involved the biggest companies such as Smit, Wijsmuller, Maersk and Bugsier.

Since the Second World War, the modern Canadian Navy has maintained a number of tugs at its principal bases at Halifax and Esquimault, BC. The war program tugs were gradually replaced by new construction. These included a new class of Villes, small yard tugs of 365bhp with twin Z-drive, as well as large, new Voith-Schneider type cycloidal-propeller driven Glens. For ship and floating crane handling the Glen class are equally adept running ahead, astern or sideways. Three new ocean-going Saint class tugs were built in the fifties for target towing. Even in the 1950s, the Canadian peacetime navy still maintained almost thirty tugs, determined not to be caught short again, but this has shrunk more recently with the rest of the fleet.

Sydney

The port of Sydney in Cape Breton has many advantages thanks to its size and location. North Sydney serves as the terminus of the ferry services to Newfoundland. However, occasional blockage of these ports by drift ice has inhibited ferry service. Major harbour facilities were largely limited to servicing the Dominion Coal Company and the steel mills. In the nineteenth century there was some local shipping activity in and out of the Bras d'Or Lakes, requiring the help of small, wooden steam tugs.

Early in the twentieth century, Dominion Coal established a distribution network along the East Coast with ships and barges, the latter usually former sailing vessels. The company maintained their own tugs for this purpose. One was *Ascupart*, a former Red Funnel tug from Southampton built in 1921. She was one of those rare, single screw tugs fitted with a war surplus engine that turned in the opposite direction to normal, as one of a pair intended for a twin screw vessel. This could be disconcerting for a new captain as, when starting astern, the propeller tended to throw the stern of the tug in the direction of rotation, in this case not the direction expected. Her sister, *Morglay*, got the other engine. (With twin-screw vessels it was necessary to have the two propellers turn in opposite directions so as to throw water effectively against the rudder.)

Under an arrangement with Canadian Pacific Steamships, the latter's large tug, *Cruizer*, registered under the name of Cruizer Shipping Company, was maintained at Sydney by the coal company starting in 1925. This was intended to assure the big steamship line of rescue tug service for their many vessels passing through the area to and from the Gulf of St. Lawrence and the Bay of Fundy. *Cruizer* was eventually sold to W.N. McDonald, an operator of a variety of small coasters and coal barges in the area, and she was last used to tow decommissioned corvettes to the St. Lawrence at war's end. She went to the breakers in 1952, feeding the steel furnaces at Sydney. McDonald also operated *Grenadier*, an ex-USN

ATR tug. Dominion Coal also used *Empire John*, of the British wartime class, for a time after the war. Then the bottom fell out of the coal market and the barging distribution network disappeared. In more recent times Sydney Tugs, Ltd. has operated *Orion Expediter*, the former Swedish *Orion*, a 3400bhp icebreaking tug. The operation ceased in 1990, the tug taken over by Secunda Marine of Dartmouth until 1994. Atlantic Towing has at times stationed a tug at nearby Louisburg, Nova Scotia.

St. John's

Possibly the first tug to be based in the harbour of St. John's, Newfoundland, was *Dauntless*, a paddler which arrived from Swansea in 1857. *Blue Jacket* arrived about the same time. *Dauntless* towed sailing vessels in and out of the narrow harbour entrance for almost twenty years. She sank in 1858 when one paddle rode up on a rock. Raised and returned to service, she was finally lost on the coast near Dildo in 1877.

When the steamship *Argo* ran ashore near Trepassey in 1859 with many passengers trapped on board, the news was telegraphed to St. John's. Both *Dauntless* and *Blue Jacket* were dispatched to the scene by the agent, Ambrose Shea, arriving in time to help get the passengers ashore before *Argo* rolled over and sank.

A Newfoundland Steam Screw Tug Company existed in 1870, operating the 216-ton *Hercules*, a wooden, 60ihp compound engined vessel built in South Shields, England. Companies like Bowrings operated steam vessels from St. John's for various purposes from about 1865. In the latter part of the century, doughty coastal and sealing steamers such as *Terra Nova* were sent out on rescue missions by their owners whenever a ship was reported in distress. Perhaps little need was seen for any specialized salvage or rescue vessel.

In the early part of the twentieth century, Bowrings had small tugs in service in the harbour somewhat like the little Thames craft tugs. In addition to helping schooners in and out, they may have helped berth the Red Cross and Irish Line sail-steamships. When large troopships could not be accommodated during the First World War, these tugs acted as tenders.

The narrow entrance that protects this fine harbour was the cause of grief for ships that missed the channel, particularly before Pancake Rock was removed. The unfortunate Canadian Pacific passenger liner *Metagama* had to come into St. John's for repairs after a collision off Cape Race in 1924. Patched up and departing, she

Vessels of the Tall Ships fleet are assisted to their berths in Halifax by ECTUG's docking tugs *Point Vigour* and *Point Vibert*. (Author's Collection)

The ups and downs of the petroleum industry and its refinery ports left these specialized tanker handlers, *Point Melford* and *Point Tupper* (300 tons, 4250bhp) temporarily idle. They have foam firefighting capacity and oil spill gear. (Author's Collection)

went aground on Pancake Rock. Local tugs and the salvage tug *Ocean Eagle* pulled in vain; *Metagama* staying put until, on a favourable tide, the Furness Red Cross Line steamer *Sylvia* pulled her off.

Another casualty occurred at The Narrows when the 7000-ton, salt-laden freighter *Marsland* came to grief in July 1933. She was entering port at dawn, tried to dodge a schooner on the wrong side of the channel by going astern, lost steerage way and drifted off the channel. Moving ahead again, *Marsland* ran on Ship's Rock right below Fort Amherst light. Two of the railway coastal boats could not get her off even after some cargo was jettisoned. Six days later

Foundation Franklin arrived, hungry for the salvage job that would keep her in business. Although determined attempts to patch the damaged vessel were made, *Marsland* tilted steeply and the Foundation men gave up. Later, the stricken freighter abruptly slid out of sight into deep water.

During the Second World War there was an influx of Canadians and Americans to the little harbour. St. John's became the crowded base for the mid-ocean convoy escorts and the railway's drydock was a refuge for damaged ships in urgent need of patching. Rescue tugs were scarce until the advent of the convoy tugs provided by the British Admiralty. These included the big, 1100-ton *Bustler*

The restored last RCN corvette, HMCS *Sackville*, is given a nudge by the stern of *Glenevis*, a modern Glen class naval tug. The five 1300hp tugs of this class operate equally in any direction, being among the earliest in Canada with twin Voith Schneider type vertical axis propulsion.

class boats, capable of 16 knots and developing 4000bhp from their twin diesels. The Assurance class rescue tug *Tenacity* (1940, 1350bhp and 630 tons) regularly operated out of St. John's for the Admiralty. The US Army also stationed a harbour tug, *ST-27*, here to assist its transports. It later became a dredging tug, renamed *Catalina* and then *Beaver Lily*, based in Halifax.

One of the RCN's wartime "long house" Glen class harbour tugs was stationed here. *Glenmont* (1943, 102 tons) stayed on to serve as the provincial government-maintained berthing tug for St. John's

Harbour, being retired only in 1987. The big ocean rescue tugs of the Soviet fishing fleet have been part of the scene in more recent years, coming in briefly for replenishment. More recently there have been oil rig anchor-supply tugs and ocean tugs on the Hibernia and other offshore projects, refuelling or waiting for jobs. The little *Glenmont* has been succeeded by a number of large tugs based on St. Johns as a result of the offshore oil projects on the Grand Banks, including six Maersk supply anchor-handling tugs.

Montreal: Head of Navigation

IN 1812 WHEN HUGH ALLAN OF THE SCOTTISH SHIP-OWNING FAMILY landed in Canada, the small Allan brig *Favorite* was as large a ship as could get upriver to Montreal. Few ocean vessels attempted the trip because the difficult and poorly marked channels made sailing fraught with perils and delays. Most overseas freight for Montreal and westward arrived by sailing barge from Quebec, or overland by sleigh from New York.

For some reason, *Favorite* was one of the exceptions. Perhaps the Allans had an interest in assessing the potential for their vessels to sail from the United Kingdom right through to Canada's metropolis. At this time, Torrance's *Hercules* was the only tug available; certainly the most powerful towing vessel. *Hercules* picked up *Favorite* from anchor in Lac St. Pierre, having bargained in proper seeker style on the price. This large but shallow lake was a great stumbling block for the sailing vessel. The navigable channel across it was convoluted and hard to follow.

The second major difficulty was the powerful St. Mary's Current, sweeping down past Montreal Island. To assist the furiously churning paddles of *Hercules*, a second towline was passed from the brig to a team of ten oxen on the towpath along the riverbank. Finally, a third line had to be run to the shore with a gang of fifty men hauling it before *Favorite* was brought in to a mooring at the mudbank below Common Street.

The Allans were apparently optimistic about the possibilities of the St. Lawrence River, for they proceeded to establish regular shipping services to Quebec and Montreal. These grew into one of the finest of the major transatlantic passenger and mail liner operations by 1900.

The Allan Royal Mail Line soon began providing its own tugs, starting with *Alliance*, a 192-ton single cylinder side wheel paddler, built in Montreal in 1843. She was followed in 1866 by *Rocket*, of 386 tons, built in Sorel. This vessel's size suggests she also served as a tender to carry passengers and mails to and from the ships. Allan tugs did roam widely between Montreal and the Gulf of St. Lawrence. Undoubtedly they could be very useful in expediting the arrival and departure of passengers and cargo crossing the Atlantic in sailing vessels and using the St. Lawrence ports. By comparison, when the great river was frozen in winter and either Halifax or Saint John was used as the terminus, the sailing ships could get in or out of port without the same complications.

A third Allan tug of this period was *Meteor*, probably built in 1873 and operated until 1889. These tugs were all built of wood, still the normal practice in Canada. British yards, however, had by now changed to iron hulls for tugs. *Rocket* was rebuilt in 1891, however, with an iron hull. The first iron hulls in Canada were ferries manufactured in Britain and assembled in Quebec. Under the name *Britannic, Rocket* continued in service at least until 1912, in later days with the Montreal and Cornwall Navigation Company.

In the 1840s when increasing numbers of timber rafts were being towed between Montreal and Quebec, the tugs of the Calvin Company near Kingston were operating out of Quebec. These included the paddlers *Chieftain* and *John A. MacDonald*. Other companies were established in Montreal to exploit the expanding opportunities for handling rafts and sailing ships in this stretch of the river. They included the long-lived Sincennes McNaughton Line and James G. Ross and Company. The tug *A.G. Nish* is recorded as towing fifty-five sail and seventeen steam

CHAPTER 10

The St. Lawrence Ports

Ocean Intrepide (Robert Allan, Ltd.)

The distinctive square wheelhouse and graceful sheer of the 1885 *Florence*, seen berthing the first *Empress of France* at Quebec City, reveal her as one of the Hackett fleet. Losing the river barge traffic, these tugs were just big enough to handle the increasingly large passenger liners of the Allan and Canadian Pacific lines. (CP Rail Corporate Archives)

vessels, plus salvage work in 1872. At that time there was a chain tug named *Minnie Parsons* in service in Montreal helping to get ships through St. Mary's Current.

The Richelieu River, flowing from Lake Champlain in New York State to the St. Lawrence, was another important water transportation link to be exploited. The Chambly Canal at St. Jean was opened in 1863 to allow small barges and rafts towed by mules to complete this route.

The Richelieu's shallows and shoals discouraged larger steamer traffic, so tugs and barges monopolized the trade. As trade in sawn lumber built up in the middle 1800s, a substantial traffic by barge from Ottawa and Quebec to New York was carried along this route. In fact, a diversified list of cargoes including hay, ice, newsprint and live eels developed. The newsprint traffic, notably, continued on into the middle of the twentieth century, latterly by self-propelled barges plying from St. Lawrence ports such as Trois Rivières and Donnacona into the Hudson River and New York Harbor.

The route began in 1845, when a group of farmers in the agricultural Richelieu Valley formed a company to carry their farm produce to market in Montreal. A major proponent was Captain Felix Sincennes. Only about 15 miles long in a straight line, the mud tracks that passed for roads were not to be preferred over the 90-mile water route via Sorel. The company bought a paddle tug, *Richelieu*, and a barge, *Sincennes*, to set up a twice weekly service. *Richelieu* made a leisurely run from village to village with passengers and freight, stopping at Chambly so the passengers could visit Fort William Henry and, on Sundays, at St. Antoine or St. Ours while passengers and crew attended Mass.

Richelieu did not have the power to negotiate St. Mary's Current with the barge, having to anchor it and serve as a lighter herself to carry passengers and cargo up to the city in several trips. Another group of farmers set up a competing service. Eventually, an amalgamation created a company that was a direct ancestor of today's Canada Steamship Lines.

In the Northwest Territories, the far north has depended upon river and lake barge traffic for basic transportation of cargo. On the Athabaska River in 1970, *Radium Prospector* follows the pioneering route north handling barges Mississippi-style. (Northern Transportation Limited)

The small tug *Peace* plied the river with her name in the seventies. Very shallow draft and multiple propellers in tunnels are the rule on the undredged northern rivers. (Northern Transportation Limited)

A large modern pusher with mast wheelhouse propels a barge train on the Mackenzie River, loaded with buildings, containers and a large drilling plant. Her wake is typical of shallow draft, multiple screws. (Northern Transportation Limited)

This Mississippi-style towboat is not on that river, but on the River Plate-Parana River traffic in Argentina. Up ahead is a small steering tug to help with entry to Buenos Aires Harbour. Such towboats have spread worldwide. (Author's Collection)

Irving Pine aims her big barge loaded with woodchips into the short, narrow Jemseg River toward the St. John, on the way from Grand Lake, NB. She has 900bhp from twin screws and is fitted with flanking rudders. (Author's Collection)

Having brought a barge through the Reversing Falls Gorge at the mouth of the Saint John River, *Atlantic (ex-Irving) Pine* hands it off to *Atlantic Teak* for passage of the rougher waters of Saint John Harbour. (Author's Collection)

Irving Pine with her bargeload of wood chips destined for a pulp mill at Saint John, having come from Chipman on the Salmon River in the heart of the province. This was likely the last of the long history of wood movement on the Saint John River system. (Author's Collection)

A prime venue for tug and barge traffic has been the intracoastal waterway of the American East Coast with its extension to the Mississippi River. Open sea barging is now common with sophisticated tug-barge linkages. An oceangoing barge and its tug with auxiliary mast wheelhouse at New Orleans. (Author's Collection)

An heroic tow was this huge bargeload of mine buildings starting off in the St. Lawrence River, heading for the far north. *Irving Elm* (3458 bhp, 1980) has the tow with *Helen M. McAllister* steering from the stern. The great "sail area" of the high buildings made handling difficult in winds. (Author's Collection)

Arctic Nanabush, seen on sea trials in 1984, was built in Vancouver. Twin fixed screws in nozzles, fore and aft thrusters, a high ice rating and 7200bhp made this a powerful, go anywhere anchor handling tug. Normal crew was twelve. (Arctic Transportation Limited, Ranson Photographers)

The large Mississippi River towboat never tows. Highly specialized, these powerful, shallow draft vessels push incredibly long strings of barges a thousand miles through the heart of America.

Margaret Hackett was a river barging tug built in 1912 with a compound steam engine. When the Hackett fleet dispersed, she went to Saint John to serve as a berthing tug until scrapped half a century later. (John Weeks Collection)

In 1849, Captain Sincennes entered a partnership with William McNaughton, a Montreal lumber broker, to operate a towing company on the Ottawa, St. Lawrence and Richelieu Rivers. The Sincennes McNaughton Line prospered with the growing business in raft and sailing ship towing between Montreal and Quebec, as well as barge service on the three rivers. The seeking operations on the broader river below Quebec were left to the larger Quebec tugs. The loaded lumber barges were generally picked up at Lachine, to which point they had been brought by Ottawa River tugs, and were delivered to ocean vessels at Quebec or to the Chambly Canal service.

Sailing ships gave way to steamers on both the inland and ocean routes in the second half of the century, and the tugs of this company shifted to the canals, towing bulk cargoes in barges. These barges were frequently hulks of retired lake and river sailing vessels. Sincennes McNaughton built up a substantial trade carrying coal from Oswego and Fair Haven, New York, to Montreal, and grain from Port Colborne to Montreal via the old Welland Canal. The

Port of Montreal was also growing and required tugs for berthing the larger ocean vessels now arriving.

By 1898 what was known as "Sin-Mac" was operating widely on the St. Lawrence-Great Lakes system, having nineteen tugs, wood and steel, registered. *Mathilda, Ethel, Azilda, Conqueror* and *Sincennes* were prominent among them. Until about 1880 they were all paddlers, then screw tugs powered by vertical steam cylinders began to replace them. As in Britain, many of the captains felt that paddle wheels were preferable for their steady bite in the water and ability to turn a large vessel when tied alongside it. The early screw propeller tugs on the rivers were shallow draft also, but this did not permit the screw to have a deep enough bite. The earlier paddlers had a single engine and poorer steering ability than those with an engine on each paddle wheel, the latter capable of running one ahead and one astern for maximum turning ability. The single engine paddle tugs were often equipped with chain boxes, moved from side to side, to assist in turning while towing. This function

was accomplished by heeling the vessel over, thus tilting one paddle deeper and the other shallower to vary their bite in the water.

The Sincennes McNaughton fleet at the turn of the century (1900) was large in numbers, but very low in power by later standards. The tugs usually had one-cylinder simple or two-cylinder compound steam engines, with or without condensers. There was at least one paddle wheeler still in service, *Conqueror*, the 1871 tug built in Renfrew, Scotland, and formerly of Quebec. Long the pride of the Montreal fleet was *Mathilda*, built by the company in 1898 at Sorel and the later personification of the saucy little harbour docking tug. She had a steel hull and a compound engine with jet condensing, and served valiantly until the 1960s. Today, *Mathilda* is preserved in a marine museum display on the Hudson River in New York State. Her sister *Ethel* later served on Lake Ontario and, after conversion to diesel, with the Hamilton Harbour Commission under the name *Argue Martin*. She was acquired by McKeil Boatworks in 1991 and had a busy career on the St. Lawrence

Seaway and in Hamilton Harbour, still at work in her second century, although recently sold to foreign owners.

Competition based at the Port of Montreal in the late 1800s and early 1900s came from the George Hall Company of Ogdensburg, New York, through their interest in the Montreal Transportation Company and the St. Lawrence Marine Railway. Their big tug, *Mary P. Hall*, was based here for some years beginning in 1898. Another operator was James G. Ross and Company, operating tugs and barges from the 1870s until well into the 1900s, including for a time the old 1865 *Conqueror*, brought out from Scotland many years before.

Blows to the prosperity of Sincennes McNaughton came with the development of the "canallers," steamships designed to fit the improved St. Lawrence River canal systems early in the century. These took away many of the bulk cargoes in coal, grain and wood. Among the leading operators of these were the Hall Company (later The Hall Corp.), who utilized their subsidiaries in Montreal and

Opposite: The Davie company's *Busy Bee* strains against the moving stern of SS *Empress of Scotland* while other tugs turn her bow in the river at Quebec, where tides and currents constantly change. (CP Rail Corporate Archives 10204)

Right: *Gopher* (1910, 222 tons) was one of several tugs operated by Canadian Pacific Steamships in Liverpool, England. She and her sister *Musquash* were relocated to Quebec in 1914 when the company set up Quebec Salvage and Wrecking Company there. *Gopher* later was taken over by the Davie shipyard of Lauzon and rebuilt as *Chateau*. (Author's Collection)

Top: In the last days of the venerable Sincennes McNaughton Line in the 1950s, it was primarily a ship berthing fleet in Montreal, some more than 50 years old. Moored in McGill Basin are the steamers *Fire Chief, Mathilda, Yvonne Dupre, Rival, John Pratt* and the now diesel *James Battle*. (Author's Collection)

Bottom: *Felicia* and *Rival* were identical steam tugs built in 1923 for Sincennes McNaughton Line and saw service up and down the St. Lawrence system. Here is *Felicia* before they were rebuilt and given diesel power in the fifties. (McAllister Towing and Salvage Ltd.)

Quebec to successfully make the transition from tugs and barges. Sincennes McNaughton did not. The coal trade also suffered by competition from oil as a heating fuel by 1930.

A change in the style and power of the SinMac harbour fleet came briefly in 1934 with the arrival of the twins *Bon Secours* and *Bon Voyage* from Scotland. These 215-ton, steel steam tugs were typical British harbour-estuary type vessels built by Alexander Hall of Aberdeen, and much bigger and more powerful (900bhp) than the existing Montreal area boats. Aside from having large fire pumps and firefighting monitors, their specifications appear identical to those of the Halifax tugs *Banscot* and *Banshee*, also built by Hall in 1934.

The new tugs were placed in service with the Sincennes fleet, although owned by the Ross Towing and Salvage Company. There was much publicity about their firefighting ability, many complaints having been made about a lack of such capabilities in the port since the deaths of several firefighters in the *Cymbeline* tanker explosion in 1931. However, they soon disappeared from the Montreal scene, to reappear at work on the Great Lakes. *Bon Secours* towed logs for a time at the Lakehead. Then in 1938 both were sold to European buyers. A viable theory pertaining to this case is that there was a vain attempt by Ross and Sincennes to secure a retainer from the federal National Harbours Board for harbour fire protection. This since has been tried by other tug companies, but over the years the Board consistently showed little interest.

By 1950, Sincennes McNaughton had shrunk to mainly a ship berthing operation in Montreal, with minor salvage and distance towing work from bases at Kingston, Sarnia and Fort William (Thunder Bay). The company had a monopoly on ship berthing in Montreal, however. Ships of over 20,000 tons, like the Cunard and Canadian Pacific passenger liners, were now entering the port and required the assistance of three and four tugs. The tug fleet at this time included one diesel (*James Battle*) and seven steam tugs, most based in McGill Basin at the lower entrance to the Lachine Canal in Montreal Harbour.

A specialized tug operation during the early and mid-1900s in the Montreal area was that of Consolidated Oka Sand and Gravel Company, major suppliers of building aggregates for Montreal and for building its port. These materials were dredged from the Lake of Two Mountains and barged through the Ste. Anne's and Lachine Canals. Early steam tugs of the company included *Glenclova* (ex-*Gwennith*) and *Glengarnock*, built in Holland in 1908. After the Second World War the fleet was replaced with five of the war program diesel tugs of the Tanac class. Several of these were still oper-

ating with McKeil Marine at Hamilton, more than fifty years later.

Not far downriver from Montreal, at the mouth of the Richelieu River, the Port of Sorel has always been closely connected with the larger port. It was also from earliest days a shipbuilding centre. Active in its development was Joseph Simard, and various tugs were named for members of his clan. Names like Pontbriand for engines, shipbuilders Shepherd and Le Claire were ultimately consolidated in the Manseau Company and more recently as Marine Industries Limited (MIL). The maintenance base and winter quarters of Sincennes McNaughton were also at Sorel.

Manseau and MIL were prominent in dredging, performing most of the progressive upgrading of the St. Lawrence River Ship Channel. They were also active in towing on the river and some salvage, but these activities declined. Tugs included several named after the Simard family, and others prominent in the company, including the well known steam tug *Capitaine Simard*, built in the Manseau yard, and *J.O. Gravelle*. Recent towing services have been provided by Les Remorquages de Sorel, Inc., with four tugs, the largest being *Omni St. Laurent* at 1500 bhp. Absorbed as a subsidiary by le Groupe Ocean (Ocean Group) of Quebec, their work includes river pilot shuttles, ship escorts and assistance.

The federal National Harbours Board operated tugs from time to time for its needs in the Port of Montreal. The most prominent was *Sir Hugh Allan*, a large twin-screw steam tug that long attended the harbour's floating heavy-lift crane. Appearing more like a yacht than a tug, the beautifully maintained *Sir Hugh* was equipped with a comfortable saloon and was used frequently to provide V.I.P. inspection tours of the harbour.

In 1959, the venerable Sincennes McNaughton Line was purchased by McAllister Brothers Inc. of New York, who have extensive towing operations on the American East Coast. This old family firm also bought into Island Tug and Barge Limited of Victoria, British Columbia the following year. Thus the historic Sincennes McNaughton name disappeared in favour of McAllister Towing and Salvage Limited, managed by James McAllister, then Donal McAllister. The old steam-powered fleet was then upgraded. The 1923 twins *Felicia* and *Rival* were converted to diesel engines, pilot house control and variable pitch propellers. The other steamers were taken out of service and replaced by new vessels and a consolidation with the fleet of the Pyke Salvage operation of Kingston, Ontario. The steam tugs that were replaced included: *Youville* (ex-*John Pratt* 1911), *Fire Chief* (1894), *Graeme Stewart* (ex-Chicago *Fireboat 42*, 1908), and *Yvonne Dupre, Jr.* (1946).

Rival (1923) shows her stuff in McAllister colours after a rebuild in 1958, including conversion to diesel, variable pitch propellor and bridge control of her engine. Her twin sister *Felicia* was similarly rejuvenated. (McAllister Towing and Salvage, Inc.)

Control of Island Tug and Barge Ltd. on the West Coast was bought by the Canadian firm of McAllister Towing in 1961, which had itself been taken over by the Belgian Sogemines Group, now renamed Genstar Corporation, established in Vancouver as Genstar Marine in 1951. The modernization process at Montreal was thereby slowed by a decision to redirect two of the newly ordered diesel tugs to join the Island Tug and Barge fleet on the West Coast. One, British-built, to become *Island Mariner*, towed the Montreal-built hull of the other to Vancouver where it became *Island Warrior*.

Significant changes in the pattern of towing requirements took place with the opening of the St. Lawrence Seaway in 1959, the end of the transatlantic passenger liner services in the 1960s, the container revolution in freight handling and the introduction of the bow thruster on ships. New opportunities arose for towing on the

Seaway system and McAllister gained business through the occasional barging of unusually bulky items. There was also a trade in handling old upper lakes ships enroute overseas for scrapping. However, there was a drastic drop in harbour berthing operations with the shift to container ships.

The modernized fleet of McAllister Towing and Salvage Inc. was later locally owned by its former manager, Donal McAllister, of the famous New York clan. The company has carried on a mix of ship berthing, distance towing in the St. Lawrence system and wide-ranging salvage work as the principal salvor based in Canada. The flagship of the fleet for a short time was the 5300-horsepower *Patricia C. McAllister* until she was tragically lost in the Gulf of St. Lawrence with heavy loss of life, apparently after striking ice. Major tows on the Seaway and river were usually han-

A move to modernization of the Sincennes McNaughton Line fleet brought the new diesel powered *Sinmac* (1000bhp) to the Montreal scene in 1959 for harbour, river and seaway work. (McAllister Towing and Salvage Ltd.)

dled by *Salvage Monarch* (219 tons), *Helen McAllister* (152 tons) and *Cathy McAllister* (225 tons) all 1440bhp, sometimes assisted by *Daniel McAllister* (286 tons, 1300bhp), stationed strategically at Kingston.

The tugs *W.N. Twolan* and *Jerry C.*, for a while competing for berthing work in Montreal, joined the McAllister fleet on the retirement of the late Donal McAllister in 1994, the company being sold to le Groupe Ocean (Ocean Group), of Quebec, which grew out of AquaMarine and has consolidated ownership of McAllister, Quebec Tugs and other towing operations along the Lower St. Lawrence. The old former steam tugs *Felicia* and *Daniel McAllister* were then retired. Tugs with new technology propulsion systems have since been acquired, raising the low power ratings that had previously been available. Ocean Group operate their own small shipyard on

Ile aux Coudres where they have built a number of the new Azimuth steering drive (ASD) tractor tugs. They operate over a large territory, as do most of the larger towing enterprises of today. Their operations include specialized notch and other barging of liquid and dry bulk cargo under the name Ocean Transport Maritime.

OLD QUEBEC

The Port of Quebec saw its first specialized towing vessel in 1823 when *Hercules* came down from Montreal to tow out the big, newly launched sailing vessel *Columbus*. This was a seeker's sort of job, taking the ship downriver to Bic where there was enough searoom for her to sail out the St. Lawrence estuary on her own. *Hercules* was Canada's first tug and her 100-horsepower, low pressure engine seems to have been in demand for special jobs like this.

The sleek *Empress of Britain II* of the 1950s turns downstream from her Montreal berth with the aid of three steam veterans, *Yvonne Dupre, Youville* (ex-*John Pratt*) and *Mathilda*. (CP Rail Corporate Archives 19951)

Quebeckers nevertheless must have put a higher priority on the ferry service across the river to Lévis, and built a steamer ferry in 1827. The service proved unreliable, however, for Captain Gabriel Chabot discovered that towing jobs were more profitable than fares from foot passengers. He was prone to abruptly dash off to help a sailing ship or move a timber raft in the coves, leaving ferry passengers waiting on the dock fuming, or even taking them with him. The same presumably applied to *New Lauzon*, which appeared a year later.

Additional ferries, *St. Roch* and *St. Georges*, built in 1845 and 1846, were very soon sold off for service as tugs. Similarly, *Queen Victoria's* owners found towing a more profitable business in the congested and tidal conditions of the port. The great timber boom was just getting underway, and in the spring rush to open up navigation, there would be as many as one hundred ships arriving from sea in one 24-hour period.

By mid-century, Quebec was a booming port as the transhipping point for the timber trade to Britain. The coves above the city at Sillery were full of timber rafts. There were twenty-five shipyards and eight or ten wooden, floating drydocks. In addition to timber coming downriver, lumber was being barged upriver to the port. François Baby held a subsidy to build tugs, tow and "relieve wrecks" between Quebec and Bic. This consisted mainly of seeking-style towing in the more difficult part of the river below Quebec. Among his fleet were: *Admiral, Advance, Napoleon III, Lady Head, Victoria* and *Druid*.

A St. Lawrence Towboat Company was running river steamers in the 1860s and 1870s, but despite the name and early expectations, was apparently engaged primarily in operating passenger and freight vessels. The name was changed to the St. Lawrence Steam Navigation Company after some years.

There were a few vessels registered as tugs at Quebec in this period, including the two *Conquerors* built by Simons of Renfrew,

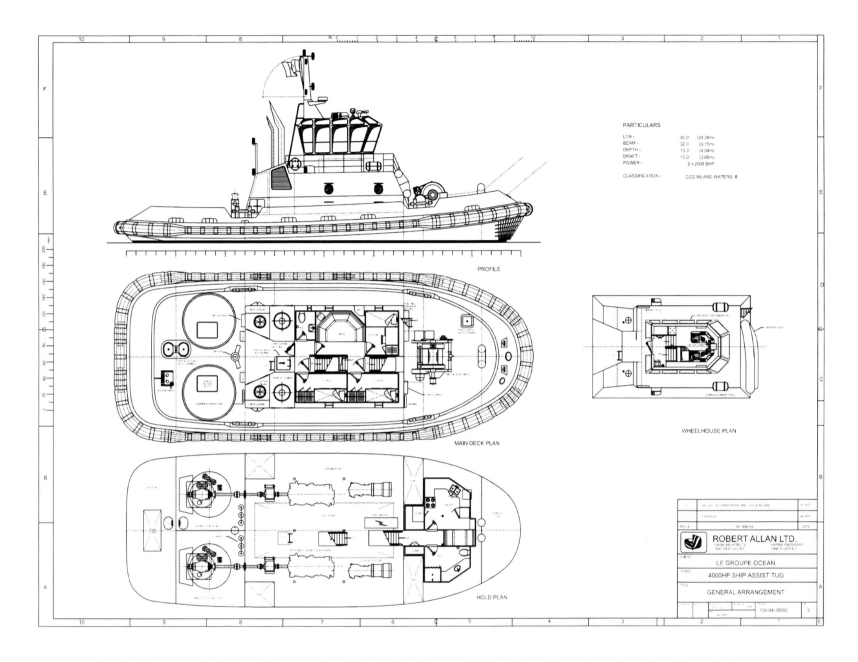

PROFILE

MAIN DECK PLAN

WHEELHOUSE PLAN

HOLD PLAN

ROBERT ALLAN LTD.

LE GROUPE OCEAN

4000HP SHIP ASSIST TUG

GENERAL ARRANGEMENT

104-94-30000

ASD tugs utilized in the recent modernization of the Montreal McAllister docking fleet, two 4000hp "ship assist" tugs *Ocean Intrepide* and *Ocean Jupiter*. (Robert Allan, Ltd.)

Scotland. The 1865 vessel was owned by James G. Ross and the 1871 tug by Michael McNamara. Three other tugs of the 1870s, *Mersey, Castor* and *Rival*, were recorded as suffering damage in a destructive river "ice shove" that damaged or sank numerous vessels at Quebec in 1874. Although there were about 250 vessels loaded with cargoes of timber for export in the coves at Quebec in 1888, the trade would be all but dead in 1900.

The timber trade was replaced on the St. Lawrence by tug and barge operations, which in turn succumbed to the success of the self-propelled canallers. At first, Sincennes McNaughton dominated the barge traffic from Montreal, but competition came both from above Montreal in the form of the Oswego-based George Hall Company and in Quebec from William Hackett and Sons. Eventually, Hall seems to have taken control of the Quebec Transportation and Forwarding Company, which operated the Hackett tug fleet. The word "Forwarding" was dropped.

In the 1890s William Hackett built a fleet of larger wooden tugs based in Quebec for river barge towing and thus, with the arrival of large passenger liners, his company was prepared to handle the ship berthing duties at Quebec. The Hackett tugs were notable for their tall funnels and stately bearing. The wheelhouses were also distinctive, having a rectangular shape with bevelled corners instead of a rounded front. *Florence* was possibly the first, followed by *M.E. Hackett* of 1894, *William Hackett* of 1900, *J.H. Hackett* in 1901 and *Margaret Hackett* in 1912. The latter two were sold to Charles Wilson in 1923 for his Saint John Tugboat Company and given the names *Ocean Osprey* (then described as a recovered wreck) and *Ocean Hawk. Florence* served for a time in Montreal, then moved on to the Detroit River area.

J.H. Hackett and *Margaret Hackett*, at 340 and 560ihp, were the ultimate in large wooden tugs for barge hauls on the St. Lawrence. It was customary to tow one or two barges at a time. Some of the canallers also towed a companion barge, increasing their competitiveness. On one occasion, in 1920, *Margaret Hackett* was towing a barge across Lake St. Peter when she ran afoul of the towline between a canaller and its barge. The tug turned over and sank, but was salvaged and went back into service. Her big (560ihp) compound engine is said to have required the largest steel casting poured to that time in Quebec. It served well, lasting until the tug was retired in 1961.

The tug *Foremost 43,* built by Alexander Hall of Aberdeen, joined the Quebec fleet for berthing operations about 1929, under ownership of F.M. Ross of Montreal, but she was sold in 1932, also

to Charles Wilson of Saint John. Apparently the Hackett and other Quebec Transportation Company tugs were sold off as Hall developed their fleet of canallers. Ship berthing operations at Quebec seem to have been shared with the Davie Company of Lauzon in the 1920s, at least for the large passenger liners, and then passed on to Davie entirely.

A major player in tug operations and salvage on the St. Lawrence and in the Gulf was George T. Davie, later Davie Shipbuilding & Repairing Co. of Lauzon, across the river from Quebec. A shipbuilding and repair business founded partly on salvage the company had acquired a salvage tug, *Lord Stanley*, built in Scotland in 1889. Thirteen years later they replaced her with the larger *Lord Strathcona*. These vessels were profitably employed on the many casualties occurring along the lower river and in the Gulf as far as Anticosti Island, as described below. They were often assisted by the larger of the berthing tugs based in Quebec.

With the dispersal of the Quebec Transportation Company tugs, Davie took on the ship berthing work at Quebec, building most of their own tugs. These included the compound steam tugs *Busy Bee* (430ihp, 115 tons) in 1919 and *Manoir,* (640ihp, 250 tons) in 1930. The company also rebuilt the 1910 Canadian Pacific tug *Gopher* (890ihp, 222 tons), renaming her *Chateau. Ocean Eagle* was registered to Davie Transportation Limited after the Second World War. These boats were eventually replaced in the 1950s and 60s with more powerful diesel tugs, including *Leonard W., Donald P.* and *Jerry G.* The Davie shipyard produced more than twenty tugs for a variety of owners among the many vessels built in their yard.

The salvage business, however, carried on with a federal government subsidy, was turned over in 1914 to the Quebec Salvage and Wrecking Company, a newly organized subsidiary of Canadian Pacific Railway Company. The new company took over *Lord Strathcona* and brought two of its parent company's British tugs from Liverpool to assist. These were *Musquash* and *Gopher*. They did not stay long, being sold in 1920 and 1923 after war service overseas. *Gopher* eventually returned to join Davie's harbour fleet under the name *Ocean King*. She was capsized while berthing the liner *Marloch* in one of the worst of Canadian tug disasters, with nine lives lost.

She was then raised and rebuilt as *Chateau.*

In 1944, Quebec Salvage and Wrecking was sold to the more aggressive Foundation Maritime Limited, who maintained a tug on station at Quebec for some years following the war. The Davie ship berthing fleet was later turned over to a new subsidiary of the

Built by the Canadian government for firefighting, icebreaking and rescue in the Quebec City area, *Citadelle* was later remodelled and spent many years as a pilot boat at Father Point on the lower St. Lawrence River. (CP Rail Corporate Archives 5452)

Canada Steamship Lines group, Quebec Tugs Limited. These included the big, 722-ton notch type tug *Capitaine Ioannis S.*, the harbour tugs *Donald P.*, *Leonard W.*, *Jerry C.* and later the notch tug *Laval*, acquired from Reed Paper, who had built her for notch-barging pulpwood on the Lower St. Lawrence.

In 1972, a diving and underwater specialist, Aqua-Marine, became Ocean Group Inc. under its founder, Gordon Bain. In 1987, Quebec Tugs was purchased, followed by acquisition of McAllister Towing and Salvage of Montreal in 1993, Sorel Tugboats in 1994, and Three Rivers Boatman in 2002. This group gained control over the St. Lawrence ports for towing and salvage. Three to four tugs each are based at Montreal, Sorel, Trois Rivières and Quebec City, operating under the McAllister name. Ocean Group provides cover-age of towing needs from the St. Lawrence Seaway at Montreal down the Gulf of St. Lawrence. They recently acquired the 5280bhp *Canmar Supplier VII* (ex-*Polar Shore*) for conversion as the ice-rated tug *Ocean Foxtrot*. Ocean Group musters a fleet of seventeen tugs, ranging in power up to 6400bhp (*Ocean Delta*, formerly *Capitaine Ioannis S.*), together with several barges.

With the outright acquisition of the towing companies in Montreal and Quebec under Groupe Ocean Inc. in 1993, many of the tugs renamed with the prefix "Ocean" except the older McAllister tugs in process of disposal. The Group's shipyard at Ile aux Coudres below Quebec City has produced the new Allan-designed tractor tugs *Ocean Intrepide* and *Ocean Jupiter* for docking service in Montreal.

The Port of Quebec has always been an important base for the marine vessels and services of the Canadian government. This resulted in a number of government tugs being stationed here over the years. Among these were *Graham Bell* (1929) of the National Harbours Board, *Lanoraie* II (1928), and *Citadelle* (1932); the last, equipped for harbour towing and firefighting, later served as the pilot vessel downriver at Father Point where her power was useful in getting through drift ice. Earlier, in 1920, the tug *Polana* (1911, 278 tons), had been refitted for the same reason, to handle this outer pilot station on the St. Lawrence under the name *Jalobert*.

When the port was operated by the local Quebec Harbour Commissioners, they acquired a British-built tug, *Laval*, along with a floating crane, grain elevator lighter, two dredges and six scows. *Laval* towed the 30,000-bushel lighter across the Atlantic in a protracted 42-day trip from Middlesborough. Her captain allowed that it was a boisterous trip. This earlier *Laval* was later sold for use in Lake Superior lumber operations.

THE LOWER RIVER

In the seeking era, Quebec tugs ventured far down the St. Lawrence estuary to the Gulf to meet incoming sailing ships bound for Quebec. The Allan tugs and *Conqueror* of 1865, imported from Britain, would appear to have worked this service. Assistance from tugs was also required so that ships could get to their cargoes in lesser ports downriver. The port of Chicoutimi on the Saguenay River suffered the limitation of shallows below the town. The side wheeler *Sampson* was built in Lévis in 1849 for the Price lumber interests to tow lighters through this stretch and help sailing ships on the river. Similarly, as late as the 1920s, an ex-steam drifter, *Two Roses*, was used to tow schooners loaded with lumber and pulp over the shoals at Outardes.

Port Alfred, just below Chicoutimi, became the deepwater port on the Saguenay and, after the Second World War, Foundation Maritime provided berthing service with two of their ex-RCN "long house" Glen class tugs. Other ports down the North Shore of the Gulf of St. Lawrence that have grown to require berthing services include Baie Comeau and Sept Iles. These are serviced by more modern tugs of Eastern Canada Towing Limited of Halifax, following on the pioneering carried out under its former name, Foundation Maritime. These powerful ice-strengthened, twin-screw berthing tugs include *Pointe Sept-Isles* (424 tons) and *Pointe aux*

Basques (396 tons), both of 5400bhp, and the 4500bhp Voith-Schneider water tractor *Pointe Comeau* (391 tons). Port Cartier is covered for Federal Terminals by the powerful Voith-Schneider tractor tugs *Brochu* and *Vachon* (1972/3, 390 tons, 3400bhp).

The large island of Anticosti stands athwart the shipping route from the St. Lawrence to the Strait of Belle Isle. Its shorelines are forbidding and there is only one harbour, Port Menier. Not only have there been many ships lost on the unforgiving headlands, but some of the extensive pulpwood shipping had to be carried out by towing chained bundles of logs out to ships at anchor. The Anticosti Shipping Company operated tugs for this purpose from the 1920s. *Hullman* (1914, 171 tons), a steamer from Britain and the diesel *George M. McKee* (1928, 221 tons), built for them by Davie, carried out this duty for some years, until replaced by *Charlemagne* (1920).

When pulpwood was handled entirely in the form of four-foot logs, the paper mills along the St. Lawrence system were supplied in part from the river by vessels like the canallers of the Hall Corporation, and from the smallest ports by the little family-run, wooden auxiliary schooners called "Goelettes." Booms and bag tows were impractical on the great tidal river beyond the mouths of small tributary rivers. Much of this pulp-log trade disappeared with the adoption of chips as the most efficient form for handling pulpwood. The large Reed Company paper mill at Quebec nevertheless continued to use logs for many years. After the Second World War four converted landing craft were used to bring logs upriver. In 1969 these were replaced by a large notch tug, *Atlantic*, built for the purpose by Port Weller Drydocks, and two large notch barges. The 438-ton tug, operated by the Reed Maritime Corporation, later became Quebec Tugs' *Laval*. Otherwise, significant regular line-haul tug and notch-barge traffic on this great river has been developing only very slowly in recent years, although some specialized cargos are carried.

CHAPTER 11

Kingston and the Great Lakes

Steam Power on the Lakes

FROM ITS EARLIEST DAYS, Kingston had been a key military base. Its harbour then grew important commercially because of its fine location at the end of Lake Ontario where the lake empties into the St. Lawrence River. Most important was the fact that a short distance down the river began the series of rapids that confounded navigation on this great river. Not until the modern St. Lawrence Seaway replaced the smaller canals built around the various rapids did the port of Kingston and its downriver satellite, Prescott, lose their significance to the Lakes-River passage.

The first experimental steamer on Lake Ontario was a primitive vessel with mechanical paddles, somewhat like that of the American, Fitch, on the Delaware. *Walk on the Water*, as the Indians named her, was understandably not in service for long. The more practical side paddle wheels were installed in *Brockville* and *Frontenac* in 1816 and 1817. These two vessels established service on the river and from Prescott along the shore of Lake Ontario to York (Toronto).

The value of the steamship in carrying commerce up the chain of enormous lakes leading right into the heart of the continent was obvious. The spreading of population upbound and the export of timber downbound promoted rapid trade development, and the succession of canals was built to circumvent the obstacles along the route. As elsewhere on the North American continent, the early steamers carried passengers and some freight aboard, but frequently enhanced their profits by pushing or towing barges at the same time. The extensive operations of D.D. Calvin at Kingston were a prime example.

One long-famous steamer on the Lakes was *Algoma*. She was built as the *City of Toronto* in 1839 for service on Lake Ontario. She had two decks and twin beam-engines driving her 26-foot diameter paddle wheels, was 147 feet long and had two smokestacks in tandem. Before long, however, she was moved to Detroit, becoming *Racine*, probably to work the Detroit River-St. Clair River stretch as a tug. This waterway between Lakes Erie and Huron was difficult for sailing vessels to ascend because of the strong currents, and there was plenty of towing to be done. To get from Lake Ontario to Lake Erie *City of Toronto* had to be disassembled and put back together above the Niagara Escarpment.

Rebuilt in 1863, this vessel returned to Canadian service in 1865 once more as *Algoma*. Running out of Collingwood to Sault Ste. Marie and on to Prince Arthur's Landing at the head of Lake Superior, she was now a packet for the Royal Mail Line. This was a key link in the route to Western Canada, until the Canadian Pacific Railway was built twenty years later. *Algoma* was retired in 1871, an achievement in longevity on the Great Lakes. The vessels were casually built, the lakes given to sudden violent storms, drifting ice and sketchy navigation aids. In 1871, a particularly stormy year, there were 1067 marine casualties, Canadian and American, reported on the Great Lakes.

Another example of the chameleon lives of mid-century vessels that makes them difficult to classify as tugs or otherwise, is *Ploughboy*. This 170-foot boat was built at Chatham, Ontario in 1851, fitted with a sidelever engine from the earlier *Transit*. She carried passengers and freight on Lake Huron, on one occasion having a close shave with disaster, when she blew onto a lee shore of Georgian Bay with Sir John A. Macdonald among the passengers. The towing opportunities in the burgeoning traffic on the Detroit River caused *Ploughboy's* conversion to a tug in 1864. After six years, however, she went back to freight and passenger service. These

Abitibi (German and Milne, Naval Architects)

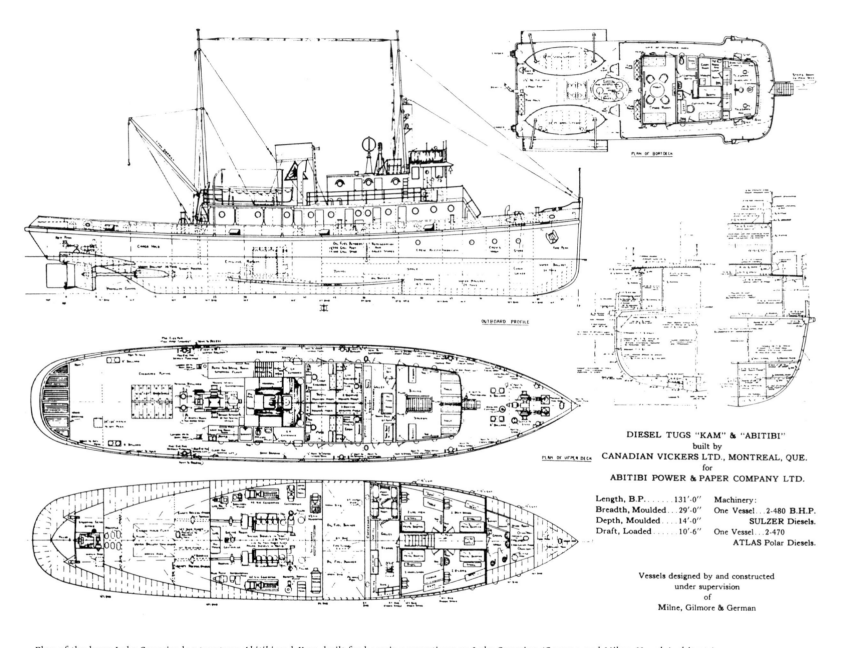

DIESEL TUGS "KAM" & "ABITIBI"
built by
CANADIAN VICKERS LTD., MONTREAL, QUE.
for
ABITIBI POWER & PAPER COMPANY LTD.

Length, B.P. . . . . 131'-0"   Machinery:
Breadth, Moulded . . . 29'-0"   One Vessel . . . 2-480 B.H.P.
Depth, Moulded . . . . 14'-0"   SULZER Diesels.
Draft, Loaded . . . . . . 10'-6"   One Vessel . . . 2-470
                                                    ATLAS Polar Diesels.

Vessels designed by and constructed
under supervision
of
Milne, Gilmore & German

Plan of the large Lake Superior log tow tugs *Abitibi* and *Kam*, built for booming operations on Lake Superior. (German and Milne, Naval Architects)

A train of four schooners leaves the Welland Canal at Port Dalhousie on Lake Ontario, under tow of a big lakes screw tug. Canals and straits between the Great Lakes made good business for tugs. (Archives of Ontario 12026-268)

The large *Metamora* was involved in numerous salvage operations in addition to long distance towing on the Great Lakes. (Archives of Ontario S5385)

conversions did not greatly affect the general lines of a vessel, the long lean hull and side wheels remaining unchanged. The need for a short, broad-beamed hull and towing bitts well forward of the rudder did not seem important elements at the time.

Champion II was one of three similar, side wheel "passenger tugs" built in Lévis, Quebec in 1877. She was converted to a passenger and freight vessel at Owen Sound in 1887 for service on the upper lakes. Perhaps this was related to the building of the Canadian Pacific Railway, which stimulated traffic to the head of the lakes at this time.

The Canals

Attempts to establish canals around the rapids on Canadian rivers began during the French regime and continued throughout the British colonial days. The first canals were only a couple of feet deep, suitable for freight canoes, and the open, flat-bottomed freight boats that were poled and sailed along the shores. With the use of larger sailing vessels on the lakes, successively larger canals were built, one section at a time along the lengthy route between Montreal and Lake Erie. These were periodically replaced or enlarged under pressures to accommodate larger vessels. The earlier canals had towpaths for horses to haul vessels through.

The Welland Canal, connecting Lakes Ontario and Erie was rebuilt four times, ranging from the thirty-nine, 110-foot locks of 1829 to the present eight locks of 859 feet completed in 1933. The third canal, completed in 1887 with twenty-six locks of 270 feet, was well suited for tugs. Many were built at Port Robinson by William Ross. These were certainly built for the job, short, beamy, and with short or folding funnels for clearing bridges. They handled a growing traffic in schooners and barges sailing between the lakes.

The series of canals on the St. Lawrence between Montreal and Kingston grew slowly. By 1847 a 9-foot-draft channel was complete

The Pyke Salvage and Navigation Company tug *Salvage Queen* at work on the raising of the tug *Dalhousie Rover*. The Kingston, Ontario based company thrived until better vessels and navigational aids cut the incidence of marine casualties on the St. Lawrence and Lake Ontario. (Public Archives of Ontario 16657-42)

and the following year D.D. Calvin was offering towing services through the canals. The system finally reached a depth of 14 feet in 1905. However, a lot of traffic passed through at the 9-foot depth on this vital link from the sea to Lake Ontario. Calvin, operating his lumber carrying and timber rafting business from the head of this system at Garden Island, off Kingston, made good use of tugs in his own business as well as towing other owners' vessels. Spotting a good opportunity, he soon promoted and secured a contract from the government for towing services on the canals.

Calvin was well connected politically with Sir John A. Macdonald and served on the government's canal commission. He opposed the deepening of the Welland Canal to take ocean-going vessels, claiming the specialized river vessels were competitive enough. In 1849, he succeeded in persuading the government to maintain tugs on station along the canals to ensure their availability to sailing vessels wishing to transit.

For this, the Government Tug Line was established by Calvin, Cook and Company. Using Calvin tugs including *Chieftain*, *William IV* and *Raftsman*, regulated towing service was provided between Prescott and Lachine. Later this service was extended to Kingston. It required four tugs, based on four stations. Rates were set on tonnage and the power of the currents in each section. Tows included

schooners, brigs and barges, the last being unwieldy and difficult to handle in the downstream runs. The usual rate for hire of a tug in 1860 was $65 a day while running or $20 on standby. This work became a major element in the Calvin towing operations, but the contract was cancelled by the Mackenzie government in 1874.

The Port of Kingston

The Kingston area harbours, including Prescott and Portsmouth, were dominated through much of the 1800s by the Calvins from their base at Garden Island, adjacent to Wolfe Island. Competition came late in the century from the big companies up-

and downstream, Sincennes McNaughton of Montreal and George Hall of Ogdensburg, both providing their own barges and tugs.

The Garden Island operation was heavily oriented to wood. It was the principal product Calvin transported, the stuff of which their tugs and barges were made and the fuel that heated the boilers. The maintenance shop is said to have built an emergency engine crankshaft of wood on one occasion. Great quantities of cordwood were amassed over the winters for each coming navigation season, brought in both by scow and over the ice. In the 1860s and 1870s the company bought about 25,000 cords annually from contractors, cut by farmers in the region. Company chits in receipt for wood circulated like money. The wood that fired the steamers' boilers was mostly hardwood, but supplies within reasonable distance were becoming exhausted at the same time coal was becoming readily available from American sources. This ended the era when steamers set out on a trip looking like floating woodpiles, every open space crammed with the quick-burning fuel of the forests.

As the century ended, the Calvin Company, as it was now named, was heavily engaged in towing of all sorts as well as salvage, or "wrecking" as it was called then. Perhaps the term indicated the rate of success in salvage attempts. The Calvins continued to build their homemade paddle tugs and adapt second-hand vessels, re-using the slow-turning engines that easily outlasted the perishable wooden hulls. *Parthia*, of 1896, was one of the last, along with the third *Chieftain*.

A typical Calvin boat was *Highlander*, a former mail packet, bought in 1865. Her outside walking-beam engine had a single steam cylinder with 40-inch diameter piston and 8-foot stroke. This and the big paddle wheels turned at a leisurely 17 revolutions per minute, producing 116ihp from 20psi boiler pressure. *Highlander* was 300 tons, 173 feet long and 24 feet in the beam, but over the paddle wheel guards she was forty feet across. She towed log rafts to Quebec. The company maintained several side wheelers on into the twentieth century for salvage and raft towing.

The last Calvin tug, built at Garden Island in 1894, was the screw propeller, compound-engined *Reginald* (265 tons, 480 bhp) reputed to be the only Calvin vessel to be well constructed and of contemporary design. The company did not survive long, though, as competition and the Calvins' failure to adapt to changing needs caused it to close down in 1914. The Donnelly Towing and

Tugs, with their tough hulls and power, often performed ice-breaking duties around harbours, as they sometimes still do. *J.S. Pratt* of Great Lakes Transportation Co. rears up in the traditional method of breaking solid ice with the weight of the vessel. (Archives of Ontario S13516)

KINGSTON AND THE GREAT LAKES

Tugs of the Reid fleet of Sarnia, on Lake Huron, muster at a log boom for a major pushing job. (Archives of Ontario 16856-2398)

Opposite: *James Reid*, a steam tug of the Sarnia Reid fleet doing the bread and butter work, taking a sailing vessel loaded with lumber into the St. Clair River near Point Edward. (Public Archives of Ontario 13097)

Wrecking Company based at nearby Portsmouth bought the Calvins' salvage gear. Captain M.B. Donnelly had become prominent in the salvage business at Kingston and operated the well-known tug *Mary P. Hall* for a time. Another long-lived river salvage tug was named for him.

In the first half of the nineteenth century there was intense competition for salvage business in the area between Donnelly and the Pyke company of Kingston. In this era, most salvage on the St. Lawrence system consisted of lightering off cargo from a grounded vessel that had wandered off the prescribed channels, then pulling her free. Pyke's salvage tugs such as *Salvage Prince* (1924, 184

tons) were low in power, but equipped with large winches and ground tackle for such pull-offs. Pyke tugs filled their time between salvage jobs towing coal barges on the river.

Sincennes McNaughton had various of their tugs based on nearby Portsmouth for their barging and other long-distance towing operations. On one of these, *Rival*, the crew had the dubious distinction of being arrested for towing directly between two American ports on the river, contrary to American regulations.

At Prescott there was for many years an important railway-car ferry across the St. Lawrence River, connecting the lines of Canadian Pacific with the New York Central system. It was part of

the famous C.P.R. "Silk Route" from the Orient, providing the link to New York City. Originally in private hands and providing passenger services as well, the two railways took it over in 1930. A new 1400-ton railcar barge, *Ogdensburg*, was provided, together with the tug *Prescotont* to handle it.

This 302-ton, 1000-bhp, diesel-electric tug was built by Davie Shipbuilding in Lauzon, Quebec, in 1930 and operated in a unique manner with the barge. The barge had its own operating bridge with a duplicate of the tug's controls, from which the engine and rudders of the tug could be handled electrically. *Prescotont* was also kept busy in winter breaking and moving the river ice as far down as the Galop Rapids in order to keep the ferry channel open. Passenger service stopped when the international bridge was opened in 1958 and rail freight service ended with the burning of the Ogdensburg terminal in 1970. The tug *Prescotont* and her railcar barge were then transferred to the Windsor-Detroit Barge Line Limited, for service across the Detroit River. Eventually this tug joined the ranks of tugs converted to use as private yachts or homes.

The Pyke company was purchased by McAllister Towing and Salvage of Montreal, who built the modern twin screw, ice-strengthened *Salvage Monarch* (1959, 1440hp) to replace *Salvage Prince*. By the late 1960s, however, she had been moved to the main base at Montreal and the Kingston station was reduced to one

tug, *Daniel MacAllister* (291 tons, 1300hp). A former government steam tug named *Helena, Daniel* was built in 1907, converted to diesel power and rebuilt in 1957. She was put on the station for salvage work using a lightering barge. Occasionally she worked berthing lakers at Prescott and on long distance tows such as hauling old lakers to the steel mills for scrapping. More recently the company's seaway station was relocated to Valleyfield, Quebec.

At the other end of Lake Ontario, the principal ports of Hamilton and Toronto appear to have had some local tug activity in the latter part of the 1800s, but with no major timber export and the small steam vessels not requiring berthing, this did not loom as important as it did in the lower St. Lawrence ports. The city of Toronto, however, was unique in maintaining tugs for its own special harbour needs. With the main waterworks production plant and a sizeable population located on the Toronto Islands, regular ferry service and maintenance facilities were required.

Toronto tugs were utilized to break ice for the ferries, handle construction and maintenance barges, to fight fires and substitute for the ferries when ice conditions were severe. Iron- and steel-hulled vessels were necessary and included locally famous steam tugs like *James Whalen* (1905, 313 tons, 660bhp), *Rouille* (1929, 214 tons, 950bhp), and *Ned Hanlon* (1932, 105 tons, 280bhp). The last, in fact, has been permanently preserved on dry land as part of

The modern, hydroconic-hulled, 600bhp diesel tug *William Rest*, built for the Toronto Harbour Commission in 1961. (German and Milne, Naval Architects, Les Baxter Photo)

the Maritime Museum of Toronto since being replaced by the diesel *Ned Hanlon II. Rouille*, built in Collingwood, Ontario, was oil fired and had large fire pumps. She had a heroic career in the Halifax Fire Department during the Second World War, then retired to mundane dredging work with the J.P. Porter company. The other two went on to work Lake Superior and the East Coast, respectively.

Commercial firms like Toronto Drydocks and various dredging contractors have maintained tugs in Toronto Harbour as well. Small tugs for ship berthing purposes came on the scene when Toronto became a port of call for ocean vessels from the St. Lawrence Seaway. Some of the better known recent tugs are *William Rest* of the Harbour Commission, *Ned Hanlon II* and *G.W. Rogers*. The last was originally steam-powered, built in 1919 in Britain under a the First World War program as *West Hope*.

The steel mills of Hamilton have been the providers of considerable business for tugs over the years. After the Second World War, in a period of active scrapping of old vessels here, there was considerable tug activity. The old steam tug *Helena* worked out of Hamilton for a time in this service. After the building of the St. Lawrence Seaway, Hamilton became the home base of an expanding general towing service under the name of McKeil Boat Works. Recently renamed McKeil Marine Limited, it was started by Evans McKeil, a former Nova Scotian with a small home-built workboat, *Micmac*, during the construction of the Seaway. The company carries out berthing operations in Hamilton Harbour, as well as long distance towing and contract work up and down the Great Lakes. More recently McKeil has spread down the St. Lawrence River and Gulf, to the Arctic and the Eastern Seaboard, with a fleet including about sixteen tugs of modest size and power and fifty barges, as well as a floating drydock at the Hamilton base, involving six companies. The smaller tugs are practical for work in the smaller waterways and range from 500 to 1200bhp. The major business of McKeil, through specialized barging in the 1980s, is now transportation, supplemented by marine construction, salvage and spill control.

The McKeil fleet of the eighties included for a time the modern *W.N. Twolan*, originally built for work in the north in federal government service, and *Argue Martin*. Although built in 1895 as the Sincennes McNaughton steam tug *Ethel*, she recently sailed off to new ownership in the Caribbean. Part of the fleet are carefully maintained tugs built in the The Second World War Canadian government programs. They include former naval war program tugs like *Glenevis, Glenside* and *Glenbrook*, *Riverton* and Tanacs

renamed *Lac Como, Lac Vancouver, Lac Erie* and *Lac Manitoba* from the Consolidated Oka Sand fleet at Montreal. *Evans B. McKeil* at 2150bhp, is retro-fitted with an auxiliary mast wheelhouse for notch barging. Major expansion at century's end included two former Moran tugs, *Point Carroll* and *William Moore* for growing barge work as well as *Otis Wack (II)*, renamed *Wyatt McKeil*.

As a link in the middle of the Great Lakes-St. Lawrence Seaway route and the focal point for iron and coal moving to the steel-making and manufacturing hub of Detroit, the Detroit River has long been one of the busiest waterways in the world. With its strong current and constant traffic, winter ice is kept moving so commerce continues year-round. The largest tug fleet on the Great Lakes is that of Great Lakes Towing, operated out of Cleveland, with more than forty tugs at various bases elsewhere.

One of the larger British war-built ocean tugs was *Empire Sandy,* seen here in her years after the war as the log boom tug *Chris. M.* of Great Lakes Paper Company on Lake Superior. Since then she has been converted into a three masted schooner for passenger cruises out of Toronto as *Empire Sandy*. (Archives of Ontario 16657-38)

Long before the automobile made Detroit a great industrial city, timber rafts, schooners, barges and brigs made their way through the river to Lake St. Clair, Sarnia and the upper lakes. When tugs became available, there was certainly work for them. The strong river current along this waterway brought about a seeking type of tug enterprise quite early. This was based primarily on the Canadian port of Amherstburg, below Windsor, still in recent years a base for the Canadian Coast Guard and some American vessels.

In the latter 1800s a large fleet of tugs scrambled for the business of towing sailing vessels up the Detroit River from as far as Cleveland and Long Point on Lake Erie, through Lake St. Clair and the rapids at Point Edward, to Lake Huron. Large wooden screw tugs like *Crusader, Gladiator and Champion* frequently towed several vessels at once. Log rafts were towed as well to mills in Michigan and Ontario. These large river and lake travelling tugs were of wood, like most Canadian tugs, long after the British and Europeans had changed to iron and steel. They were evidently capable of carrying considerable freight aboard and, with their enclosed main decks, did not look much like the modern idea of a tug.

After 1900, the more specialized tug shape became the norm, the Quebec style of tug appearing in the form of *Florence*, which served under the Hackett name in these parts. The distinctive high bow and low profile tug built for getting under bridges on the canals and rivers along the American side of the lakes also became a common sight. Seeking-style towing faded away with the coming of self-powered steamer traffic on the river after the turn of the century, leaving the growing traffic in ore, coal, petroleum and chemical barges, mainly on the American side.

Rail links between Windsor and Detroit have required rail car barges that cut across the main river traffic on a steady basis. Canadian Pacific's *Prescotont* worked here for a time, but the more recent style is the square-bowed push type towboat, secured firmly to the stern of the car barge. One pushes upriver from the American terminal to the Canadian terminal while, simultaneously, a second towboat backs her barge down on the current in the other direction.

Captain Earl McQueen, operating out of Amherstburg for many years, was a colourful if unorthodox salvor and tug operator. He encouraged the annual international tug races held on the river during the 1950s. These became more organized after a few impromptu races. McQueen's *Atomic* was naturally winner of the first race. Tugs were raced in classes by steam or diesel type and by horsepower. Otherwise it was an anything-goes race, with tugs cutting each other off and an occasional bumping.

With the decline in marine casualties in the middle of the century, salvage no longer helped support operators like McQueen. His company's last tug was apparently the 2920bhp, twin-screw *Amherstburg*, built in 1965, but sold ten years later to J.D. Irving's Atlantic Towing Ltd. for operations around Saint John, becoming *Irving Poplar*, then *Atlantic Poplar*.

The Windsor-Detroit area is a crossroads where tugs and towboats seem to complete the great circle of eastern North America. The large American companies, Great Lakes Towing and Hannah Marine, maintain numbers of tugs at various ports on their side of the lakes. Major push tows have come up from as far as the Gulf of Mexico through the Mississippi, Illinois and Chicago Rivers. Descending the Great Lakes, they cross the path of the occasional ocean notch tug and barge that has come up the Atlantic from the Gulf or Eastern Seaboard, through the St. Lawrence Seaway and Welland Canal to the Detroit River.

An example of a tug and barge from the Atlantic Coast would be the 4800-bhp *Gaucho*, locked by a sophisticated hydraulic coupling into the notch in the stern of the 385-foot, carbon tetrachloride tank barge *Pampa*. Normally working out of Philadelphia to New Orleans, disdaining the sheltered intracoastal waterways for the open sea, this pair came around to the petrochemical port of Sarnia, Ontario several times a year, a harbinger of things to come.

With a strategic location at the entrance to Lake Huron, Sarnia has been the base for a few tugs looking for jobs along this busy route. A well known salvage operator, Captain Thomas Reid, ranged far and wide from Sarnia at the beginning of the twentieth century with steam tugs such as *Sarnia City, Smith* and *James T. Reid*. Reid was bought out by Sincennes McNaughton Line of Montreal, who operated a base here for their upper lakes runs as well as continuing in salvage work. The Sincennes tugs *Rival* and *Bonvoyage* were stationed

Opposite top: Two fine Lake Superior log boom towing tugs of Abitibi Paper Limited were the 388-ton, 140-foot, *Abitibi* and her twin, *Kam*, built by Vickers in Montreal in 1938. In addition to her crew they carried woods workers and their supplies to the remote north shore of the lake. (German and Milne, Naval Architects)

Opposite bottom: The river log drives delivered the wood to the booms at the Lake Superior shore. *Abitibi* waits to commence the long open lake tow to the mills. She later worked on the Pacific coast as *Gulf Ivy* and *Swiftsure*. (Abitibi Price Limited, Lockwood Survey Photo)

#28454~JUNE 28, 1938.
140ft. ABITIBI TUG "KAM."
SHIP 127.

KAM
TORONTO

Sister ship to *Abitibi, Kam* nears completion at Vickers' yard in Montreal in 1938. The early Kort nozzles and bar guards protect the twin screws from logging debris. These tugs were powered by two 480bhp Atlas Polar Diesels. *Kam* was a pilot boat at Halifax during the Second World War. (German and Milne, Naval Architects)

Opposite: For the first half of the twentieth century a mainstay of Upper Lakes log towing was the large former American coastal bargehaul tug. *Sulphite* was typical of the Driftwood Land & Timber Ltd. of Port Arthur. She was 433 tons, built in Elizabeth, New Jersey in 1919. (Archives of Ontario S1308)

Similarly Purvis Marine has operated since 1967 a dozen tugs of up to 5500bhp out of Sault Ste. Marie, currently operating the larger *Anglian Lady* (1972, 398 tons, 3500bhp), *Avenger IV* (1962, 293 tons, 2400bhp) and the ice-rated notch-suitable *Atlantic Cedar* (renamed *Reliance*), acquired from Atlantic Towing. As with other Lakes tug operators, Purvis offers barge services.

here for a time in the 1930s. A converted diesel Bangor class minesweeper, *Lachine*, served as his salvage vessel after the end of the Second World War. In the 1980s and 90s Sandrin Brothers operated tugs at Sarnia for general towing services, *Glenada* and *Tusker* of 1400 and 1600bhp. Similarly Purvis Marine has operated since 1967 a dozen tugs of up to 5500bhp out of Sault Ste. Marie, currently operating the larger *Anglian Lady* (1972, 398 tons, 3500bhp), *Avenger IV* (1962, 293 tons, 2400bhp) and the ice-rated notch-suitable *Atlantic Cedar* (renamed *Reliance*), acquired from Atlantic Towing. As with other Lakes tug operators, Purvis offers barge services.

Head of the Lakes

As the farthest point west in the great water route running into the interior of the continent, Fort William, at the head of Lake Superior, became a point of commercial significance in the days of the fur trade. This commanding position as the gateway to the vast western plains also made the twins, Fort William and Port Arthur, now amalgamated as Thunder Bay, a vital port. Chiefly, it is the railhead for the outpouring of prairie grain to the cheaper water transportation available at this point.

Today, berthing and general towing services are provided by local companies, including Gravel and Lake Services Limited, with several harbour tugs, including *George N. Carleton* and *Robert John*, both 1250bhp. But the golden age of towing was in the lumber and pulp movements carried out along the Canadian side of Lake Superior in the first half of the twentieth century. In the earlier years, large quantities of pulpwood were cut along the lake for the pulp and paper mills at Thunder Bay and Sault Ste. Marie.

Large tugs, suited to the broad waters of this inland sea, carried pulp cutters to the woods in the autumn, together with horses, pigs and other supplies, often a trip of several days. *Gargantua* and *Reliance* were two of the pioneering tugs in this work. The former had been an unfinished American first world war production vessel. She was completed in Sault Ste. Marie in 1923 and worked out of there, a 150-footer with two Scotch boilers and a crew of fifteen. Built of fir, her hull was hard to maintain in fresh water.

After the winter's cutting, log drives on rivers like the Pukaskwa brought the logs to collecting booms at the lakefront. Here the tugs took over, towing huge bags of pulp logs along the shore to the mills. Lake Superior is well known to mariners as a big and dangerous sea. Lee shores were a major peril for the pulp tugs. Abitibi Paper Company tugs handled 10,000-cord tows, moving at about one knot, taking a week or ten days to get from the northeast shore to Sault Ste. Marie. The break-up and loss of an occasional towing boom was not unexpected.

The tugs were usually over 300 tons, and the early fleets operated by the pulp and lumber companies were collected from a wide variety of sources. The Great Lakes Lumber Company of Fort William made it through the restrictions of the Second World War with some very old boats. These included *Lawrence H. Shaw* (289 tons, 1900) and *W.E. Hunt* (388 tons, 1913), built in Camden, New Jersey. An unusual vessel was *Oscar Lehtinen*, a 582-tonner built in New York in 1903, having propellers fore and aft and quadruple expansion engines. A modern tug, *Abele* (1942, 861 tons), was an American wartime diesel-electric wooden vessel. Another end-of-war acquisition was Great Lakes Paper's *Chris M.*, built in 1943 on the Tyne as *Empire Sandy*, one of the larger (479 tons) Empire war service steam tugs. She regained her original name in the 1980s when rebuilt as a three-masted schooner to carry 250 passengers on sailing cruises out of Toronto.

Abitibi Power and Paper Company operated a considerable fleet of tugs before and after the war, including several built just before and after, resulting in a modern roster of mainly twin-diesel powered vessels in the 1950s. Canadian Vickers built the splendid *Abitibi* and *Kam*, of 386 tons in 1938, fitted with two 480bhp Sulzer and Atlas diesels respectively. They were early examples of use of Kort nozzles. Russel Brothers built *Clarke B. Davis* and *T. Gibbens* after the war. An older steam tug that lasted a long time was *Strathbogie*, originally the British *Laval (I)*, built in 1914 and brought to Canada earlier by the City of Quebec Harbour Commissioners. Abitibi also operated the 1938 *Nipigon* and *Orient Bay*, 90-foot, twin diesel boats, on Lake Nipigon. These were built at Sorel, dismantled and shipped in parts to Lake Nipigon, with *Nipigon* eventually turning up on the West Coast.

Sincennes McNaughton Line of Montreal maintained *James Whalen* and *Bonsecours* in wood-towing work in the Lakehead area in the middle to late 1930s as part of their declining long range operations. The British Alexander Hall-built *Bonsecours* and her sister, *Bonvoyage*, were operated by Sincennes, but owned by Ross Towing and Salvage of Montreal. They were sold overseas in 1938.

CHAPTER 12

Seeking and Logging: The West Coast

Early Days

THE NORTHWEST COAST OF NORTH AMERICA HAS TWO DISTINCT SECTORS. The American shore, running south from Cape Flattery, is open and exposed to the storms of the Pacific. There are few good harbours, and those at river mouths generally have perils for the mariner in the form of violent and capricious waters over bars at the entrance. North of Flattery's stormy corner on the Strait of Juan de Fuca is the Canadian coast, marked by the sheltered passages behind the long bulk of Vancouver Island and the many smaller islands of the Inside Passage running north towards Alaska as well as south into Puget Sound.

But this shelter from the long Pacific swell and storms with thousands of miles of momentum behind them is not all placidly safe. The very configuration of the waterways among the islands results in powerful tides and rips that kill unwary ships and men. The periodic rushing tidal currents, whirlpools and huge standing waves on the Seymour Narrows and Yaculta Rapids rival the Reversing Falls on the Saint John River in New Brunswick. Like the latter, they dictate when waterborne traffic may pass. Winds roar down passes and sea inlets from the coastal mountain ranges to menace unwary passing vessels.

These perils notwithstanding, the multitudinous passages behind British Columbia's islands have long been frequented by swarms of tugs, barges, coasters and, more recently, by cruise liners. They brave the fogs, snows and rain, their masters kept constantly on alert by the density of traffic. The need of the pioneers for transportation by water was not substantially diminished by railway and highway construction as it had been in the east. The rugged mountain ranges, rising right out of the sea, have preserved the competitive existence of the tug and barge, making the coasts of British Columbia, Washington and Alaska what local enthusiasts have described as "tugboat heaven."

When steam powered vessels first appeared, the Canadian West Coast, unlike the East, was in no position to design and manufacture its own steamers. In 1835 there was little on the B.C. Coast but a few posts of the Hudson's Bay Company. However, the company could see the usefulness of a steamer to get among the islands and up the long fjord-like inlets to carry on its trade. That year, a paddle wheeler named *Beaver* was built in Britain to penetrate the Columbia and Fraser Rivers carrying trade goods to barter with the Indians. As in so many other cases, however, it was soon learned that the versatility of towing would extend her usefulness. In fact, a goodly part of her 53-year career would be spent functioning as a tug.

Beaver sailed out from Britain by way of Cape Horn and Hawaii, but was not the first to make such a heroic passage. The first steamer on the Pacific was probably the Spanish paddler *Telica* on the Mexican coast around 1825. Two paddlers, *Australia* and *Surprise* were delivered from Britain to Australia in 1830 and 1831. All of these very early vessels made their journeys either entirely or primarily by sail.

Beaver set sail from Gravesend on 27 August 1835 with her paddle wheels stowed on board. To spend her life on a primitive coast she was heavily built of teak and oak, close-ribbed with greenheart, and bolted and sheathed with copper. Her two vertical, single cylinder engines of 35nhp each, drove 13-foot diameter side wheels. Steam was provided by a rectangular, low pressure boiler set on a brick firebox.

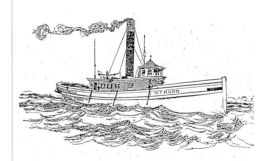

W.T. Robb (German & Milne)

Above: First powered vessel in the Pacific Northwest was the tough little paddler *Beaver*, which sailed around the Horn from England in 1835. The Hudson's Bay Company ordered her for carrying fur trade goods but she spent most of her 53 year career towing ships, barges and timber rafts. (Vancouver City Archives)

Opposite top: A sort of *Great Eastern* among tugs was the 1875 vessel *Alexander*, a huge 180-foot side wheel seeker out of Victoria. This tug carried out long coal ship tows between Cape Flattery and Nanaimo and salvage operations like this one, but was expensive to operate. (Archives of British Columbia 17-6771)

Opposite bottom: One of the long-lived tugs of the Northwest Coast was the steel-hulled screw, *Tepic*, built at Blackwall on the Thames in 1883 for the French Panama Canal project. She worked mainly in the building supply and coal trade until decommissioned in 1938. (Vancouver City Archives BON 332.P665)

This hardy pioneer of the Pacific Northwest stopped in at Madeira, Trinidad, the Falklands, Juan Fernandez, and Honolulu (the best sailing track), sailing into Fort Vancouver on the Columbia River, arriving on 10 April 1836. She was a good seaboat and handled well under sail for Captain David Home and his twelve-man crew. At Fort Vancouver *Beaver's* engines and paddle wheels were hooked up and trial runs proved her ready for duty. Soon she made a trip up the B.C. coast, exploring the Inside Passage until turned back by the Russians, who then owned Alaska.

Beaver played an important role in the early history of British Columbia and is well known to every school child in that province. She performed a variety of duties from routine trading and supply missions to locating the site for the City of Victoria. She carried the governor to Alaska for a parley with the Russians and surveyed the coast for the Royal Navy. In the 1850s, other steam vessels began to arrive to share the load. *Beaver* consumed huge amounts of wood for fuel and carried a crew of wood cutters for this purpose. She simply put in anywhere along the shore where the tall timber grew right down to the water's edge.

On long expeditions these "wooding-up" interruptions were very time-consuming. It took two days to cut the forty cords of fuel required to steam 30 miles on the following day. The problem disappeared very quickly in the 1850s when high quality coal deposits were discovered near Nanaimo on Vancouver Island. This led to fuel conversion for *Beaver* and others like her, as well as a whole new industry. Coal joined timber as a major export for the region.

The coal trade out of Nanaimo for the west coast of the United States flourished, calling for sailing ships to work through the tricky passage of the Gulf of Georgia and the Strait of Juan de Fuca. The burgeoning lumber trade also faced this gauntlet for shipping headed to and from distant markets. The result was a golden age for seeking tugs from Vancouver, Nanaimo, Victoria and Seattle, running out Juan de Fuca Strait as far as notoriously stormy Cape Flattery on the Pacific Ocean.

After a varied career with the Hudson's Bay Company, *Beaver* was sold in the seventies to a Victoria group for use as a full-time tug, joining others in an expanding trade. She towed lumber vessels in and out of Burrard Inlet, the main harbour at Vancouver, hauled logs on Puget Sound and worked in the Stikine River, as well as serving as a seeking tug between Nanaimo and Albert Head.

When, in February of 1883, *Beaver* ran ashore in the entrance to Vancouver Harbour, the press noted that, "The *Beaver* has had many experiences with rocks during her long career in these waters." It was certainly true, as she had frequently nosed ashore to load in the days when there were no wharves. The tough little vessel was not much harmed and, in September, the Victoria *Evening Post* was reporting, "*Beaver* arrived from Chemainus with probably the largest boom of logs ever seen here or on the Sound, 800 feet long and 100 feet wide." She was owned by the B.C. Towing and Transportation Company at that time.

Five years later, though, on 26 July 1888, the most famous vessel in British Columbia history ran heavily ashore at Prospect Point while heading out of Burrard Inlet at Vancouver. She was a victim of the lethal tide eddies in the First Narrows and the unresponsive steering of the early side wheeler. She lay impaled for four years, unmercifully scavenged for her metals and teak, before sliding off into the depths.

The gold rush of 1857 boosted trade generally, including the need for tugs. Purpose-built tugs appeared on the Pacific Coast at San Francisco in the fifties. The first was probably the side wheeler *Goliah*, claimed to be the second real tug in the United States and the largest in the world, although she was only 136 feet long. Her intrepid crew made off with her from a threatened sheriff's auction on the East Coast to join the California Gold Rush. They made their way around Cape Horn to San Francisco to work towing and carrying passengers. Eventually, in 1871, she was a sawmill logging tug on Puget Sound, the first in a succession of

Opposite top: The northwest coast from Puget Sound to Alaska became prosperous for the towing trade and tugs abounded in the ports. Here are some of the numerous small wooden steam tugs, all screw type, that worked log rafts, barges and sailing ships around Vancouver early in the twentieth century. (Vancouver City Archives 1210)

Opposite bottom: A breed of large wooden single screw tugs was developed to perform long distance seeking and raft towing in the inside waters of the Northwest. The territory of vessels like Young and Gore's 200-ton *Sealion* included Cape Flattery, Victoria, Seattle, Vancouver, Nanaimo, the Inside Passage to the Queen Charlotte Islands and ports between. She was built in 1905 with a triple expansion engine. (Archives British Columbia HP 53171)

Labyrinthine passages, murky weather and tidal currents made the deceptively sheltered coast of British Columbia treacherous for the unwary tug handling a long ungainly raft of logs. (Archives British Columbia HP53176)

Goliahs in this part of the world. An earlier gold rush tug on Puget Sound was *Resolute* from Philadelphia in 1858, smaller at 90 feet and a logging tug as well.

West Coast Seekers

In the 1850s Puget Sound tugs were towing sailing vessels in from Cape Flattery, a lucrative and important service to a growing economy that was based on exports. They were joined sometimes by the Canadian *Beaver* and *Otter*, although it was not until later that *Beaver* became a serious seeker, hanging about Albert Head looking for incoming ships. Victoria was a good base for seeking and for towing out sailing ships, being astride the routes from Flattery to Vancouver, Seattle and Nanaimo. An early tug built in Victoria in 1866 was *Isabel*. The Victoria firm of McAllister Brothers built a large vessel on the Skeena River in 1875 that was a *Great Eastern* among tugs. A very large side wheeler of 180 feet, she was expensive to run and thus not profitable. Named *Alexander*, this seeker towed sailing ships between Flattery and Nanaimo.

The early Victoria tugs were heavily occupied with towing ships to and from Nanaimo. In proper seeking style, they towed a coal-laden vessel down to Cape Flattery and loitered there while waiting for an incoming ship. Experienced sailing ship captains carefully considered the weather, hoping to get as far in as possible towards Nanaimo, 150 miles from the open sea, to reduce the towing cost. Sometimes they made it all the way without help. But the treacherous winds in Juan de Fuca Strait, in the shadow of the Cascade Range, made it a gamble to argue too long over a towing fee. Even far at sea off the Cape, ships often looked anxiously for a tow to keep them off the infamous lee shore.

The tugs eventually developed into two sizes; very large, long and lean for seeking, and small and manoeuverable for harbour work. Some of the major shippers and owners maintained their own tugs. The coal baron Robert Dunsmuir had built the ultimate among ship-towing tugs in *Lorne* of 1889 to handle his coal traffic. This fine boat was 150 feet long, powered at 14 knots by Scotch boilers and a 1250ihp, triple expansion engine, said to be the first triple built in Canada. *Lorne* had a crew of seventeen, carried 150 tons of coal in her bunkers and was equipped with a 16-inch manilla towing hawser with capstan. She carried 150 tons of coal fuel, had a coppered bottom and cost $60,000. The smaller *Active* (150

Crew take it easy, except for the fireman below, as *Wireless* (1910, 330hp) plods along at the usual 2-3 knots with a large raft of logs in tow. (Pacific Coast Tug Society)

tons), built in the same year, and the later *Sealion* were similar vessels, though they were built firstly for log towing. By now they were all screw propeller driven vessels. *Active* was a prototype for long distance log towing tugs, with low power at slow speed for economy of fuel. Her engine was triple expansion, locally built in New Westminster, lasting until 1956 when replaced by a diesel.

In 1891, a consortium of Puget Sound mills put together the Puget Sound Tug Company with a fleet of four large seeking tugs to establish a rational towing service from Cape Flattery. Later on, the Canadian *Lorne* and *Sealion* also served with this fleet. At the turn of the century the company had four tugs cruising off Flattery as much as 15 miles out. Outbound, they took their charges 10 to 20 miles out to sea. Such was the appreciation of the dangers to sailing vessels of this main passage to the ports of the inside waters.

The Americans generally called the seeking tugs that were engaged in bringing ships through the difficult entrances of their

west coast rivers "bar tugs." The problem for ports like San Francisco and Portland, Oregon, was not a long narrow channel, but difficult and sometimes violent currents off the sea entrance. This was caused by tidal and river flows over the shallowing water offshore; in effect, underwater deltas. The shallow bar at the entrance to the Columbia River is notoriously hazardous, while San Francisco's is a serious threat. Once across, sailing ships had an easy 100-mile tow upriver to Portland. At San Francisco's Golden Gate, tide races and fogs were additional perils. These locations, therefore, had their "bar tugs" that ventured out to sea to solicit the business of incoming vessels whose captains had to weigh the risks carefully before haggling.

The seeking business faded with the decline of sailing ships on the world's oceans during the First World War. A few ships clung on in bulk trades such as lumber and grain. The Strait of Juan de Fuca saw classic square-riggers towed through by tugs as late as 1946,

Running light, with a bone in her teeth, *Seaswell* hurries to another job. She was built in 1922 for Mowat Towing. (Public Archives of British Columbia)

when *Island Commander* did the honours by taking the famous four-masted barque *Pamir* out to Flattery on her last trip in these waters. This *Island Commander* (217 tons, 1912) was famous for her time supplying small ports along the coast with line-haul barge service. She was also distinctive for her odd whaleback forecastle, derived from her original incarnation as the trawler *Andrew Kelly*. During the Second World War she was under American charter for defence work in the Aleutians, and still registered in 2002.

The Logs

What is now Vancouver's downtown harbourfront was once tall timber right to the water's edge. Trees could be felled right into the water and floated conveniently to Moody's and Hasting's sawmills close by on opposite shores of Burrard Inlet. The rich forest resource was exploited with a vengeance by the entrepreneurs and soon the prime logs had to be towed longer and longer distances. As the distances grew, so did business for tugs. Various forms of rafts were devised to make up the tows. The mill owners had their own tugs built, but eventually needed the help of the independent tug operators.

The earliest log towing was done by primitive steamers like *Beaver*, followed by increasingly sophisticated boats particularly suited to the requirements. The early tows were for short distances, but they lengthened with the search for fresh wood supplies. The sheltered waters made this work easy as long as a sharp eye was kept on the possible quirks of weather. The Moodyville mill on Burrard Inlet in the 1880s was using local small tugs to bring in logs. Among these were *Etta White*, the first screw-driven tug in the area, and the little British-built *Tepic*, an iron-hulled vessel that had been ordered for the ill-fated French Panama Canal project.

The small raft-towing tug continues to have its place to the present day. The big mills that surrounded Vancouver have all gone, but a few tugs, small by later standards, less than 1000 horsepower, still tow rafts of logs for export up Burrard Inlet past the berths of the gleaming cruise ships to the ship-loading berth at Port Moody. Most tow or sort logs on the Fraser River nearby for the remaining sawmills there, led by Westminster Tug Boats, the pioneer log handler on the river.

By 1890, large and graceful steam tugs had appeared to preside over the more glamorous long distance log tows. *Active* was built for the Moody company to assist the smaller *Comet* and *Belle*, presumably with longer tow runs in mind and the Hastings Lumber Company built the long famous *Haro* and *Czar*. At this time, enterprising independent log towing specialists began to pick up enough business to start building sizeable fleets. The first may have been Captain George French with his tugs *Huron, St. Clair* and *Superior*.

One of the earlier harbour tugs in Canadian waters with Voith-Schneider type propulsion was ice- strengthened *Pointe Comeau* of Eastern Canada Towing in 1976, destined for service at Baie Comeau, Quebec. Her twin rotors are seen under the head end, with a fixed skeg at the stern. (German and Milne, Naval Architects)

The salvaged cruise ship *Sundancer* enters Vancouver Harbour in 1984, in tow of *Seaspan Mariner* with a Crusader class tug steering astern, having been raised by McAllister of Montreal at Campbell River. (Seaspan International, Commercial Illustrators Ltd)

In 1988 azimuthal steering drive tugs had reached the port of Buenos Aires. Twin screw *Ona Temple* undocks a cruise ship, her high broad stern housing the Z-drives. (Author's Collection)

Above:
A jack-up drill rig is towed out of Saint John by *Irving Elm* and *Irving Cedar* together with one of the new anchor handling tugs when these began to assume major long distance tows and before the development of semisubmersible barges to carry drill rigs more efficiently. (Author's Collection)

Left:
A semisubmersible drilling platform, SEDCO 708, with two Seaspan tugs in attendance. The rig is riding high preparatory to towing out to sea. (Seaspan International)

Semisubmersible drilling platform under tow by one of the larger Smit tugs, *Smit London*, with smaller steering tug astern. (Seaspan International)

A semisubmersible rig sits parked on the bottom of Halifax Harbour at sunset in 1986 while Ectug's *Point Vibert* passes by. (Keith Vaughan)

C.H. Cates brought ASD "Z-Peller" drive tugs to Canada and its Vancouver docking operations starting with its *C.H. Cates I*, *II* and *III* in 1983, 1986 and 1988. These high power-to-length, 2400bhp boats feature a hydraulic crane forward for ease of passing towlines up to ships' decks. (Author's Collection)

In the year 2000 the Halifax docking tug *Point Chebucto* (1993, 4300 bhp) showed at the tall ships gathering in her new Wijsmuller livery of blue, white and black, ECTUG and their British owners having been absorbed by the venerable Dutch firm. (Author's Collection)

Cabot Sea is one of the many purpose-built offshore petroleum support vessels to displace the traditional tugs that first assisted this industry. Now the anchor handling service tug competes directly with the seagoing tug. (Author's Collection)

Arctic Shiko, an Arctic Class II anchor handling tug of 12,280bhp for floating drill rigs, departs Okpo, Korea, in July 1983 on a long haul to the Canadian Arctic. Her tow is a saltwater treatment plant, the voyage a challenge to even the traditional oceangoing tug. (Arctic Transportation Limited)

The first powerful new generation docking tug of Seaspan's Vancouver fleet was *Seaspan Discovery*. She was built in 1984, is 104 feet long with a 35-foot beam. The broad stern shows her purpose is to push and pull with her bow using a towline winch and plenty of rubber fendering. (David Baird)

A hydraulic winch has been added to modernize a tug for bridge control of the towline length and more truck tire fendering added in the newly versatile push and pull or tractor handling of ships. (Author's Collection)

In ECTUG colours, *Point Valiant*, end-on,
illustrates the current preference for maximum
wheelhouse visibility all around, overhead and
down on the tug's deck. The superstructure slope
also avoids contact with overhanging ship's sides.
(Author's Collection)

One of the Ocean Intrepide class of ASD tugs built at Ocean Group's Isle aux Coudres shipyard is Ectug's *Point Valiant(II)*. She has Niigata propulsion from two Mitsubishi diesels for 4000bhp. Others in the class include McAllister Towing's Montreal docking tugs *Ocean Intrepide* and *Ocean Jupiter*. (Robert Allan, Ltd.)

One of a series built in the Irving East Isle shipyard in Georgetown, Prince Edward Island, ASD tractor tug *Atlantic Hemlock* (1996) rates 4004bhp (50 tonnes BP) with Aquamaster drives and two Caterpillar diesel engines. Here she pulls back while turning a ship at Saint John. (Author's Collection)

A promotion for a children's television series, the wooden hulled *Theodore* has also promoted water safety for children up and down the eastern seaboard of Canada and the United States, proving everyone likes tugs. (Author's Collection)

River barge-pusher *Atlantic Pine* plays another role barging a heavy process vessel out of Saint John Harbour, assisted by *Atlantic Alder*. Delivery by barge makes practical the convenient factory fabrication of such bulky objects. (Author's Collection)

Seaspan Hawk and *Seaspan Falcon* are 3000hp tractor tugs built for the company's entry into ship berthing and escort activity in Burrard Inlet, Vancouver. (Robert Allan Ltd.)

Ajax is a powerful, 10,000bhp VSP escort tug of advanced design by Robert Allan, Ltd., of Vancouver, and constructed in Spain for service in Norway. (Robert Allan Ltd.)

Ocean Jupiter, one of two modern ASD tractor tugs placed in service by Ocean Group for ship berthing at Montreal by McAllister Towing. She is one of a number produced in the Ocean Industries yard at Ile aux Coudres, Que. (Robert Allan Ltd.)

A liquid bulk carrier, *McCleary's Spirit* is an example of the new breed of specialized notch barges appearing on the Seaway canals and Great Lakes. She is seen being steered through the Welland Canal in McKeil service by *William J.Moore*. (McKeil Marine)

Representative of the late twentieth century versatile anchor-handling tugs (AHTs) scattered about the world is *Naftegaz*, a Russian boat operating in Greek service and seen on charter in Canada. The standard rescue pickup point is seen marked on her side.

In 1905, he had built what is considered by many to have been the classic among large log towing steam tugs on the West Coast, the 218-ton, 130-foot *Sealion*. Powerful and well fitted, she had commodious facilities for her crew. She was renowned for having a piano in her spacious saloon and a whistle that could play tunes like a slide flute. When in the 1950s she was converted to diesel with an 800bhp engine taken from *Active*, her flute whistle continued in use on compressed air and was used to serenade fascinated passengers on cruise ships.

Sealion was soon sold to the British Canadian Lumber Company, which was setting up its own tug operation, but this venture foundered and she went to the Young and Gore fleet for a long and successful career. The short-lived British Canadian operation was run by Claude Thicke, who went on to buy the Progressive Steamboat Company in 1920, becoming a well-known and innovative tug operator with his Blue Band Navigation Company. He began the trend to diesel propulsion in West Coast tugs in the 1920s, very early by world standards.

While the lumber and pulp mills eventually gave up running their own tugs for the most part, a couple defied the trend to turn over log towing to the growing specialists in this field. Instead they maintained their captive towing operations right into the recent and much changed era. These were Kingcome Navigation Company, first operated by the Powell River Company then by MacMillan-

Nanoose was a well-known B.C. tug in the barge towing trade for Canadian Pacific. She was one of the earlier steel hulled tugs built in British Columbia, built in Victoria in 1908, with a compound engine (630hp, 166 tons, 116 feet long). She lasted 38 years. (CP Rail Corporate Archives)

One of a couple hundred little log sorters on the British Columbia coast moves a raft of logs in Burrard Inlet near Vancouver. Most of this work moved to the Fraser River. (Author's Collection)

Bloedel, and Canadian Tugboat Company, subsidiary of Canadian Western Lumber Company. Kingcome, particularly, perfected a two-way service for its owners—barging supplies in for their isolated mill towns and hauling product out.

The greatest turn of events in the wood industry of the West Coast occurred around the turn of the century. On the one hand, freewheeling cutting of the forests in eastern Canada was becoming significantly restricted by governments. Then the American government imposed similar restrictions. The result was an influx of American lumber and pulp producers into British Columbia. This expansion brought with it a new era of large scale woodlands operations using logging railways and donkey-engine-powered tramlines to haul the big logs to water. There inevitably followed a boom in business for the tugs in the 1920s. The expansion of sawmilling promoted development along the Fraser River for mills and traffic in rafts and barges.

Another leap in development came during the First World War. High quality spruce was in urgent demand for the aircraft industry.

The American market purchased all of the normal production, so British and Canadian requirements had to be sought farther afield. It became necessary to tap the forests of the Queen Charlotte Islands, until then considered too remote for practical lumbering purposes because of the open and frequently rough seas of Hecate Strait. Under the encouragement of the British government, a fleet of eighteen tugs was drawn together. The Imperial Munitions Board supplied *Massett* and *Moresby*, tugs they had built for log towing purposes. Log rafts of a type that would stand up to the Pacific swells were needed. The problem had been addressed before, with varying degrees of success. Now, solutions tried under wartime pressures were to open up a new phase of expanded log towing, bringing vast new areas into the realm of regular transportation by tug.

The traditional West Coast rafts had been made up of basic boomstick sections about seventy feet square, the outside logs chained together and the inside logs held in place by cross logs on top. These single layer raft sections were joined together into large tows that gradually expanded as techniques improved and the power of tugs grew. *Beaver* was a pioneer in handling boomstick tows. In later years tows grew to sixty or eighty sections. They were suited to sheltered waters and slow towing. Heavy stresses caused logs to slip out and the rafts to break up. It was necessary, therefore, to keep a weather-eye out even in the more sheltered waterways. There were many recognized, sheltered locations where tug captains waited out bad weather and tides with their charges.

These rendevous even had beer parlours to help the crews while away their time.

The essential approach to a rough-water raft was to bundle logs together in a mass, often with a sharp-ended, vessel-like form. The earliest successful major attempt on record seems to have been the Joggins Raft, built on shore in the Maritimes about 1880 by Hugh Robertson of Saint John, and launched like a ship. It was about 600

Log tugs like *Robert Preston* (1923, 510hp) of Preston-Mann in the forties worked with rafts in many remote places without wharves. The raft was the mooring point, keeping the tug in deep water away from the shore. (Pacific Coast Tug Society)

The British built 332-ton *William Jolliffe* had a varied career in towing and salvage in British and British Columbian waters, including a period handling barges for Canadian Pacific under the name *Nitinat*. She was built in Britain in 1885 and had a 164nhp compound engine, the most powerful of her time. She was wrecked in 1925. (CP Rail Corporate Archives 22164)

feet long, somewhat cigar-shaped and consisted of 22,000 logs chained together. It was towed to New York by two schooners, but there is no record of the system becoming common usage on the East Coast. Much earlier, in 1824, a contraption made of sawn timber, described as half-ship and half-raft, was sailed from Quebec to England and then disassembled.

Robertson is thought to have built similar rafts in Washington and Oregon. Histories of the C.H. Cates Company state that the father of Charles Cates, the founder, worked with Robertson on his Joggins Raft and tried similar rafts in British Columbia. In any event logs were bundled together en masse in various experimental ways with varying degrees of success, including a type called the Davis Raft. This was, in effect, a mat of logs woven together with chains and cables that was then wrapped around a mass of logs and tightened using donkey engines. These rafts were simply large bundles of logs assembled from logs brought to a convenient site in bags or square rafts.

The Davis Rafts measured from about 200 feet in length to an eventual 500 feet, drawing over twenty feet of water and containing as much as 2.5 million board feet. They were comparatively rigid and could stand fairly heavy swells. American attempts with similar rafts off the coast sometimes met with disaster when they were caught by bad weather far from any shelter.

First used before the war, the Davis Raft came into its own with the opening up of timber cutting operations in the Queen Charlotte Islands. The bigger tugs towed them across Hecate Strait when the weather was favourable. The first such tow was in 1917 by *Progressive* with her 300bhp, triple expansion engine. The big old seekers like *Lorne* found a new lease on life with this work. The system involved making the two-day tow as often as possible across the Strait when weather was good, and parking the rafts at various points on the mainland shore to await the next stage. When the weather was rough outside in the strait, the rafts were picked up again and taken the rest of the way to mills anywhere from Prince Rupert to Vancouver using the more sheltered inner waters. This might be done by the same tug or a smaller one.

Such methods extended the range of logging and retrieval of logs over water to all of the British Columbia coast. After the Second World War, a cheaper, simpler method came into common use. This was the use of bundle booms, in which small cabled bundles of logs were boomed together as though they were individual logs in a flat boom. Eventually, bundles would be hoisted onto barges for speedy hauling over long distances and through open waters. This method has culminated in the modern seagoing tug-and-barge team, capable of hoisting 10,000 tons of log bundles aboard the barge with its own cranes, then sailing at about eight knots to a distant mill. There, the barge is partially flooded, tipping itself and dumping the load in minutes.

Cannery Tugs

Another great British Columbia seacoast resource is fish, used most notably in the salmon canning industry. Beginning in the early 1880s, the processing of salmon grew to something over 100 cannery operations up and down the coast. But it centred upon the greatest salmon rivers, the Skeena and Fraser. Surprisingly, as this industry expanded, its logistics called for a very substantial amount of work by tugs.

First, there was the regulation stating that fishermen could not use powered boats to catch the salmon, a conservation measure. This resulted in the use of tugs to tow the small open sail-powered fishing boats out and back from the fishing grounds each week, with as many as thirty boats in a tow. Then there was the daily collection of bargeloads of fish to be towed to the canneries. Many cannery boats had holds for transporting salmon and there was sometimes little difference between a tug and a "fish packer." The latter carried salmon to the cannery, but they sometimes towed as well.

The canneries owned many of each vessel type themselves, while others were hired. About one hundred tugs worked for this industry early in the century. One of the most famous was *Tyee*, not only unusual in appearance with her carved, pointed bow, but one of those legendary tugs with an engine that rotated in the wrong direction. She was a single-screw vessel fitted with an engine that

was one of a pair intended for a twin-screw vessel and had to rotate the propeller counter to the normal direction for a single screw. Tugs, with their large propellors, on going astern, tended to have their stern thrown sideways. Captains understood and made use of this propeller characteristic, but could be fooled by one that "threw" the wrong way. *Tyee's* fancy bow is said to have suffered as a consequence.

The tug early proved to be a vital factor in the economic development of the West Coast. Its role has continued strong although roads and railways have diminished the early importance of these doughty vessels elsewhere. Key elements in their endurance are the mountainous and indented coastline of British Columbia, and the sheltered inside passages.

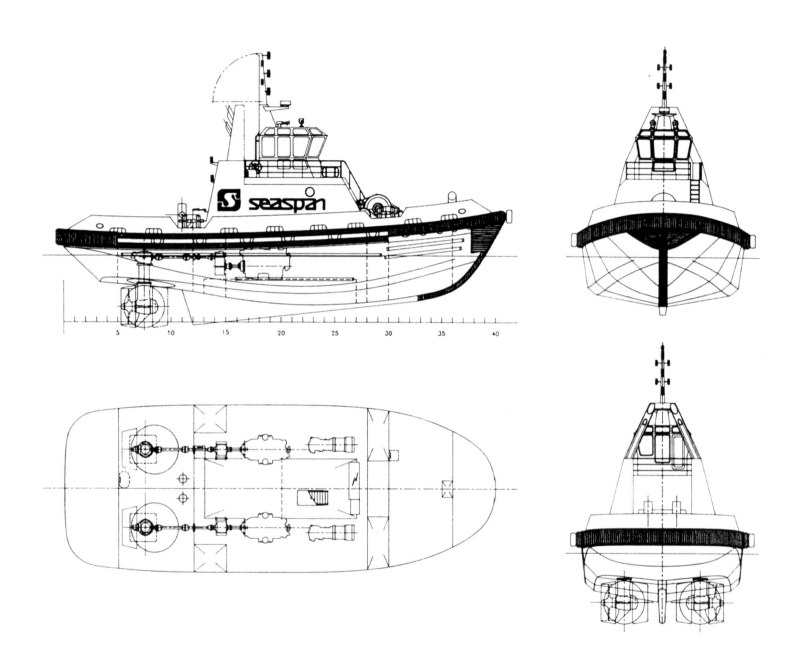

General arrangement plan for *Seaspans Hawk* and *Falcon*, twin ASD, 3000bhp tugs with winch forward and towing hook aft, part of Vancouver docking fleet. (Seaspan International, Washington Group)

Vancouver: "Towboat Land"

BURRARD INLET, the spectacular main harbour of Vancouver, was still forested to the water's edge until the mid 1880s. Only a couple of early sawmills and the lumbermen's settlement of Granville, or Gastown, broke the continuous wall of forest. When the decision was revealed that the new transcontinental Canadian Pacific Railway would have its terminus at the Gastown site, frantic construction began on a booming new city.

Vancouver's seacoast location in a paradise of magnificent timber, logs and lumber was the impetus for burgeoning commercial enterprise. Naturally, the new city was built from the handy material. In fact, tree clearing operations for the railway facilities resulted in a fire that burned it all down two months later. This was but a momentary interruption. The combination of unlimited high quality timber, railway transport and a splendid harbour ensured the destiny of Vancouver as a world seaport. Because of the rugged, mountainous coastline, it was also to become the hub of a unique, localized, seaborne traffic, secure from serious competition by rail or road.

Although Vancouver was born when the world was well into the age of steam navigation, ocean shipping of bulk commodities like lumber was still by sailing ship. The supply of logs for the mills came from the immediate neighborhood, pulled overland by oxen or floated along the shoreline by kedging, or even pulled by rowboat. The first tugs, brought to the harbour by the mill operators, were used to assist ships in and out of the harbour and through the straits as far as the open sea. They were wooden, steam-powered screw boats and, for the day, were often very powerful at 1000ihp or more. The notorious tidal currents of the First Narrows on Burrard Inlet apparently discouraged ships from passing through under sail, even in the best of weather. There seems to have been little discussion over whether to take a tow.

On the Vancouver side of the harbour, Stamp's Mill, soon to be the Hastings Mill, had the first real Canadian West Coast-built tug. This was *Isabella*, a side wheeler constructed in Victoria in 1866. She looked much like the versatile combination passenger, freight and towing vessels sometimes used on the Great Lakes in this era. Ten years later, the Moodyville Sawmill Company on the north shore, exporting many shiploads of lumber, brought in the 97-foot *Etta White* from Puget Sound for this seeking type of work and the moving of logs. These were not the first towing vessels serving a West Coast harbour. Two small steam vessels were assisting ships in and out of the long Alberni Canal on Vancouver Island in 1862.

The port grew, led by development of the Canadian Pacific rail and steamship interconnection, the importing of coal from Vancouver Island and local shipbuilding. The 1880s saw a rapid build-up of the nearby shoreline. This process and the appearance of deeper draught vessels necessitated a shift from parallel wharves to finger piers, with a need for tug assistance to berth ships of increasing size. As well, loading of lumber was slow and it was more convenient to load ships at anchor from barges rather than tie up expensive berths. Logs had to be floated longer distances to the local mills, bringing a new need for booming and sorting at suitable locations close to Vancouver. There was a need for tugs of lower power than the big seekers that were now becoming long distance raft haulers. The venerable paddler *Beaver* and the little, iron-hulled screw tug *Tepic*, of Panama Canal fame, worked these local raft tows.

CHAPTER 13

West Coast Ports and Fleets

Jervis Crown (Robert Allan, Ltd.)

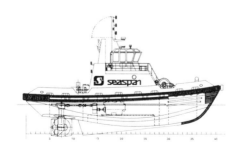

Seaspan Hawk (Seaspan Intl., Washington Group)

An assortment of funnel markings shows a variety of ownerships in this flock of tugs in Vancouver harbour circa 1913. Small Christmas trees at their mastheads have long been an annual custom with tug crews. (Pacific Coast Tug Society)

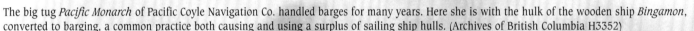

The big tug *Pacific Monarch* of Pacific Coyle Navigation Co. handled barges for many years. Here she is with the hulk of the wooden ship *Bingamon*, converted to barging, a common practice both causing and using a surplus of sailing ship hulls. (Archives of British Columbia H3352)

These factors resulted in smaller tugs being brought into service specifically for harbour work and the birth of independent towing companies unconnected with the mills. One of the first of these was the Burrard Inlet Towing Company, operators of the tug *Skidegate* in 1886. As in earlier days in other ports of the world, this company also carried passengers on local trips. It was soon reorganized as the Union Steamship Company, becoming a long-time, major coastal passenger and freight carrier in British Columbia.

It was in the middle of this decade, 1885, that a Nova Scotian stevedoring entrepreneur arrived to establish his name as synony-mous with towing in Vancouver Harbour. He was Charles Henry Cates, an energetic character who began transporting materials needed in the young and burgeoning city. For this he acquired a clumsy 240-foot, self-propelled barge with derricks, dubbed after its builder, *Spratt's Ark*. The *Ark* was twin-screw and sometimes towed barges. Cates also acquired a small tug, *Swan*, and in a winner-take-all race with a rival owner, doubled his towboat fleet by winning *Stella*. Several of Cates' brothers arrived on the scene as well, one becoming a shipbuilder on False Creek, others owning tugs of their own.

An epic tow starts out from Seattle heading for Buenos Aires, 20,000 miles away in 1947. Delivery of the six American war surplus tugs by Island Tug and Barge's *Snohomish* was so impressive, the Argentinians bought her too. The large tug had been built in 1918 for the U.S. Coast Guard. (Author's Collection)

Charles Cates was lured away to the Yukon Gold Rush in 1898, but eventually returned to Vancouver to start a pile-driving business. With this he became highly involved in the activities of the harbour, including wharf building. By 1913, he was back in the towing business with *Gaviota*, later named *C.H. Cates III*. Concentrating on expertise in towing in Vancouver Harbour, Cates prospered. The company was family run, with three sons, Charles, John and Jim, together with in-laws and daughters, involved in all aspects. The company operated a pioneering excursion steamer line, Terminal City Navigation, later sold to Union Steamships. At the end of the First World War the enterprise took the present name C.H. Cates & Sons, Ltd. Afterward, it grew steadily to gain total dominance in ship berthing work in Burrard Inlet until the 1990s, when Seaspan International entered the field.

The invasion of British Columbia by American owned sawmill companies began around 1900, with a great number moving in around Vancouver. The Fraser River was opened up to navigation with dredging, and logs were brought down from its upper reaches. Further up, spring log drives and specialized shallow-draft tugs came into use, sternwheelers being used on Harrison Lake. Vancouver Harbour activity expanded to False Creek and English Bay. The Fraser proved a good storage and sorting ground, the fresh water being proof against the damage caused to timber by teredo worms in salt water. New Westminster became a deepwater port and the company Westminster Tugs took on the ship berthing work along with log and lumber handling.

Canadian Pacific Railway bought up the Esquimault and Nanaimo Railway in 1905. This brought them into the business of

The big salvage tugs *Sudbury* and *Sudbury II* helped earn their keep between jobs by towing barges. *Sudbury II* was built for Pacific war salvage service by the U.S. government, later acquired by Island Tug and Barge. Here she has the purpose-built barge *Island Exporter* in hand. (Pacific Coast Tug Society)

handling their own rail car and coal barges, utilizing the railway's tugs, *Czar and Escort No 2*. Later, under the name *Nitinat*, they used *William Jolliffe*, the veteran British-built two-stacker, bought from B.C. Salvage of Victoria. Canadian Pacific was building up a large fleet of coastal passenger and freight packets at the same time, in its B.C. Coastal Service subsidiary, dominating this service between Vancouver and the Island until 1959, when the British Columbia government moved into the ferry business. CP's barging continued, but using independent towing companies after the railway's own tugs were phased out. Eventually, self-propelled barges took on the bulk of the railway's island-mainland rail and truck traffic.

With burgeoning opportunities for working in and out of Vancouver in the decades surrounding 1900, and the decline of mill-owned tugs, a number of independent towing companies came into being. Turn of the century tugs were mostly no more than 300hp, a little later acquiring steam winches and steel towing hawsers. Some were the direct antecedents of today's large operators by way of numerous amalgamations. The predecessor of one

major player was set up by Harold Jones with *OnTime* and *Uncle Tom* in 1898. On closing the operation in 1912 he gave his son, Harold Jr., the tug *Rosina K*. which the younger Jones parlayed into the rising Vancouver Tug Boat Company, starting in 1924. Preston and Mann, George H. French, and Young & Gore were also familiar names in Vancouver towing circles early in the century. Senator Stan McKeen joined his Standard Towing with Union Tugboat, then took them into the larger Straits Towing Co. in 1943.

Other prominent companies set up in Vancouver included Greer and Coyle, which started with six tugs and through amalgamations became a very large operator by 1926. In that year it absorbed Pacific Tug and Barge to become Pacific Coyle Navigation, picking up the big *Pacific Monarch* together with *Pacific Imp, Pacific Foam* and *Earl*. The company also took over Hecate Strait Towing which had the famous *Lorne* and British Pacific Barge Company with numerous ex-sailing ship barges. With the first of the large mergers in the industry, this company came to dominate it in this decade of expanding barge traffic.

Railcar barges have formed an important part of freight handling on the British Columbia coast, both for connecting railway systems and to permit loading from the mills directly into the rail cars at the wharf. *Iris G. Slocan* handles local traffic at Vancouver Island. (CP Rail Corporate Archives M6853)

Another well-known towing entrepreneur was Claude Thicke, who took over the Progressive Steamboat Company with its fleet of "Pro" steam tugs such as *Progressive* (1935, 300bhp) *Pronative, Prosperative* and *Projective*, creating the Blue Band Company. Thicke had pioneered conversion from steam power to diesel starting in the early 1920s, then on a large scale with these *Progressive* series boats, changing engines even when the steam engines were still in good shape. The economies in fuel and manning with the diesel were important in the competitive West Coast situation, so others followed, putting the western tug fleets far ahead of the East in this respect.

The first diesel tug on the coast came as early as 1912. Some owners converted directly from steam coal burners to the slow semi-diesel engine, usually American-made types such as Washington, Atlas or Union. Others went through a period of firing their steam boilers on oil first. After the Second World War the high speed, geared diesel arrived in the postwar-built fleets.

Also unlike the East Coast ports, Vancouver's major tug fleets, except for Cates, have always roamed far from the harbour waters, following the traffic demands along the sheltered waterways up and down the coast. Even the smallest boats could do this. On the East Coast, towing operations beyond local, sheltered waters were

WEST COAST PORTS AND FLEETS

TRANSFER Nº4

VICTORIA BC

The veteran first world war Admiralty tug *Kyuqout* of Canadian Pacific (*St. Florence* until 1925) brings a transfer from Vancouver Island to Vancouver with a mix of rail cars and highway semi-trailers. The barge is a converted second world war tank landing craft, and the tug was the last owned by Canadian Pacific on the coast. (CP Rail Corporate Archives 13840)

inhibited by the harshness of Atlantic weather, including the limitations imposed by ice in rivers and estuaries. The British Columbia tugs were built of wood like most of those on the East Coast until after the war. Many of the craftsmen came from small ports in Nova Scotia where the fishermen built their own wooden vessels, and fleets of great square-riggers had been turned out for a century. The steam engines had been largely imported from Scotland and assembled locally.

For many years, Cates have operated their large fleet of highly visible tugs with yellow deckhouses, built in the 1920s and 1930s, and uniquely specialized for ship handling work. All have traditionally been named *C.H. Cates*, followed by a Roman numeral; They are small, highly manoeuverable and with a high power-to-length ratio. The 1980s brought to this fleet the first in a new style of docking tug in *C.H. Cates I, II and III*, (1982, 1983, 1986,) radical in their twin-screw, azimuth steering drive (ASD) or "Z-Peller" configuration and high power-to-displacement ratio. In a different approach to the same performance as the Voith-Schneider system (VSP), these pioneering tugs had twin screws that could rotate through 360 degrees. Rated powerful for harbour tugs then, at 2400hp, they also had a hydraulic boom forward to lift the tug's towing line to a ship's deck. The booms became largely redundant with the recent advent of new lightweight, fibre towlines. They had both a forward towing winch and a towing hook aft, making them among the earliest tractor tugs in Canada.

Cates's amalgamation into the Washington Marine Group brought a major upgrading of the fleet with five ASD tractor tugs for shiphandling and a change in colour scheme to match the red Seaspan livery, eight of the older tugs supporting them in miscellaneous duties. The new tugs' wheelhouses have clear all-round visibility and a setback to clear the flare of a ship's bows overhead and are the forerunners of the turn of the century tug, considered in more detail in Chapter 15.

Typical of the old Cates fleet are *C.H. Cates V* to *VIII*, twin-or triple-screw tugs, developing 1800bhp in a 60-foot hull of 66 tons. With a crew of two and well fendered with tires, they can either push, or pull with a quick-release towing hook aft. They pioneered the concept of the "day boat" built without living accommodation and not straying far from home.

In recent times Cates remained unchallenged in their specialty, until the 1993 entry of Seaspan International into harbour shiphandling with the new ASD tugs *Seaspan Falcon* and *Seaspan*

Hawk, of 3000hp. These were built in the company's own Vancouver Shipyards, next door to their tug terminal in North Vancouver. Seaspan already had the docking work at Roberts Bank coal terminal, bringing together numbers of tugs, led by the resident Z-drive *Seaspan Discovery* (1984, 4000hp), to handle the very large colliers berthing there. In Burrard Inlet, Seaspan International's shiphandling has been directed at the largest vessels and in escorting tankers.

The only major Canadian competition to these Washington Group companies today, Rivtow Marine had been founded in 1939 at Hope, B.C. with one tug for log towing on the Fraser River. Rivtow grew to wide ranging towing operations on the coast and entered the ship assistance competition in Burrard Inlet in 1997 using one tug. That was followed soon by five others operating under the name Tiger Tugz, including ASD tugs *Tiger Spirit, Tiger Pride* (1994 and 1997, 3000hp) and *Tiger Sun* (1999, 3000hp).

To cap the great changes in the industry on the West Coast at the end of the century, in mid 2000 the world-wide Smit organization gobbled up Rivtow Marine and its associated Westminster Tugs. This move established for them a Canadian West Coast operation, placed under the direction of Captain John Cosulich, whose family had founded Rivtow in 1939, as general manager.

Victoria: Seeking and Salvage

Although very much part of the west coast, timber-oriented maritime scene, the port of Victoria has always demanded a different kind of towing job. From the gold rush days of the 1850s, it was a busy port for ocean sailing ship traffic. For tugs it became a base for the big seeking tugs that shepherded the square-riggers and schooners in and out among the islands and through the tricky waters of Juan de Fuca Strait. As a natural parallel service, it became the headquarters for salvage and rescue tugs. As elsewhere, the big drydock built at adjoining Esquimault was a stimulus to salvage services and port business generally.

In the beginning, the ocean ships braving the run through Juan de Fuca to the inland waters of Puget Sound and Georgia Strait were assisted by the tug consortium of the American mills. When industry began to thrive in the Victoria area, based on lumber exports, shipbuilding and the coal trade from the mines at Nanaimo, locally based seeking tugs were acquired. One of the first was the huge *Alexander*, so costly to operate that she bankrupted

Canadian National Railways operated the 1918 *St. Catherines* as *Canadian National NO.2* in the railcar barge trade. Part of the first world war program in 1918, she was later rebuilt as the diesel powered *Gulf Freda*. (Pacific Coast Tug Society, Bob Martin)

her owners. The former Hudson's Bay Company's *Beaver* first operated as a fulltime towboat out of Victoria in the 1870s and did some seeking as well.

Robert Dunsmuir, king of the coal business, bought *Alexander* to tow coal ships to Nanaimo for loading. He also bought *Pilot*, another seeking tug, and had *Lorne* built for him in 1889. This fine 150-foot vessel became a fixture on the B.C. coast, serving as a ship and log-raft hauler for many years. Her 1250hp triple expansion engine was built by Albion Iron Works, and could drive her at 14 knots when running light.

The Dunsmuir operations grew very large and local independent tug operators, like B.C. Towing, worked for them much of the time, along with some speculative seeking in the strait. The first tugs were operated by the mill and coal companies, but, as in Vancouver,

the work was gradually handed over to the independent entrepreneurs in towing. Another famous and long-lived tug was *Czar*, built in Victoria in 1897 for Hastings Mills. She was sold to Dunsmuir for towing coal ships and barges, then was inherited along with the Esquimault and Nanaimo Railway by Canadian Pacific in 1905.

For a time, from her base at Victoria just across Juan de Fuca Strait from the Puget Sound Tug Boat Company fleet, *Czar* gave the Americans stiff competition in the rescue of sailing ships in trouble. In traditional seeking style, these tugs cruised the strait looking for ships in need of a tow. They went out whenever there was a likelihood of ships having difficulty with adverse winds and currents, which was most of the time.

A serious, full-time salvage enterprise was established at Victoria in 1900, under the name B.C. Salvage Company. The first salvage vessel was *Salvor*, the converted freighter *Danube*. She was joined by the tugs *Maude* and *William Jolliffe*. The *Jolliffe* was a Scottish-built two-stacker, claimed to be the most powerful tug in the world in her day.

In these days before wireless, salvage was largely a matter of spotting and pulling ships off after they had run aground. There was seldom any effective way of knowing a vessel was in distress until wireless came into use.

Reorganized in 1916 as Pacific Salvage Company, this operation became the major salvage firm for the whole Pacific Northwest coast. The business belonged to Burdick Brothers, owners of Pacific

Drydock Company, later sold to Burrard Drydock which eventually became North Vancouver Ship Repairs. It is possible that, like the East Coasters, the salvors thought they and the drydock would bring each other business.

One of the company's salvages, the steamer *Tees*, became a salvage vessel under the name *Salvage Queen,* and *William Jolliffe* was repurchased from Canadian Pacific to become *Salvage Chief*. To these vessels were later added several more salvage tugs, including the fine, large *Salvage King* (1925, 1164 tons, 3960bhp) from Britain. The company was later merged with the rival Straits Towing Company.

Gulf Freda

In modern times, with the boom in barging of the 1920s, the port of Victoria saw the beginning of a new company that would dominate the local towing scene and set the pace for Victoria's role in ocean rescue and long distance towing. In 1925, seeing the bright future of barge towing, Harold Elworthy left his job with Pacific Salvage to start his new company called Island Tug and Barge. He began with one 60-foot tug, *Quinitsa*, (1914, 30 tons, 50hp) which he renamed *Island Planet*. His intention was to concentrate on local barge towing, but he saw his family concern grow to include deep-sea towing and salvage on a large scale. In 1942, several smaller companies were absorbed and Island Tug was briefly owned by Elworthy, Stan McKeen from Standard Towing and

Henry Foss, president of Foss Launch and Tug Company of Seattle, the biggest and one of the oldest owners on the U.S. Pacific Coast. But Elworthy's partners soon departed, in 1947.

Barging on the Ocean Highway

With the spread of towns, canneries, and paper and lumber mills along British Columbia's rugged, roadless coast, the need for large scale water transportation was clearly evident by the turn of the century. Steamers were fine for passengers and express freight, but the sailing vessels that normally carried bulk cargos more economically could not manage the intricacies of navigating the narrow channels and inlets. Barges were the answer. They could also

Opposite and right: Two-man crews operate their small tugs on a twelve-hour shift, juggling the many barges handled in ports such as Vancouver. The deckhand climbs aboard the barge and reaches down to the tug with a pikepole for the ready connected towlines he needs. (Author's Collection)

For long tows, the medium tug *Seaspan Champion* (ex-*Island Champion*) has the usual large winch and steel towline. The captain operates this and his tug's engines from the auxiliary control position above the lifeboat. (Author's Collection)

be left for loading and unloading while the power plant, a tug, was off on another run. This type of operation also fitted well with the advantages of lightering cargo directly aboard ships at anchor.

In this advantageous climate, a number of prominent tug and barge operations were established early in the century. James Greer and E.J. Coyle saw the opportunities and, in 1905, founded Greer and Coyle Towing with its six tugs. In 1912, the owner of the Vancouver Machinery Company, George Walkem, found he had "inadvertently become the owner" of a somewhat used scow. Without hesitation, apparently, he plunged into the lumber lighter-

ing business, adding a couple of tugs and founding the very successful Gulf of Georgia Towing Company. This was the same year that the Vancouver Tugboat Company was established.

The enterprising Claude Thicke, founder of Blue Band in 1921, is credited with selling the mill owners on the use of "hog fuel," the waste wood product from the sawmills, to fire their boilers. This spawned a lucrative trade in towing barge loads of the former waste, now a marketable commodity. In the mid 1920s, what were to become major operators emerged, based on the two principal ports of British Columbia. These were Harold Jones' Vancouver

Tugboat Company (1924) and Harold Elworthy's Island Tug and Barge Company (1925). Both looked to the expanding barge traffic as opposed to the traditional reliance on raft towing.

Jones built up his fleet on a wide variety of commodities: wood chips, lime rock, pulp, newsprint, salt, lumber and chlorine. Subsidiary shipyard operations were added and a specialized barge fleet built up. The tugs were acquired from various sources or built by the company. They were given French names such as *La Pointe*, the converted steam trawler formerly *Kingsway* that became a successful 800hp diesel tug. *Le Beau II* was a British first world war boat and the later *La Brise* was the renamed *Sea Giant* from the Dolmage fleet, a 1943 wooden tug of 675bhp.

The company expanded to 24 tugs and 160 barges by the late 1960s, led by the flagship *Harold A. Jones*, a 3500hp, twin-diesel, ocean-going tug with a 9000-mile cruising range. She was built in 1966 and named after the now deceased founder of the firm, but later renamed *Seaspan Monarch*. It would be hard to overestimate the importance of the woodpulp chip trade to both towing and the pulp and paper mills. The merger of Vancouver Tugboat and Vancouver Island Tug as Seaspan brought about three-quarters of this trade into the hands of one hauler. Straits Towing Company's merger with Rivtow held the balance.

The family-run Island Tug and Barge operation was also substantially involved in log towing. However, with the traditional Victoria outlook on the sea, this company developed an interest in long distance towing and took on the primary salvage and rescue function. In addition to their roster of barging tugs, scows and barges for local and B.C. coastal work, there were a few large ocean-going tugs. For some years the flagship was *Snohomish*, originally an east coast U.S. Coast Guard vessel. This very large steam tug was built in 1908 (549 tons, 1120 bhp). She got the company into real ocean towing in 1947, when she carried out a 20,000-mile tow from Seattle to Buenos Aires with a barge on which were loaded six war surplus American yard-tugs. However, on arrival, *Snohomish* was apparently admired by the Argentines and they bought her along with the bargeload. A wrecked U.S. Army tug was repaired as the new flagship and deepsea vessel, *Island Sovereign* (2400hp and 117 feet long).

Then, in 1954, Island Tug and Barge purchased their far-famed ocean towing and salvage tug *Sudbury* (2750bhp, triple expansion engine), an ex-corvette of the same name from the Canadian Navy. She captured headlines with her exploits recovering stricken vessels from Pacific storms. A later acquisition and replacement was the larger *Sudbury II*, the former *Cambrian Salvor* (1943, 1219 tons, 3800bhp), a wartime British-designed but American-built salvage tug. She had been bought by L. Smit & Company for use in a joint enterprise with Island Tug in 1961. Using *Island Sovereign*, Island Tug and Barge led the field in long distance tows and salvages from the Northwest Coast in the 1960s, including transpacific voyages.

The Modern Barge Trade

From open scows and flat-topped barges, a variety of specialized carriers evolved on the coast. Petroleum products, chlorine, mineral concentrates, railway cars, pulp, hog fuel and newsprint all had special barges tailored to their use. One of the most useful carriers has been the closed deck barge, like a warehouse afloat. Using the post second world war forklift and pallet system, these barges efficiently carry newsprint and pulp down to the major ports from the isolated pulp and paper mills, under cover from the elements. The barge then returns with supplies for the mills and their townsites, performing a warehouse function at either end while loading. Meanwhile, the tug is off on its way with another barge. A well-known application of this method was the Island Express, a regular barge haul by Island Tug and Barge up the east coast of Vancouver Island, servicing small ports as far around its tip as Quatsino Sound and Port Alice.

As time went by and log rafts of a number of types were being towed longer and longer distances, the idea of carrying raw logs on barges had to be tried. Log haulers in the 1920s were finding handling Davis Rafts and their equipment to be expensive. Hecate Strait Towing, a creation of a great Vancouver maritime figure, Barney Johnson, pioneered raft and log-barge towing from the Queen Charlotte Islands using *Lorne* and *Cape Scott*. The four Gibson brothers, self-educated and innovative log haulers, acquired the old lumber schooner hulk, *Malahat*, which they converted into a log carrier; then others did the same. The big Pacific Coyle merger of 1926 took in ten log barges from the British Pacific Barge Company. These were all old wooden ship hulks. Many once-proud sailing ships ended their days as barges on the British Columbia coast.

Newer barges were built specifically for logs, carrying them as a deckload for easier loading and unloading. This led, after the Second World War, to the self-unloading barge. In 1954, Island Tug and Barge sent *Sudbury* and *Island Sovereign* to Venezuela to bring back four old oil tankers for conversion. This they did, in a unique

Above: The modern self-loading, self-dumping log barge *Seaspan Forester* flips its 20,000 ton load of logs on arrival at the sawmill, while the tug keeps clear. Heeling and other functions aboard the barge are controlled from the tug. (Seaspan International Ltd., Commercial Illustrators)

Opposite: The numerous small, specialized ship handling tugs of the Cates Vancouver fleet are all named *Charles H. Cates*. Classed as "day boats," always operating close to base, they have little accommodation but plenty of engine-room. (Author's Collection)

tandem tow of 5000 miles. Soon three more followed. The resulting log barges could be flooded on one side so that they would tip sufficiently for the deck load of log bundles to slide off into the sawmill's receiving pond. Pumped out again, the barge was ready to be towed away for another load in short order. A tricky situation would occasionally arise, however, if the barge was tipped to the maximum degree and the load did not slide. The solution was to gingerly pull off bundles until the load did let go, a potentially dangerous piece of work for those involved. Sometimes, a sharp bump against the barge with a tug or a big log, or even explosives, would do the trick with less risk.

The latest evolution of the barge was the present self-loader-unloader. These huge barges are loaded in about ten hours with their own cranes, operated by a crew of skilled loaders flown into the remote loading sites. The world's largest such log barge is *Seaspan Forester*. She is towed by a powerful ocean tug such as the 5750bhp, twin-diesel flagship *Seaspan Commodore* on the end of a 2½-inch diameter towline. *Forester* carries a 20,000-ton load that can be dumped in about an hour. Like many large, specialized barges for long distance hauling, this state of the art carrier is fitted for remote radio control of her navigational lights and anchors by the tug.

When loading, the bundles of logs are pushed within reach of the cranes' grabs by a pair of little dozer boats, the smallest of all tugs, that are carried aboard the barge. The tug crew members actually get paid to operate these marine versions of amusement park

bumper-cars. Seaspan International operated four of these log carriers. *Seaspan Commodore* came to these routine hauls from assignments in the North Sea oil drilling play in its early phases when traditional tugs were predominant, returning home by way of the Suez Canal, the Arabian Gulf, Japan and Valdez, Alaska.

The most prominent company that ran counter to the early move of the lumber and paper mill owners to get out of tug operation was Kingcome Navigation, a subsidiary of MacMillan Bloedel. It was established by the Powell River Company in 1910 and managed for a time after the Second World War by Bill Dolmage, who had built up and sold his own successful log towing company. Kingcome evolved into a successful transportation company, with representative modern barging facilities.

In 1967 the company put into service the powerful 140-foot, 3500bhp *Haida Brave*, built by Halifax Shipyards, to tow newsprint cargoes from Port Alberni to Long Beach, California to feed the voracious appetites of Los Angeles newspapers. Together with the smaller tugs *Harmac Pine* and *Harmac Spruce*, she replaced an older generation of tugs such as *Haida Monarch*, originally *St. Faith*, the British Admiralty first world war rescue tug. The company also built a new *Haida Monarch*, a 15,000-ton self-propelled barge for the Queen Charlotte Islands trade. They acquired *Haida Transporter*, a self-propelled barge for carrying railway cars loaded with newsprint from the Powell River Mill to the railhead at Vancouver. A new *Haida Brave*, a 10,000-ton self-loading, self-dumping log carrier for the west coast of Vancouver Island, took the name away from the namesake tug. A few very large woods operators, like MacMillan Bloedel, operate large numbers—some more than fifty—of small yarding tugs to handle logs at their booming grounds and millsites. Understandably, they have no proper names and are identified simply by numbers.

The railcar barge has long played an important role in coastal traffic, particularly between the mainland railheads and Vancouver Island. The ability to carry loaded railway cars from the end of track to the beginning of track on the other side of the water without any reloading was even more advantageous before the advent of containers, pallets and fork-lift trucks. The Vancouver Island service was started in 1900 by the Esquimault and Nanaimo Railway with the steam tug *Czar* becoming their main source of power. With the purchase of this line in 1905, Canadian Pacific expanded it over the years. The last of half a dozen C.P. operated tugs was *Kyoquot*, originally the Admiralty's *Saint Florence*, finally removed from service in 1957. The company then switched to charter services by Island Tug and F.M. Yorke Co. as well as ferries and self-propelled railcar barges.

Even without any length of railway line to deliver rail cars to a millsite, it has been advantageous to carry them to the exporting mills to directly load pulp, paper and lumber products. This, in effect, brought these big freight producers into the sphere of operations of various railways. The Milwaukie Road made use of this method to link their Seattle terminal to lumber sources in British Columbia. Foss Launch and Tug Company of Seattle, the biggest towing company in the American Northwest, pioneered the use of the Inside Passage between Seattle and Alaska with all kinds of barging, railcar, bulk cargo, tankers and, in the 1960s, containers. The same and similar barges, towed and self-propelled, are used by a number of companies to carry cargo containers and highway transport trailers up and down the B.C. coast. Barging is still the lifeblood of both the coastal communities and the towing industry of British Columbia.

The practical advantages of marine cargo transportation of all kinds by barge over long distances was firmly established by the heavy traffic up the west coast from the United States and lower British Columbia during the Second World War. Modest-sized tugs such as the celebrated U.S. Army Transport Service Mikis carried on such services after the war in the private sector. They served with major American companies like Foss Launch of Seattle and Canadian companies who purchased some of these durable vessels. Foss did not let even the broad Pacific stop them, carrying out supply contracts in support of the Korean and Vietnam wars, still using retreaded single-screw Mikis and twin-screw Mikimikis.

Canadian postwar long distance barge towing on a regular basis has involved cargos of newsprint, pulp and other wood products and limestone down the American West Coast as far as Los Angeles, and the import of salt from California and Mexico. Special projects have been highly varied. Major water-borne supply projects have been involved in the building of mill towns like Kitimat.

Vancouver Tug's *La Belle* took two barges carrying a school complex to Alaska with the same aplomb as their local tugs delicately pushed the tall spans of Vancouver's Second Narrows Bridge into place. The latter included a lift span 500 feet high and weighing 2400 tons. It was towed, perched on two barges, a distance of five miles from the point of erection to the bridge site.

Island Tug's bigger boats, the 2400bhp *Island Sovereign*, and the two *Sudbury*s performed both salvage and long barge-hauls. *Island Sovereign*, the former American army tug, made some transpacific runs before the long distance towing business fell off in the 1970s and the new breed of anchor-handling tugs arrived on the scene.

End of Century Fleet Consolidations

A major shakeout in the towing fleets of British Columbia came following the mid-century mark. After the postwar replacement of worn-out vessels with cheap, war surplus tugs came the need for greater efficiency due to rising crew and vessel costs. Unfortunately, new-built tugs were also escalating in price. Many new and re-engined diesel tugs, now all built of steel, appeared in the 1950s only to receive serious criticism in terms of their safety and comfort. Numerous casualties were occurring in both American and Canadian fleets. New tugs packed more powerful, high-speed diesel engines into existing and smaller hulls with smaller crews. A strike of tug crews in B.C. in 1970 demonstrated the vital nature of the towing industry to British Columbia and brought about new rules. This was followed quickly by a series of amalgamations of fleets that left two large companies dominating the coast, Seaspan International and Rivtow-Straits.

The combinations that went into the creation in 1970 of these two giants were complex. One was Rivtow Group, whose ancestry included the names River Towing, Pioneer, B.C. Salvage, M.R. Cliff, Westminster and Straits Towing. Rivtow is described as a loose family organization run by the Cosulich brothers, Cecil and Norman, longtime veterans in the towing game, who were followed by the succeeding generation. The second largest fleet on the coast, Rivtow Marine Limited, operates over one hundred barges and tugs, with experience in long distance ocean work as well as log sorting and other local services. The merger of the two major components, Rivtow and Straits Towing, has been described as a marriage of two relative equals and as a pivotal event in British Columbia towing history.

Left and opposite: On the end of a long steel hawser while at sea, the huge log barge *Seaspan Forester* is winched snug up to the stern of *Seaspan Commodore* when mooring. The tug controls barge navigation lights, anchors and heeling by radio. The control station is located in the wheelhouse on more recent tugs. (Author's Collection)

When a giant like *Hyundai Giant* arrived at the Vancouver bulk cargo port of Robert's Bank, a platoon of Seaspan tugs, led by 4000bhp *Seaspan Discovery* at left, was marshalled to help in the berthing operation. Today additional powerful ASD tugs like her are available. (Seaspan International Ltd., Bob Clarke Photo)

The larger of the two mergers occurred when Vancouver Tug and Barge joined with Island Tug and Barge to become Seaspan International Limited. Shortly before, the Dillingham Group in Hawaii had bought the combination of Foss Launch and Tug of Seattle and its subsidiary Pacific Towing and, in 1969, snapped up all of Vancouver Tug as well. Seaspan International, known briefly as Vanisle, was initially under the ownership of Genstar Marine of

Montreal and Vancouver, running a fleet of 65 tugs and 250 barges. The new company was headquartered in North Vancouver where the subsidiary Vancouver Shipyards was available to build and maintain the fleet. Another considerable fleet that joined this mix later (1977) was Gulf of Georgia Towing. Seaspan became involved in long distance ocean towing work, notably in supplying Arctic and North Sea oil rig exploration and other offshore related jobs. At

Island Commander had a long career barging supplies to the ports on the British Columbia coast and was famous for the regular 700-mile "Island Express" run to small ports. She was originally built in Britain as a trawler. (Author's Collection)

any given moment their tugs and barges would be at work all up and down the Pacific Coast of North America.

The advent of international free trade and recent emphasis on size for success in any business has not left the towing industry unscathed. Consolidations have taken place on both the east and west coasts of Canada, in Europe and around the world. On the North American West Coast, the American Washington Marine Group, an association of Washington State companies, has absorbed Seaspan International, Kingcome Navigation and even C.H. Cates in 1992, although each of these units continued to operate under its own name. Some thirteen companies involved in towing, barging, a railway, forest products terminals and shipping, shipbuilding and repairs, and related fields are in the Washington

Marine Group; their operations extend from Alaska to California and around the world, with headquarters in North Vancouver.

Consolidations did not stop there. Rivtow Marine joined the Dutch Smit Group in 2000, giving the global Smit organization a base on Canada's West Coast. Rivtow's John Cosulich remained as manager of the B.C. operation. Of the numerous divisions of Smit the key towing elements were Smit Wijsmuller for long distance towing and Smit Harbour Towage, handling docking in ports around the world. Control of these companies would then be taken over by the Svitzer division of Danish A.P. Moller (Maersk). To further confuse us the name Island Tug and Barge has been bought for a new specialty barging operation.

In 1878 the Canadian Pacific transcontinental railway was still under construction and Winnipeg was supplied mainly by barges and paddle wheelers. Much like her contemporaries on the Mississippi River system, *Pluck* is shown here on the Red River with a load of steam traction engines and harvesting machinery from an American railhead. (Manitoba Archives Transp Boat 2)

Towboating "Down North"

IN THE NINETEENTH CENTURY, steam-powered water transportation was so superior to ox-wagons pulled through mud tracks that even the unpromising rivers of the Canadian Prairies were exploited. The Red and Saskatchewan were no Mississippi, Missouri or Ohio Rivers, but steamboats in the same style did ply the Canadian prairie country. Service was very much subject to erratic cycles and seasons that determined water levels. Nevertheless, palatial stern wheelers, with all the features except the fabled riverboat gambler, did travel on occasion from St. Paul, Minnesota, via Winnipeg and Lake Winnipeg, as far as Edmonton. Along the way, the usual barge push was a feature of freight traffic. Perilous and unreliable though it was, there existed at times a continuous water route from the ocean on the Gulf of Mexico to Edmonton and beyond.

Before the first Canadian railway crossed the rugged Canadian Shield to join the Prairies with the East, the easiest way to get to Fort Garry (later Winnipeg) was northward down the Red River from American railheads. The first steamboat to navigate this route was a crude, boxy little vessel called *Anson Northrup* that arrived in Fort Garry from the U.S. in 1859. Little more than a barge with a paddle wheel, engine and a cabin, this craft was still a vast improvement on open boats. J.C. Burbank bought her in 1861 and gave her the name *Pioneer*.

By the time the Canadian Pacific Railway was under construction in the 1870s, Winnipeg was a busy town. Railway construction had started at numerous points along the transcontinental route, including Winnipeg. To this end, in 1877, the first locomotive and several cars arrived in a barge pushed by the large stern wheeler *Selkirk*. There were small push tugs here as well at that time, such as *Pluck* of 1878, a side wheeler riverboat in the Mississippi style.

At various times until early in the twentieth century, steamers were pushing barges in Western Canada. They were on the Red River, the Nelson and the two Saskatchewan rivers, braved storms on vast Lake Winnipeg and provided the freight connection to Prince Albert until a railway arrived there in 1890. The posh, passenger-carrying steamer *Marquis*, 200 feet long and with a draft of 18 inches to 4 feet operated in these far reaches of Saskatchewan. Because these rivers were unreliable, however, waterborne commerce did not stand up to the competition of trains when the rails came.

By the 1880s, in the pursuit of further new frontiers, more promising rivers for navigation were being discovered far to the north. Steam-powered towboats were being built at Fort Smith on the great Mackenzie River in 1886. Braving the little-known sandbars and rapids, *Wrigley I* reached the Arctic Circle in 1899. The Athabaska River, Lake Athabaska, the Slave River and the Slave Lakes also began to hear the slap, slap, slap of paddle wheels in these days. Steamboats in the hands of nervy pilots pushed barges eastward up the Yukon River from the ocean before the turn of the century to supply the gold rush towns. Canadian Pacific built six of these Mississippi-style stern wheelers at Vancouver for the Klondike boom, but it collapsed before they were ready.

Until the age of air travel provided a preferred means of carrying passengers and express freight in the 1950s, the stern wheelers were still the main line of communication "down north." It was a reincarnation of what had been the system on the great American rivers before the 1880s and railroads. The cry, "Steamboat!" closed the businesses of the river communities and the whole population ran to the riverbank.

CHAPTER 14

Northwest Passages

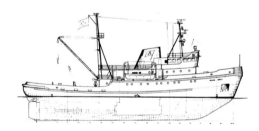

Irving Birch (German & Milne)

Arctic Nanook (Arctic Transportation Ltd.)

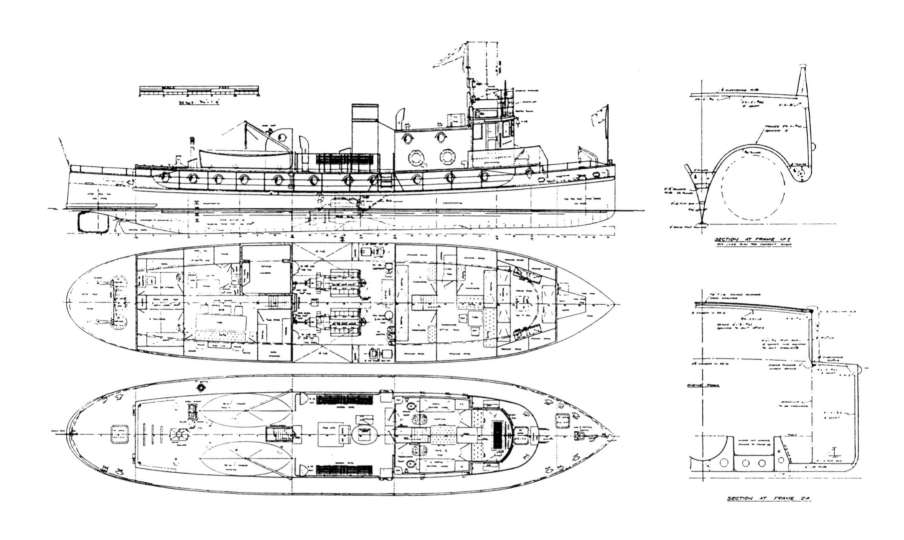

Plan of *Radium King*. Her two V-engines were 240bhp each. The two shallow draft tugs also carried passengers and were built by Marine Industries of Sorel for Northern Transportation Company. Propellers are in tunnels. (German and Milne, Naval Architects and Maritime Museum of the Great Lakes)

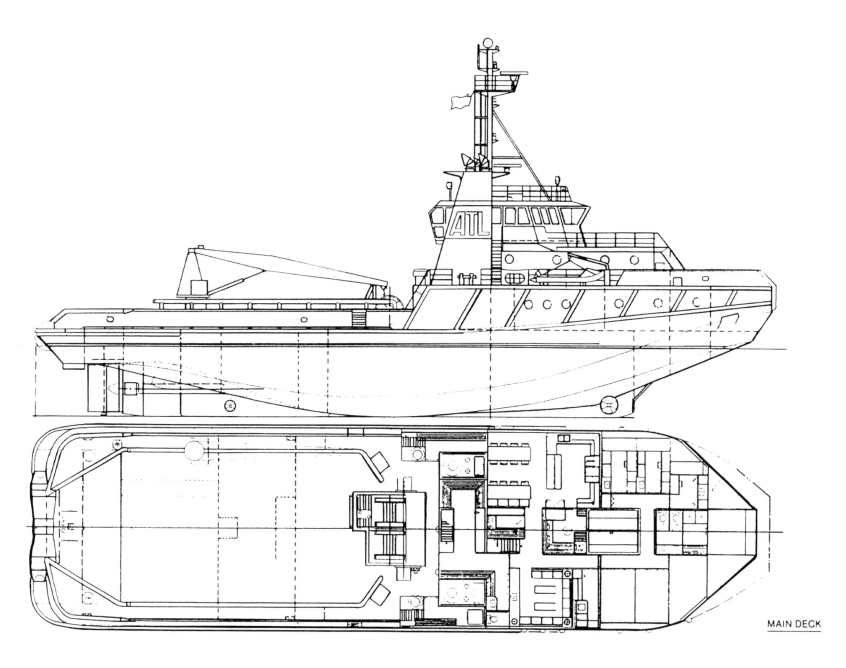

MAIN DECK

An anchor handling tug of 6440bhp (80 tonne BP) with ice-breaking capability, *Arctic Nanook* was built in 1982 with twin CP screws in nozzles and bow and stern thrusters. (Credit Arctic Transportation Ltd.)

The Hudson's Bay Company operated four paddle steamers in the North through the 1930s and 1940s. *Athabaska River* and *Northland Echo* ran on the Athabaska River and Lake Athabaska. These connected with the two Mackenzie River boats, *Distributor III* and *McKenzie River*, providing a link between the railhead at Waterways, Alberta, the old town of Aklavik and the newer Tuktoyaktuk on the Beaufort Sea. These steamers also pushed barges to supply the many communities, missions and mines along the northern rivers. Cargo space on the steamer was restricted due to the large amounts of wood carried to feed the boilers. Like the old *Beaver* on the West Coast, a ten-man crew was needed to load wood every day or two along the rivers and to carry freight over gangplanks to shore at the way stops.

As commerce grew, notably when the Second World War brought military developments to the north, the steamer's liner runs were supplemented by a variety of push tugs and barges carrying freight. This included trucks, bulldozers, mining machinery, building materials, foodstuffs, the ubiquitous drums of gasoline

Above: Between the two world wars, the radium mining fleet was the major operator on the Long Mackenzie River System. *Radium Queen* was 86 feet long, with a draft of 1 foot, 9 inches, and was powered by two 160bhp diesels with propellers in tunnels. (German and Milne, Naval Architects)

Opposite top: The Canadian Prairies saw tugs and fairly palatial steamers like *City of Selkirk* on the major lakes and rivers, but navigation was tricky and unreliable. The growing railways put them out of business. (Manitoba Archives N1287 J.H. Clarke)

Opposite bottom: Stern wheelers were utilized on northern rivers like the Mackenzie, the northern lakes and the interior lakes of British Columbia. This is SS *Moyie* of 1898 (130hp) with a railway car float on Lake Kootenay. She lasted almost sixty years, until 1957, and was bought by the Village of Karlo from the CPR for $1.00. She is now a designated National Historic Site. (CP Rail Corporate Archiives M4246)

and oil, and, heading south, furs, reindeer hides, mineral concentrates and fish. From Fort Smith on the Slave River at the Alberta border, to Great Slave Lake and Aklavik or Inuvik in the Mackenzie River delta, there are 1400 miles of varied navigational situations. It was easy to run up on the sandbars that shift and change constantly, as they do on the Mississippi River. The skipper usually had to find his own way off again, although with luck another boat might come by eventually. Help was always offered in such cases, as it could be the passing vessel's turn to need help next time. Left alone, the boat could try to get off on its own by running the engines until the propellers scoured away the sandbar and winching off with a cable tied to a tree or large rock on shore.

The Mackenzie River's one thousand navigable miles range in width from five miles down to a mere hundred and twenty feet at the San Sault rapids. Its depth varies from three to three hundred feet. According to one anecdote, a deckhand was once knocked overboard. His captain, apparently not familiar with the river shouted "Man overboard!" and ran to throw a life ring to the drowning hand. Looking back, much to his amazement, he saw the missing sailor standing there, the water only knee-deep in the channel they were passing through.

The relatively primitive towboats of the 1930s were diesel-engined and twin-screw with shallow draft, pushing a motley assortment of wooden barges. Improving technology for very shallow draft vessels on the northern waterways brought triple-screw boats with quadruple rudders, standardized pushing posts between tug and barges, and comfortable accommodation for the crews. Dredging, buoyed channels and radio also helped. The first large dredge made its way to the Mackenzie by the perilous route around Alaska through the Bering Strait.

Above: The superstructure of *Radium King* is unloaded at the railhead. *Radium Queen* has been assembled. The former was intended for service on the Mackenzie River and Great Slave Lake, the latter on the Athabaska and Slave Rivers. (German and Milne, Naval Architects)

Opposite: *Radium Queen* is seen here with her sister tug *Radium King* in parts at the Waterways, Northwest Territories railhead. Both were built at Sorel, Quebec in 1937, knocked down and transported in parts more than 4000 miles by rail, water and tractor train to be reassembled on the northern river system. (German and Milne, Naval Architects)

A small U.S. Army towboat with the Corps of Engineers symbol on her funnel brings in a bargeload of highway construction equipment during the Second World War. The large American presence in the northern waterways during the war disappeared later, forbidden by American legislation. (National Archives of Canada, PA 101816)

Tows, as the push-tug people have always insisted on calling them, increased to as many as eight barges. The longer strings of barges, however, would have to be split into smaller groups to go safely through some sections of river. The ice-free season lasts from June to September, but there could be problems with ice runs in June and it was a difficult decision as to when to stop in the autumn. Tugs and barges usually wintered at Hay River where they could be refitted conveniently for the next year and be protected from ice runs in the spring. The other end of the line at Tuktoyaktuk provided a reasonable refuge, but there were no other good wintering spots. Crews on the boats in the short northern season—the summer sailors—traditionally included a mix of three disparate types: those from the Mississippi, the Great Lakes and "salties" from either coast. All brought their own views on how the job should be done.

A major fleet of tugs of earlier days were the "radium" tugs of Northern Transportation Limited, dating from prewar uranium ore cargoes carried on the Slave and Athabaska Rivers. *Radium Dew* was the largest of the eight tugs at 289 tons and rated as a semi-icebreaker. *Radium King's* photo was frequently published before the Second World War as an example of a modern tug on the northern frontier. It had twin screws in tunnels driven by two 240bhp diesels. This boat was 95 feet long and had a draft of 4 feet, 3 inches. *Radium Queen* was twin-screw, 86 feet long and had a draft of only 21 inches. She was rated as a tug and passenger vessel for the Slave and Athabaska Rivers. These two vessels were built at Sorel, Quebec in 1937, knocked down and shipped 4000 miles by rail, water and tractor haul to be finally welded together again on a riverbank. Uranium ore was barged south then and supplies brought north. One special barge put into service some years ago carried a swimming pool and was used to teach northern native children along the Mackenzie to swim.

Arctic Transportation Limited emerged as the major river carrier in the oil exploration boom of the 1960s and 1970s, greatly expanding river operations. The company was a consortium of Canadian

The larger post-second world war towboat *Radium Dew* is being launched in 1955 with encouragement from bulldozers. Her four rudders may be seen. She was 120 feet long and 289 tons. (German and Milne, Naval Architects)

and American tug and barge operators and maintained a large fleet of tugs and barges on the Mackenzie River and Beaufort Sea.

The most modern of the shallow draft, river push-tugs, up to 4500bhp, were introduced by Northern Transportation after construction in Vancouver in 1973. Boats of the *Jock McNiven* type are 777 tons and 143 feet long, with a draft of only 3 feet. Built in 1973 in North Vancouver, they sailed or rode on barges through the Bering Strait around Alaska to the Beaufort Sea as part of a great northern supply convoy. Such shallow draft boats are useful along the shallow Beaufort Sea coast as well as in the river.

In the 1970s oil boom, competition appeared in the down north traffic. American carriers, inhibited in international trade by the U.S. Jones Act, tended to take everything they needed for North Slope exploration around through the Bering Strait. The bulk of Canadian supplies have gone by the Mackenzie route, although Arctic Transportation Limited used both routes. The Canadian and American companies making up this Canadian consortium gained experience between 1958 and 1967 with northern supply, principally in the construction of the DEW Line early warning radar system. They were then well placed to participate in the Beaufort Sea oil exploration play.

After 1967 the group established barge routes from Yellowknife and Hay River, from the railhead on Great Slave Lake, down the Mackenzie and eastward along the Arctic coast. An affiliate, Moosonee Transportation Limited, established tug and barge routes along both shores of James and Hudson Bays. The later slump in oil prices and resultant exploration cutbacks have, of course, pulled back drastically the ambitions of all these companies for northern water transport. There can be no doubt, however, that the flexibility and viability of the tug-and-barge method is well established as the prime means of freight commerce for the Far North.

On the Mountain Lakes

Another area of inland tug services developed in the long narrow lakes lying between the mountain ranges of British Columbia. Canadian Pacific Railway built a number of branch lines to serve the mountain valleys, but in some spots the valley was occupied for its full width by a lake. The solution was to operate steamboats for the length of the lake, connecting with rail lines at either end. Typical late nineteenth century stern wheelers were placed in service, and frequently pushed railcar barges so that loaded freight cars could go through without any reloading. These paddlers included *Okanagan*, of 1000 tons, and *Sicamous*, (1914, 1787 tons), both running on the 90-mile run down Lake Okanagan from Okanagan Landing to Penticton. On the Arrow Lakes there was the famous *Minto*, built in one thousand parts in Toronto to be assembled in Vancouver in 1897 for the Klondike gold rush run on the Stikine River. Too late, the delivery was rerouted to Naskup for assembly on Upper Arrow Lake. A sister ship was similarly diverted to Kootenay Lake and sailed there for fifty-eight years.

When replaced, these old sternwheelers were succeeded by screw steam tugs and barges. On the Okanagan there were *Castlegar* in 1911, *Naramata* (built in Port Arthur in 1914, 270hp) and, in 1947, the diesel tug *Okanagan II*, prefabricated in Vancouver for handling two railcar barges on the lake. Canadian Pacific had their own shipyard on this lake. The lake service ended in 1972. On the Arrow Lakes, there were the *Columbias I, II* and *III*. The last was wooden and diesel-powered (120hp, 1920), coming from service as *Surfco* on the Alberni Canal, Vancouver Island, and operated until 1968. Sunk in that year, she was raised and carted back to Vancouver for further service by other owners.

Other tugs served the C.P.R. on other lakes. Early vessels were wooden and usually built on the spot. The later steel diesel tugs were often prefabricated elsewhere. All the lake tugs were screw propeller driven. *Granthall* had the distinction of being built four times. At 164 tons and 92-foot length, she was constructed in 1928 by Vickers in Montreal, disassembled and carried out west on ten flatcars. After plying the lake between Kootenay Landing and

Opposite: Railway cars were carried the length of the British Columbia lakes on car floats, in this case by *Sandon* (97 tons, 1898). (CP Rail Corporate Archives 3701)

Right: *Naramata* was a barge tug for Canadian Pacific Railway's British Columbia Okanagan Lake service. She was 150 tons, was built in Port Arthur, Ontario in 1913 and had a 270hp compound steam engine. (CP Rail Corporate Archives 11520)

Procter until 1957, she was sold to Edmonton owners, ultimately to be reassembled twice again for service at other locations before ending her career.

Opening the Eastern Arctic

Tugs ventured north around Labrador into Hudson Bay when the port of Churchill was improved and dredged. Federal Department of Marine tugs operated there during the construction of deep sea grain shipping facilities. *G.W. Yates* (1913, 111 tons) worked here tending dredges in the early 1930s. The former Admiralty *St. Arvans*, renamed *Ocean Eagle*, made a pioneering barge-towing expedition to Port Burwell in the Northwest Territories in 1927, without benefit of ice protection. More recently, *W.N. Twolan* and then *H.M. Wilson* successively have been the resident tugs here.

After the Second World War, in the 1950s, serious charting of ice formations and channels for navigation was undertaken. Then, the building and resupply of the DEW Line early warning radar system, northern mining projects and oil exploration opened up the eastern Arctic to commercial supply operations. For heavier freight, this task has been accomplished mostly by tug and barge.

For a time the only large ocean-going, Canadian tug with reinforced Ice Class I rating was Atlantic Towing's 800-ton, controllable-pitch single-screw, *Irving Birch* (I). Built with considerable foresight in 1967 by Saint John Shipbuilding and Drydock Company, she was 827 tons, with a single 3750bhp Nohab Polar diesel engine. This tug carried out contract tows with oil barges to the eastern Arctic, which helped her owners develop experience in towing in the far north. On the first tows, retired Canadian Navy Commodore O.C.S. Robertson, the pioneer Arctic ice mapper, went along as ice advisor. The smaller tugs *Irving Maple, Irving Elm* and *Irving Cedar*, the last the most powerful at 5600bhp, have lesser ice ratings, but have been involved in northern supply and winter operations in the Gulf of St. Lawrence.

Most of this fleet built by Saint John Shipbuilding and Drydock Company were provided with Kort nozzles and controllable-pitch propellers (these are discussed in Chapter 15).

Typical of many of the northern supply expeditions was the voyage of *Irving Elm* (1980, 3458bhp, 427 tons) to Saglek in northern Labrador in 1986. Taking a large open barge loaded with construction equipment was only the first challenge. As is so often the case in the north, a second challenge was finding a way to get the cargo, in units of up to 50 tons, onto the shore with nothing to serve as a wharf. In this case, after preliminary surveys, a small pier face was built using an abandoned landing barge and rock bulldozed over it from the shore. The barge was anchored against this makeshift structure and the bulky construction components hauled ashore while the tug stood by for an emergency pull away if the weather turned sour.

A more spectacular delivery to the North by Atlantic Towing's tugs was the transport of an entire lead-zinc ore processing plant from Trois Rivières on the St. Lawrence River to Little Cornwallis Island, a journey of 3000 miles to the north. The main element in this tow was the huge process building, a structure seven storeys high, built onto a barge. Much as the Dutch had found out long before with their drydocks and dredges, delivery in one piece was calculated to save $80 million and a year's time by not having to re-build the plant at its destination.

The 420-foot barge was built by Davie Shipyards at Lauzon and the processing mill added at Trois Rivières, the combined structure displacing 13,200 tons. The greatest worry was the "sail area" of the tall building, a wind catcher like the floating drydocks. The barge was fitted with an external pushing notch on the stern for steering by a second tug. Atlantic Towing, with its ice-rated fleet, won the contract. *Irving Cedar*, with her power and tower-mounted auxiliary wheelhouse for good visibility over ice conditions ahead, took the tow. Her Captain, Peter Garnham, was towmaster. *Irving Birch*, under Captain Albert Myalls, took the notch at the stern. Naval Captain Tom Pullen, another Arctic specialist, was ice advisor, the position he had held on the famous cruise of the tanker *Manhattan* through the Arctic. The 294-ton, ice-strengthened coastal tug *Irving Beech* went along as escort. Captain Pullen has described the arduous trip in *Canadian Geographic* magazine.

The expedition left Trois Rivières on July 24th, 1981, proceeding downriver at seven knots, with the giant tow shorthauled on 400 feet of *Cedar's* 2$\frac{1}{2}$-inch towing wire and *Birch* steering astern. The towline would be let out to 1800 feet when at sea. The awkward tow yawed and steered poorly, according to Captain Pullen. Risks expected ahead included pack ice and rough water in the Labrador Sea, but it turned out to be rougher below Anticosti Island, heading toward the Strait of Belle Isle. In 20-knot winds and 10-foot seas, the seven-storey building pitched and rolled. Steering problems in *Cedar* necessitated bringing in *Beech* to tow her until repairs were effected. At times, when it was too rough for

The steel tug *Okanagan,* successor to the earlier *Naramata,* operated on Lake Okanagan until suspension of the CPR lake rail service. (CP Rail Corporate Archives 8087)

notch work, *Irving Birch* scouted ahead for ice obstacles. On reaching the Strait of Belle Isle, the smaller *Irving Beech* turned for home.

After taking refuge from further high winds, the tow moved up the broad waters of the Labrador Sea, Davis Strait and Lancaster Sound, near the top of the world. Ice conditions were light, fortunately. In Barrow Strait, the Canadian Coast Guard icebreaker *John A. Macdonald* met them, escorting them through pack ice and fog to their destination on August 13th. There, at the Polaris Mine on Little Cornwallis Island, the mill on a barge was settled onto a prepared gravel bottom in a lagoon and closed in.

The steel B.C. Lakes service steam tug *Granthall* had the distinction of being disassembled and reassembled four times for use in different locations. She was originally built in Montreal for Canadian Pacific, launched in Lake Kootenay in 1928 and laid up in 1957. (CP Rail Corporate Archives 3140)

The Scramble for Northern Oil

The northern oil exploration boom in the Western Arctic, including the Alaskan and Canadian coasts, called for extraordinary efforts in transportation. The rail and river route through Canada via the Mackenzie River had its limitations and the Americans were restricted from using it by the Jones Act. Major expeditions involving a consortium of American and Canadian towing companies were mounted to convoy supplies through the Aleutians and Bering Strait, around Alaska's tip at Point Barrow, seldom free of ice, to Prudhoe Bay and the Beaufort Sea.

Individual towing companies had gained considerable experience in towing far out along the panhandle coast of Alaska, with Foss Launch of Seattle prominent. Foss supplied the building project at the Amchitka nuclear test base and, in 1964, resupplied the western DEW Line, using barges, shallow draft tugs and small lighter-barges. Many of the earlier long tows were taken by the stalwart wooden, wartime-built Miki and Mikimiki class tugs, daring work for such unprotected vessels in ice conditions. A new breed of high-powered steel tugs was used by the large consortium organized for northern supply projects to the high Arctic in the later oil exploration boom. Most of the tugs were not ice-strengthened, but the two Canadian ice-rated, ocean-going tugs *Arctic Hooper* and *Arctic Taglu* (1976, Ice-class I, 2250bhp, 395 tons) were designed and built for this kind of service in British Columbia. Their partly squared off bows made them suitable for pushing barges and they led the way for numerous Arctic vessel designs.

From the early 1970s, there was an annual sealift around Alaska to the Beaufort Sea. The Canadian group, Arctic Transportation Company Ltd., was organized for this work by

In the postwar push to develop navigation in the northern ocean waters of Canada, ice was a preoccupation. Here the U.S. Coast Guard tug *Ojibwa* is seen heading north following the experimental ice-cutter *Alexbow* in 1967. The floating cutter later sank in heavy ice. (German and Milne, Naval Architects)

Genstar Marine (then owners of Seaspan International), Federal Commerce and Navigation Ltd. of Montreal and Crowley Maritime Corporation, an international tug and barge company based in the United States. Probably the greatest effort mounted by this group was the 1975 sealift. It involved twenty-three American and Canadian tugs and forty-seven barges in the transportation of 160,000 tons of material to Prudhoe Bay and Tuktoyaktuk. Included were complete buildings, construction vehicles, boats and large oil refinery separation towers.

A Canadian contingent set out from North Vancouver, including fourteen barges and the 1700bhp Seaspan tugs *Navigator, Commander* and *Mariner*. They sailed together with four large shallow draft push tugs just completed in Vancouver for service in the Canadian North. This group made rendezvous with the Americans for the critical dash around Point Barrow, Alaska, the point where

ice flows were certain to be a problem. Air reconnaissance was used, but the normal, brief, annual period of open water did not occur. Over a period of time, groups of tugs and barges fought their way through heavy ice in what turned out to be one of the worst seasons for ice in the area. Many got through; some had to turn back and wait for a better season. By the mid-1970s, the new breed of much more powerful offshore and ice-rated multipurpose tugs would take over, many built in British Columbia.

The large-scale Arctic supply operations declined along with the high price of oil worldwide, contributing to a slump in the tug industry generally. Another area of promise that slumped temporarily was ventures into transoceanic towing, using new technology in barges and tugs. The same group of companies also operated under the name Global Transportation Organization. They towed barge loads of large bulk cargos, from roll-on-roll-off vehi-

cles to dredges and drill rigs anywhere, world-wide, notably to the Near East petroleum producing countries during their boom time.

The reduction in oil prices and trade added to a decline in demand for the oil exploration drill rigs and their servicing. Then the North Sea oil play took up the slack in the latter 1960s. In the beginning, the ocean rigs were towed into position and serviced by the existing types of ocean-going tugs provided by the towing companies. These were predominantly American, with long experience in offshore oil drilling in the Gulf of Mexico, though not with the rougher North Sea. The bigger Canadian West Coast tugs joined in. *Gulf Joan*, Gulf of Georgia Towing's 3000bhp ocean-towing tug tended the first large drill rig off Canadian shores. *Gibraltar Straits* of Straits Towing and *Seaspans Commodore* and *Regent*, both 5750bhp, and *Seaspan Royal*, of 7000bhp, tended rigs in the North Sea during the beginning of these operations. The work included delivery of barge loads of supplies from Scotland, the Hebrides and the Netherlands, as well as anchor-handling for the floating drill rigs and for pipelaying operations. *Seaspan Royal* was later sold on

Right: A complete ore smelter plant starts off in the St. Lawrence River, headed for the high Arctic in 1981. The seven storey structure had a large "sail area" like a floating drydock. It is under tow by the 5600hp, 491-foot *Irving Cedar* (ex-*Sinni*), with *Irving Birch*, 3750hp, steering in a notch. Both Atlantic Towing vessels are ice strengthened. (Atlantic Towing Limited)

Opposite: Built for northern government service in 1962, *W.N. Twolan* (299 tons, 2200-bhp) served in Hudson Bay from Port Churchill for some time, then was sold for operation on the St. Lawrence and Great Lakes. (German & Milne, Naval Architects)

the North Sea slump to Mexican owners as too large for the company's normal coastal trades at home.

The North Sea and a New Breed of Tug

The stormy North Sea and other open ocean locations have proved rough for the traditional tugs. As well, the supply and anchor-handling functions attendant upon oil rig service called for a new kind of performance. The resultant design was the anchor-handling vessel, or AHV, a vessel with its superstructure crammed well forward, leaving a long clear afterdeck for transhipping drill pipe and other deck cargo. Facilities included tanks for drilling mediums, winches suited to laying out and retrieving heavy drill rig anchors for semisubmersible drill platforms, and sophisticated propulsion and positioning capabilities. Higher power and bollard pull were also found necessary.

The British, Norwegian, Dutch and German tug and petroleum industry companies quickly produced numerous supply and anchor-handling vessels on the new lines and boosted engine power. By the early 1970s, the supply and anchor-handling vessels and the traditional ocean tugs came together in a hybrid vessel, an anchor-handling tug of 3000 to 10,000bhp. Features were double-drum anchor winches, open sterns with rollers for anchor cables and a propulsion system permitting precise positioning (GPS) near drill platforms. This left the traditional ocean and salvage tugs with the long distance towing of drill rigs and semisubmersible drill platforms.

As early as 1965 a new Canadian player with British connections, Canadian Offshore Marine, designed a tougher supply boat for North Sea service and the company brought out a series of vessels with that capability in the Shore class, including *North Shore, East Shore, Island Shore, Channel Shore* and *Nova Shore*. Anchoring and handling for the large semisubmersible rigs that were now appearing called for powerful tugs to assist the supply vessels. This resulted in new supply boats with higher power. The company built and registered a tug/supply vessel, *Atlantic Shore,* in 1968. This tug's first assignment was to proceed from Rotterdam to the Gulf of Mexico to tow the Shell rig *Sidewinder* 3500 miles to the Bay of Bengal. *Atlantic Shore* made five knots enroute, put out eight anchors, serviced the rig for six months, then picked it up and towed it to Singapore. Vessels like this were running 6000 and 7000 horsepower with a bollard pull of around 70 tons. The threat to traditional deep sea tugs was clear.

By 1970, almost all towing, anchoring and supply of the semi-submersibles exploring off the east coast of Canada was being performed by combination tug/anchor/supply vessels carrying most of the towing accoutrements of the regular ocean-going tug.

The various types of jackup drill rigs that stood on legs extended to the sea bottom and semisubmersible ocean platforms that were heavily anchored, proliferated and were moved about the world on a fairly routine basis, usually towed by ocean tugs of very large power. More recently, however, movement of these rigs was expedited with the use of a new breed of semisubmersible barges capable of lifting them out of the water completely. This method, called "dry towing," which doubled transit speed on long voyages, was first tried in 1976 by Global Transportation Organization, (Crowley Maritime, Federal Pacific and Genstar Overseas). Later, semisubmersible lift barges that were self-propelled would eliminate many of the towing jobs. Seaspan (Cyprus) Limited is among the companies recently specializing in heavy lift, self-propelled and semisubmersible ocean-going barges out of the West Coast of Canada. Another division of the Washington Marine Group is Norsk Pacific Steamship Company, providing coastal covered and open barge services and terminals for the forest industry.

Permanent offshore oil and gas production platforms of gargantuan size for the North Sea and Canadian East Coast oil production and delivery systems have been constructed in Britain, Norway and Canada. Displacing hundreds of thousands of tons, they have had to be mated to enormous superstructures, towed out to sea, placed and held in a precise location at sea using the most sophisticated satellite navigation systems. Then they are sunk to stand permanently on the ocean floor.

An example is *Statfjords A, B* and *C*. Displacing up to 824,000 tons, these three-legged, concrete tower structures were towed out of Yrkes Fjord near Stavanger, Norway, to the oil fields 250 miles at sea. *Statfjord C* is 250 metres high, floating with about half of this height out of the water. It was towed out in 1984 by five of the world's first rank conventional ocean tugs, with three others helping maintain control astern. *Smit Singapore* (22,000hp), one of the most powerful in the world at the time, was the control tug, responsible for navigation. Total towing power was 77,000bhp, some 500 tons of bollard pull. The towing contractors were Smit-Wijsmuller of the Netherlands and United Towing of Britain. Speed of the tow was one knot in the fjord and two knots at sea.

Just as impressive was the more recent tow-out of the Canadian Hibernia platform from Newfoundland to its position in the North

Atlantic. This 600,000-ton structure, built to withstand not only the stormy North Atlantic but encounters with the icebergs that drift regularly down from Greenland, took five years to build. The concrete base was poured within a cofferdam at remote Bull's Arm, Newfoundland, floated and towed out. Numerous tugs from several operators found employment here, including McKeil Marine's from Lake Ontario. The seven-storey superstructure and towers above it were built in sections in Korea and brought by barges around the world to be floated precisely over the base and the whole combined assembly floated up. All this was tugs' work. The final, critical job brought in nine powerful anchor handling tugs from a new division of the veteran Maersk shipping interests of Denmark, with a base in St. John's. Six pulled ahead and three helped maintain steering control from astern as the great structure was moved out around the Grand Banks and, again precisely, placed in its designated permanent place.

The newer Sable Island *Thebaud* gas platform involves a seabed pipeline laid to the mainland shore in Nova Scotia. In this case, a superstructure built in Teeside in Britain was hoisted onto a platform structure prefabricated in Dartmouth, Nova Scotia and assembled on site off Sable Island. This was achieved by the use of the huge self-propelled barge *Saipem 7000*, carrying a two-crane combined lifting capacity of 14,000 tons. The tugs' work needed was handled through the supply vessels of offshore specialists Secunda Marine in Dartmouth, including *Terra Nova Sea* and *Triumph Sea*. These two had seen regular service in North Sea contracts in the mid 1990s.

The particular needs of anchor-handling and the supply of pipe, muds, cement and other materials in seas noted for rough weather had inevitably led to the special type of vessel for the purpose. The anchor-handling supply vessels were the result. Experience brought further evolution of their distinctive configuration of a long, flat afterdeck and a superstructure with twin funnels well forward on a raised forecastle. Their featured pilothouse with dual fore-and-aft facing control positions, ASD steering propellers, thrusters for automatic GPS position control and sophisticated navigation systems are now commonplace for a new generation of tugs for all uses.

The higher powered anchor/supply vessels or ASVs, with multiple towing winches and high power, have proven a tough competitor for the traditional ocean tug, towing large rigs about the seas and, on occasion, picking up vessels in distress in their vicinity. The owners of these boats are shipping companies, tug companies and others, all working under contract to the oil exploration and operating companies. The later oil exploration slump added a glut of these vessels to the over-supply of regular tugs, causing layups and a shakeout in ownerships until markets improved and worldwide oil exploration with long distance movements of drill rigs restored demand. *Polar Shore* (1971, 5280bhp) became *Canmar Supplier VII* in 1977, then in the nineties was acquired by Les Remorqueurs du Quebec (Quebec Tugs) for service as the tug *Ocean Foxtrot*. Capable of heavy ice-breaking work for the far north, she would be at home in the Gulf of St. Lawrence in winter. Atlantic Towing and McKeil Marine also operate AHVs.

Meanwhile in the 1980s and 1990s older-technology ocean tugs were disposed of in favour of the new breed of towing vessel bearing a strong resemblance to the anchor handler. They picked up the innovations derived from the ocean oil boom and can be capable of effective work in both fields when classed as anchor-handling tugs. Even harbour tugs would make use of the new ideas, especially in the technology of propulsion affecting their manoeuverability and consequent ship handling ability. Harbour ship handling and other close quarter work has stimulated a brisk Azimuthal Steering Drive tug-building splurge in the 1990s worldwide. Irving Shipbuilding's East Isle small vessel yard at Georgetown, Prince Edward Island and Ocean Industries yard on Ile aux Coudres, Quebec have produced them serially, for their own needs and for sale. These are harbour docking tugs built to successful designs by Robert Allan of Vancouver. The Marystown, Newfoundland yard, longtime builders of fishing vessels, has turned to construction of supply tugs for Maersk and big VSP tugs for Whiffen Ltd. to berth large tankers in Newfoundland waters.

In spite of dire predictions in recent years that the towing industry has a dubious future, all the signs now point to an optimistic adaptation to changing conditions.

The efficiency of the propeller was increased in many post-second world war tugs by the addition of the Kort nozzle, a ring around its perimeter. The high tides of the Bay of Fundy provide a free drydock for an inspection of the twin-screw *Irving Beech* II (1969, 2700bhp). (Author's Collection)

An Application of Power

THE PRIMITIVE ANCESTOR OF THE MODERN, HIGHLY SPECIALIZED TUG was the hull of a small sailing vessel in which were mounted a square, low-pressure boiler, engines and paddles. It was wooden, long and narrow, had no superstructure and frequently sported a vestigial bowsprit or, more often, the broken stub of one. The master shouted engine orders to the engineer down through a scuttle while trying to avoid the towline which was underfoot as he handled the tiller.

The side paddles were mounted on a single shaft at first. They could not turn at different speeds or in opposite directions, capabilities that permitted great manoeuverability when separate shafts and engines were adopted later. Greater power could also be obtained with two engines. With the single shaft, steering by rudder was unresponsive. A device sometimes adopted to help in turning with a tow was the chain box. It was a wheeled box loaded with a heavy weight and pulled from one side of the boat to the other in order to heel it over. This lifted one paddle out of the water and made the other bite more deeply. Another device was the cant hook, mounted at the side of the superstructure. When the towline was hooked to it the boat could be heeled and veered to one side.

The original side lever engines had the piston at the bottom, the piston rod rising from it to drive a crosshead and the various levers connected to the crank on the paddle shaft overhead. Increasing engine size led to mounting the pistons on an angle and this was the long term style in British paddle vessels. In North America, the overhead rocking beam with a very long piston travel was adopted following its development by Robert Stevens circa 1822 in New York. It was based on the early Boulton and Watt beam pumps. All sorts of side wheel vessels, from the tug to the great Mississippi packets, had this slowly working beam and very large steam cylinders, the beam usually in the open and plainly visible above the superstructure. Such engines had the virtue of mechanical parts that moved very slowly and, as shown on the Saint John, St. Lawrence and other rivers, often outlasted several hulls.

Tugs working in sheltered waters with a strong current such as the Mississippi, Columbia, Klondike and other rivers, favored the single stern wheel and pushed their "tows" from behind. Better steering control over a string of barges resulted. Their horizontal engines were also very slow turning, on the order of ten or twelve revolutions per minute.

The British adopted iron hulls for tugs early, then exported some to North America. Canadian and American builders, with their plentiful wood supply and skill in its use were very slow to abandon this readily available material. The earliest boilers, operating on as little as two or three pounds pressure, were rectangular and of rivetted iron. In only one decade, from 1823 to 1833, engine horsepower jumped threefold, whereas boiler pressures increased more slowly to about 40psi. Cylindrical boilers and steel, then, were necessary for greater strength and the ubiquitous Scotch boiler took over with its more efficient water-immersed fire boxes and return fire tubes. Pressures climbed by the 1880s to between 175 and 250psi.

A crude engine room telegraph was invented in the 1820s, but simple bell-pull signals sufficed for most small tugs until overtaken by diesel engines controlled from the wheelhouse. One clang meant "go ahead" or "stop" (whichever the engine was not doing at that moment). Two was for "astern" and three meant "slow." Four pulls, or sometimes a separate, distinctive bell was the signal for the engineer to "pour it on."

CHAPTER 15

The Evolution of the Modern Tug

Ajax (Robert Allan, Ltd.)

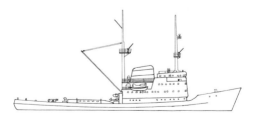

Pacific (Author's sketch)

While the paddle wheel had a solid but shallow bite in the water, the screw propeller called for a substantial change in hull design. The propeller worked much better when set deep in the water, calling for a deeper-draft boat. The hull also became shorter and broader to compensate for losing the stability of the paddles on the sides. Thus the screw propeller brought an abrupt move toward the more familiar modern squat, fat tug shape. Although the strong turning effect of the broadly set paddles was lost, a propeller set at the stern just ahead of a large rudder resulted in strong, rapid steering characteristics.

The deep-set propeller shaft was now set low in the hull, calling for an inversion of the engine, putting the pistons on top. The engine was set in a fore-and-aft configuration and the very large valve gear disposed of. The two-cylinder compound engine, utilizing the expansion of steam twice, was invented in the mid 1850s and some two-cylinder, single expansion engines were converted to compound so as to gain this efficiency. Paddle vessels also were built with compound engines. The triple expansion engine first appeared in the early 1870s in Europe. In either three- or four-cylinder form, this became a highly efficient and reliable engine for vessels large and small. The later, more efficient and powerful marine steam turbine engine was never practical for small vessels like tugs, notably because of its slower starting, stopping and reversing capabilities.

The German engineer Dr. Rudolph Diesel installed one of his compression-ignition oil engines in a boat for service in Russia in

The pair of vertical axis (or cycloidal) propellers of the Voith Schneider type that propel the Gulf of St. Lawrence tug *Brochu* permit the application of power in any direction. This is a great asset in berthing tugs, but requires greater draft than traditional propellers. (German and Milne, Naval Architects)

1904. It was diesel-electric drive because his early engines could not reverse. The world was quite happy, however, with the very effective steam tug for a long time. The drawback of the reversing or semi-diesels was that they had to stop and then start again promptly, and reliably, to reverse direction. Nevertheless, their fuel efficiency and the elimination of firemen and boilers eventually produced strong interest. Coal bunkering was dirty and facilities were inconveniently located. Reversing, slow, semi-diesel engine powered tugs, including conversions from steam, appeared on the west coast of North America from the 1920s to the Second World War. But the large wartime steam tug production in Britain kept tug operators happy with coal- and oil-fired steam in the East well beyond the end of the war. By the 1960s however, powerful high-speed geared diesel engines, coupled with economies in crew numbers, provided the push to abandon steam everywhere. Some were conversions, but many new boats were built and with them came better crew accommodations and safety measures, satisfying a growing clamour from seamen's unions.

The modern steam tug had achieved near perfection, given the available propulsion technology, in the British-style berthing or docking tug. This was a squat, stable, manoeuverable hull with its superstructure well forward. The single large slow-turning propeller had a strong bite in the water and strong pulling power at slower towing speeds. The design permitted the towing hook to be located about one-third of the length from the stern and well ahead of the propeller so the tug could turn easily on the end of the towline.

Until recent times, most ship handling was performed with tugs at the bow and stern on towlines passed down from the ship to the tugs and attached to their after towing hooks. The stern tug was particularly useful for steering control and braking. The system involved the risk of "girding," the tug being pulled over sideways and capsized, or of being run down by the tow when coming too close under the ship's bow to pick up the forward towline. Ample fenders had to be provided for the pushing and jockeying that were also part of the ship-moving job. These were usually of wood or rope until old automobile tires became plentiful.

The American approach to handling ships and barges more frequently involved control from a point alongside called "breast towing." This aided the tug's ability to work in narrow slips between piers and was safer for the tugs. As a result, American harbour tugs traditionally have had longer superstructures and towing bitts further aft. More crew accommodation above decks was a benefit of this arrangement.

The introduction of the variable pitch propeller was a great aid in the effective control of engines from the pilothouse, allowing the tug master to immediately apply the power he needed. The Kort nozzle is considered one of the greatest contributions to efficient propulsion. Proposed in 1930 by an aeronautical engineer, Ludwig Kort, to solve the problem of propeller wash eroding canal banks in Germany, it soon turned out to have greater benefits. Simply a ring or shroud around the perimeter of the propeller, it acts as a nozzle to substantially enhance the efficiency of the jet of water pushed out by the propeller. It also gets rid of the propellor side-bias and improves steering when going astern. The Kort nozzle may be fixed, with the usual rudder behind or, better, may itself turn like a rudder to provide steering. It took a long time to catch on, but today many tugs and other vessels have been fitted with it. A fully steerable propeller would be the next step.

A unique type of propulsion useful for some tug applications is the vertical axis propeller, usually referred to as Voith-Schneider propulsion (VSP) after the principal builders. A more generic American term is cycloidal propulsion. J.M. Voith first produced it in 1930 in Germany. This drive consists of four to six vertical blades rotating on a centre and oscillating on their own axes. By changing the pitch of the blades, as with aircraft propellor blades, the propulsion force can be aimed in any direction through 360 degrees. A tug with this system, single propeller or twin, forward or aft, can pull or push equally well in any direction. Vessels so equipped are deep draft with this system of blades projecting underneath and a deep pivot-skeg, or keel, at the other end of the hull, and thus are not useful in shallow waters. The blade function is not unlike that of a helicopter and is fully controlled from the bridge. Examples of earlier Canadian Voith-Schneider tractor tugs are Alcan's *Grand Baie* (1973) at Port Alfred, Quebec, ECTUG's 4500-horsepower *Point Comeau* (1976) serving on the Gulf of St. Lawrence North Shore; *Brochu* and *Vachon* (1973, 3600hp) built for docking at Port Cartier, Quebec; and the five Canadian naval tugs of the Glenevis class stationed at Halifax and Esquimault. Larger and more recent examples are *Placentia Pride* and *Placentia Hope* (1998, 5000hp) of St.John's, Newfoundland, built at Marystown.

A competing system with similar high manoeuverability and ability to push side-on appeared in the early 1980s and has become the more popular choice. This is the twin-screw, Z-drive or Azimuthal Stern Drive (ASD), also known as a "Z-peller." Tugs with such a system are steered by wheelhouse control levers that permit rotation of the propeller's direction of discharge, much the way an outboard

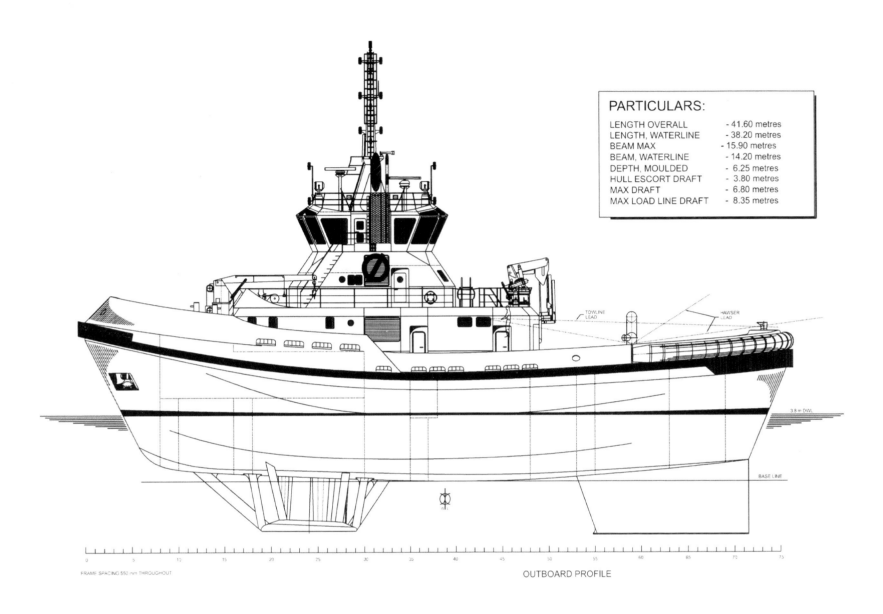

PARTICULARS:

LENGTH OVERALL — - 41.60 metres
LENGTH, WATERLINE — - 38.20 metres
BEAM MAX — - 15.90 metres
BEAM, WATERLINE — - 14.20 metres
DEPTH, MOULDED — - 6.25 metres
HULL ESCORT DRAFT — - 3.80 metres
MAX DRAFT — - 6.80 metres
MAX LOAD LINE DRAFT — - 8.35 metres

TOWLINE LEAD

HAWSER LEAD

3.8 m DWL

BASE LINE

FRAME SPACING 550 mm THROUGHOUT

OUTBOARD PROFILE

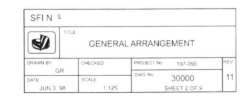

SFI N º				
	TITLE	GENERAL ARRANGEMENT		
DRAWN BY GR	CHECKED	PROJECT No 197-090		REV.
DATE JUN 3 98	SCALE 1:125	DWG No 30000 SHEET 2 OF 9		11

The 10,000hp VSP-drive, escort tug *Ajax* represents the ultimate in tug technology. (Robert Allan, Ltd.)

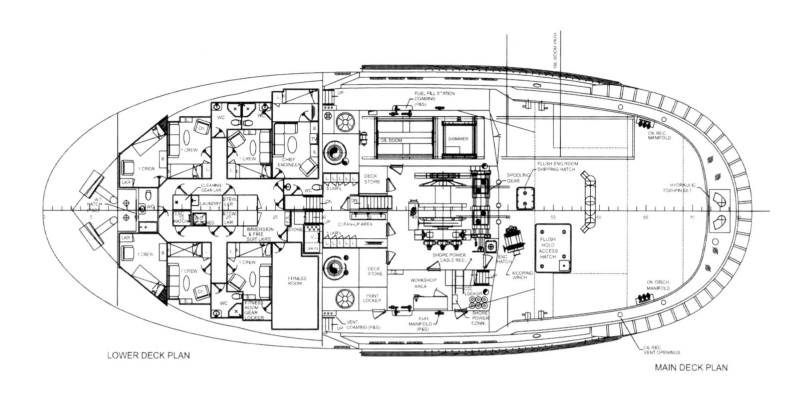

LOWER DECK PLAN

MAIN DECK PLAN

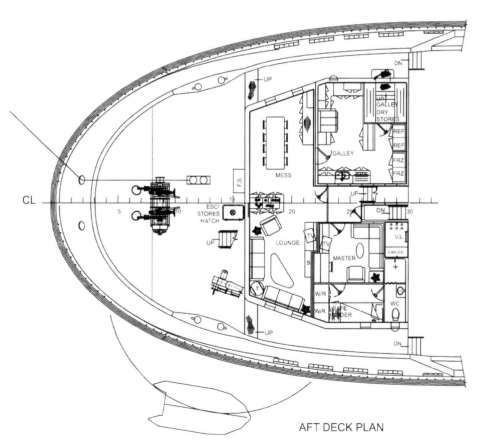

AFT DECK PLAN

SFI N º				
	TITLE	GENERAL ARRANGEMENT		
DRAWN BY	CHECKED	PROJECT No	197-090	REV
GR				
DATE	SCALE	DWG. No	30000	11
JUN 3 98	1 125		SHEET 4 OF 9	

Drawing of a large triple expansion steam engine. The steam expands three times in cylinders of increasing size for maximum efficiency. These engines reached a high state of reliability and efficiency. (Author's Collection)

motor is steered, but through 360 degrees. Appearing first in the 1950s, it was adopted slowly at first. It proved to be ideal for the precise positioning of oil rig supply vessels, and so it caught on. By the latter 1990s tug fleets worldwide were re-equipping with this type of drive for the docking tug, working with a towline over its bow.

Azimuth propellers, working on a right-angle drive and shrouded within Kort nozzles, turned through a full circle, thus capable of pushing sideways or reversing direction altogether in seconds. They are generally mounted in pairs at the stern (ASD) or sometimes forward near the bow of the vessel (Schottel type). The latter

include types that are retractable within the hull, particularly when fitted supplementary to stern propellers. Pioneering and principally used types were made by Niigata in Japan, Schottel in Germany and the British Aquamaster by Ulstein-Vickers (Rolls Royce), the last manufactured in British Columbia. The result has been a revolution in docking technique in the 1990s. Some veteran tug masters and ships' pilots have had difficulty adapting to the radically new capabilities and dynamics in vessel handling at first.

These new forms of tug operation introduced the concepts known as the tractor tug and the reverse tractor, depending on where on the tug the propellers and the towing winch are located. With greater control of movement in any direction, the risk of the tug being run down by the ship or girted (pulled over) can be virtually eliminated. These faults were the cause of many earlier sinkings and lives being lost. The new tugs now generally pass their own towline up to the ship from a wheelhouse-controlled tensioning winch on deck and can change the length of the line at will. The tug can thus push or back off and pull on demand. A tug is functionally in the tractor mode when it connects to the tow with one end while its multidirectional propulsion is at the other end. Thus many of the newer docking tugs have stern drive, but bow towlines and winches. Some have a traditional towing hook aft as well. A few tugs have their propulsion at the forward end. A retractable ASD propeller may be added forward as a supplement to traditional fixed propellers aft to modernize an older tug by improving steering and increasing power.

The Canadian Navy's little Ville class yard tugs introduced ASD Z-drive in Eastern Canada and were followed by *Point Halifax (1986), Point Chebucto (1993) and Point Valiant II* (1998) of the ECTUG fleet at Halifax. Its use has since spread rapidly, along with higher engine power, in recent docking tugs that handle large container ships and automobile carriers, at 3000 to 5000 horsepower. Both Atlantic Towing and Ocean Group have built ASD tugs on the Robert Allan design for their own use, such as *Atlantic Hemlock, Atlantic Spruce, Atlantic Willow* (1996/7/8, 4004bhp); *Ocean Intrepide, Ocean Jupiter,* (1998/9, 4000bhp). In the Port of Vancouver in 2000, ten docking tugs, four with Cates, four with Rivtow Marine and three with Seaspan were in service equipped with ASD propulsion systems, starting with the 2400hp tugs *Charles Cates I* (1983), *II* (1986), *III* (1988), and *V* (1990), and *Seaspan Discovery* (1984, 4000hp*), Hawk* and *Falcon* (1990, 3000hp). Westminster Tugs had one ASD tug on the Fraser River.

The new harbour subsidiary of Rivtow Marine of Vancouver, Tiger Tugz Inc., operates z-drive tractor tugs for harbour work in Burrard Inlet: *Tiger Sun* (1999, 5000bhp in a 70-foot hull), and *Tiger Wolf, Spirit and Pride* (1996/7, 3000bhp), all with twin Detroit Diesels. As with many modern harbour tugs, they are day boats with two-member crews. The wheelhouse contains the whole crew accommodation, including limited galley facilities. With a beam equal to one-half of her length, *Tiger Sun* is in a class sometimes referred to as a ship-docking module, and capable of moving sideways at eight knots, two-thirds of her forward speed.

Along with new propulsion and higher power in a small package, the turn-of-the-century docking tug design produced a vessel arranged to move in any direction, with heavy rubber fenders all around. Consequently there is usually a midships wheelhouse with 360-degree visibility and a rounded, bathtub-shaped hull that makes it hard to tell which end is which, because it makes little difference. Funnels are very short or skinny pipes to improve visibility astern. Pushing and pulling with the use of a tensioning winch and lightweight towlines allows a tug crew of two to do the job, requiring fewer crew on the ship being handled as well.

At sea, the vessels introduced for anchoring and supplying ocean oil rigs and the deep-sea towing tugs have learned and copied from each other, producing a versatile hybrid in a new form for long distance rescue, salvage and barging tugs.

Their features include a wheelhouse that is a complete control centre for the vessel, including coffee-maker, located near midships; full fore and aft visibility using paired funnels and fore and aft facing control positions in the wheelhouse; in ocean tugs long, low after decks with raised forecastle and the superstructure pushed more forward; precise maneouvering with GPS, and automated steering.

The People Aboard

There may be spit and polish on naval tugs in peacetime, but generally on commercial tugs it is rarely to be found. Tug crews are, above all, practical working people. Relations among the men (and the occasional woman) have to be easy-going and flexible. There is not much room on board a tug and the hours and work are varied. Danger is always nearby. Frequent shift changes tend to reduce the cohesiveness of crews, although it is likely to be first names all round and all sit around the same mess table. However, no one else sits in the captain's accustomed seat. For all the informality and the dictates of the union contract, it is understood that the master of the vessel is still someone apart. He is the traditional master of all he surveys and the one upon whose judgement and decisions everyone's life may depend. In the new high-tech tug, the master no longer slouches against a window with one hand on the wheel; he may be forced to sit hemmed in by controls and gauges, both hands on the joysticks, with everything at his fingertips and full visibility all around.

As in every line of work, it was harder in the old days, despite the larger crews. The big steam tugs had seven to nine member crews. Now, firemen shovelling coal and ashes are no more, and the engineers do not maintain continuous watch in the engine room. Harbour tugs often operate with crews of two to four; a long distance tow takes seven to nine for shift rotation. A tug will accom-

The traditional steering wheel has disappeared for many vessels in favor of joystick controls. Captain Rose handles steering of the two Z-drive propellers in *Point Halifax* (5300 bhp, 417 tons) of the ECTUG fleet. The system results in a very high degree of manoeuverability. (Author's Collection)

Opposite: One of the great salvage tugs of the Pacific coast was *Salvage King* of Island Tug and Barge at Victoria. She was repossessed by the British government for service in the Second World War and lost overseas. Here she stands by as harbour tugs ease the damaged *Prince Rupert* into drydock at Esquimault. (Archives British Columbia D-1361)

modate additional personnel for salvage work or log-loading. Since tugs serve other vessels' needs, they may spend long periods awaiting their pleasure. At the opposite end of the scale, there are periods of urgency and danger when everyone aboard concentrates mightily on keeping a tow, or the tug itself, clear of impending disaster.

Tug crews working in and around harbours today will work a twelve hour or perhaps twenty-four hour shift, preparing their own meals with a microwave oven instead of a cook. On long hauls they may work six hours on and six off for two weeks, then have two weeks off. Crews change strictly on schedule and are often relieved wherever the tug happens to be. Individually, these seamen are likely to have served in a variety of vessels, though they tend to stay with tugs and usually come from the coast where they are working. Newfoundlanders are predominant on the east coast of Canada and are found everywhere vessels work. Identified by their accent and their good-humoured, fatalistic attitude, they

accept the rigours and discomforts of the sea in small vessels. Similarly, up and down the St. Lawrence the French-speaking sailors know those waters and the Gulf from long family tradition in small coasters.

The Changing Face of Salvage

The introduction of wireless radio early in the twentieth century made possible a system based on salvage tugs kept on station at strategic ports. These were maintained ready to dash to sea in the worst of weathers in answer to an SOS. The motives were primarily commercial, and competition was keen, but the need to save lives was also served. In the First World War many enemy-damaged ships were towed in to be patched and sailed again, particularly in the vicinity of Britain. Numerous rescue and salvage tugs built in the world wars found their way into private hands afterwards, boats of improved seaworthiness and power.

THE EVOLUTION OF THE MODERN TUG

Salvage on the St. Lawrence River and Seaway system is frequently a matter of lightering off sufficient cargo to refloat the vessel. McAllister Towing and Salvage of Montreal unload scrap steel from the freighter *Monty Python*, aground on St. Helen's Island in 1985 within sight of their base.

In the 1920s, British and Dutch towing and salvage companies had tugs on station in the most lucrative North Atlantic perimeter. Key stations included Falmouth, Brest, Queenstown (Cobh), Gibraltar, Horta, Bermuda, Halifax and St. John's. Salvage tugs were capable of braving the storms that had crippled the ships they meant to rescue and carried the pumps, compressors, diving and other gear for temporary repair and recovery. These were the rescue tugs for immediate response to vessels in trouble. The salvage vessels were also capable of towing but had larger holds and specialized more in hauling ships off their groundings and restoring damaged ships to seaworthiness.

Life for the salvage tug crews consisted of long periods of inactivity or routine work in harbour followed by short, intense and risky activity. The salvage tugs sometimes abandoned their stations to take on longer towing contracts in order to ease the costly overhead of waiting. The practice of keeping tugs exclusively on station all but disappeared by 1970 with the increased cost of maintaining the tugs. Today, some are kept on station at strategic ports between other major towing contracts, or are contracted as "intervention tugs" on call for marine casualties and potential oil pollution accidents. Fewer marine casualties are occurring thanks to better-built postwar ships and greatly improved navigational aids. More large tugs capable of performing rescues are plying the sea and are available on short notice.

The big rescue tugs attached to the Russian fishing fleets, for example, were often on the spot when an emergency tow was needed by any vessel. Many of them are now in commercial contract service. An even more serious competition for specialized salvage tugs was the presence about the oceans of the anchor-handling vessels attending oil platforms. They were capable of heavy towing with big winches and long hawsers, and are often readily available close to a vessel in distress. The distinction between the two types of towing vessel has become blurred into the AHT, an anchor-handling tug.

On the northwest coast of North America, Victoria was for a long time the principal base for salvage. Pacific Salvage maintained its specialized tugs at this strategic point facing the treacherous

A tougher salvage followed the capsizing and fire involving the package freighter *Fort York*. The 1895 harbour tug *Mathilda* and a lightering barge of McAllister Towing and Salvage prepare the ship for righting, 1965. (McAllister Towing and Salvage Ltd.)

N.H.B.M. No 71. OF. MONTREAL

Juan de Fuca Strait. As elsewhere, the viability of a salvage tug came to depend on taking other business to meet the overhead. Island Tug and Barge Company held this key in the post Second World War period. Their long-distance tug *Sudbury*, a converted corvette, and her successor, *Sudbury II*, gained headlines in salvage, rescue and long towing voyages. They were well known to the public for their adventures on the Pacific, as were the *Foundation* tugs on the East Coast.

Early in the twentieth century the Canadian government provided subsidies to some companies to maintain salvage and rescue ser-

vices in the St. Lawrence River and the Gulf of St. Lawrence, possibly also on the east and west coasts. Canadian Pacific Steamships, with numerous ships, including large passenger liners plying routes into the east coast ports of Halifax, Saint John, Quebec and Montreal, were somewhat concerned about having adequate salvage tugs available. They had, after all, suffered one of the worst of all sea disasters in the sinking of the passenger liner *Empress of Ireland* in the St. Lawrence in 1909. The Davie shipyard at Lauzon, Quebec, held the federal subsidy at the beginning of the century, maintaining salvage vessels there. Local tugs were brought in to assist as

Foundation Maritime Limited was a major post-second world war operator of salvage tugs on station on the Canadian East Coast before this became uneconomical. The 3000-horsepower *Foundation Vigilant* (ex-*Abeille 26*), seen passing Quebec, was built in 1952. (Maritime Museum of the Atlantic N,11,235)

needed. The second of the company's vessels and longest in service was *Lord Strathcona*, a Scottish-built two-stacker.

Canadian Pacific took over the government subsidy of $25,000 a year in 1912, including *Lord Strathcona*, bringing out from Liverpool the large harbour tugs *Gopher* and *Musquash* from their subsidiary Mersey Towing Company. C.P. had acquired this company when they bought out its parent steamship line. *Cruizer* had been brought out earlier, working out of first Halifax, then Sydney, under different companies on Canadian Pacific's behalf.

The new Quebec-based salvage operation was set up under the name of the Quebec Salvage and Wrecking Company. It carried out numerous salvages, mainly on the ice-clogged and hazardous St. Lawrence River to Anticosti Island route and was eventually sold to the rival Foundation Maritime Limited in 1944. Foundation had done well out of the war and in the 1950s had tugs on station from Quebec City to Bermuda. This practice petered out, however, with the decline in marine casualties.

The type of casualty still occurring with some frequency on the St. Lawrence River and Seaway system is somewhat different from the coastal and ocean salvage problem. Here, the main problem is ships wandering off the channel and going aground. The normal salvage procedure is simply lightering out enough cargo to refloat or haul off the ship. Sincennes McNaughton Line of Montreal specialized in this work for a long time. The company had lightering barges with cranes stationed in strategic locations. The successor company, McAllister Towing and Salvage, has continued this service to recent times and added a new dimension.

The new style of salvage enterprise allowed McAllister to maintain an impressive salvage record when all but minor competition faded from the Great Lakes and Eastern Seaboard. In addition to tugs, barges and lighters on the St. Lawrence system, the company introduced a highly mobile inventory of salvage gear at Montreal. This could be trucked or flown almost anywhere for salvage and marine firefighting operations. Local tugs would be hired on the scene as needed.

Working with other tug companies near the casualty, McAllister's specialized equipment and, more importantly, the expertise of specialized teams, have been brought to play on the east and west coasts, the Gulf of Mexico and in the North. This is common practice now, McAllister joining forty-four large, specialist, international companies and consortia working worldwide in the prestigious International Salvage Union. Floating cranes strong

A classic deep sea salvage involved the long search for and recovery of the Liberty ship *Leicester*, whose ballast had shifted in the North Atlantic. Here she is finally brought into Bermuda by *Foundation Josephine* (ex-*Samsonia*, 1942), a 4000hp, 1120-ton Bustler class wartime vessel October 4, 1948. (Foundation Co. of Canada)

enough to lift smaller vessels right out of the water are on call. Although some large tugs are on station at strategic ports, they are also available for other work that may come along. Ocean Group have wisely retained the McAllister name.

Modern professional salvage is a blend of expertise, gambling instinct and computer calculations, with towing and salvage forces coming together in joint endeavours. The professionals still prefer to work on the famous "No cure, no pay" Lloyd's Open Form contract. Under this system, the salvors are paid only if they succeed and the amount is decided by a court. Nevertheless, depending upon the complexity of the job, many other tug operators engage in salvage if an opportunity arises. This is particularly true when the work consists primarily of towing.

The Shrinking World

The international scene in the last decades of the twentieth century has exhibited an ebb and flow of international towing ven-

tures. Very large companies coming together in a consortium to gain the resources to tackle changing markets has been a key feature. Historic companies including Smit and Wijsmuller, the German Bugsier, the British Cory and United Towing, and new companies capitalizing on the oil plays such as the Danish Maersk shipping line and offshore exploration specialists team up in various combinations. Together they handle oil platform tow-outs, barge goods to oil-rich but port-poor Middle East countries, and they brave the ice of the northern seas. A barge-mounted smelter is built in Korea for use on the Arctic coast. The Canadian anchor handling tug *Arctic Shiko* performs the tow without fuss. Interestingly, her port of registry is the inland city of Edmonton, Alberta. The leaders of the towing business are exploring work in Asia, the deepwater oil fields of Brazil, Mexico and West Africa.

Dutch, British, German and Russian tugs work together on major projects, the last-named including a fleet of seven 15,000hp vessels liberated from their Cold War support missions on the

A major effort is mounted to raise a holed ore carrier in the Lower St. Lawrence, involving *Foundations Vigilant, Vera* and *Josephine II*, the floating crane *Foundation Scarborough*, and smaller tugs. (Foundation Co. of Canada)

world's oceans for commercial enterprise in salvage and towing around the world. Another example of these Russians are the world's most powerful tugs, the sisters *Fotiy Krilov* and *Nikolay Chiker*, operated in a joint venture of the Russian Navy and the Greek-based Tslaviris Salvage Group's international towing and salvage organization. The pair are 99 metres long and rated at 40,000hp or 250 tons bollard pull, with impressive salvage, firefighting, rescue and medical facilities aboard.

Dutch and British tugs are stationed on contract in the busy English Channel to defend the environment as much as to save stricken vessels. Canadian tug operators send their bigger boats to participate in the various theatres of action, including the North Sea, Near East and transpacific, as well as at home in the Arctic and on the East Coast Hibernia and Sable megaprojects.

Tough, innovative tugs have been designed for the Arctic Ocean and operated by Arctic Transportation Ltd., such as the 1976 Vancouver-built *Arctic Taglu* and *Arctic Hooper*, and 1984 *Arctic*

Nanabush (7200 horsepower and Ice Class 1). These multipurpose vessels, after heavy ice work on the Arctic oil explorations, wandered off to other projects, possibly in the North Sea where they were based in Scottish ports, then returned home again to Vancouver for coastal work.

Anchor supply tug vessels designed specifically for the job have also followed the opportunities in the oil supply service field, such as the offshore specialist Secunda Marine's *Breton Sea, Cavendish Sea* and *Terra Nova Sea*, based on Dartmouth Nova Scotia, and active notably on the East Coast Sable Island gas project.

Beginning the twentieth century, the Wijsmuller group of IJmuiden, The Netherlands, assumed control of the large British Cory Group, which included ECTUG of Halifax, establishing a fleet of over a hundred and fifty tugs and other vessels in twenty-one countries. ECTUG funnels were repainted in Wijsmuller livery. In 2001, Wijsmuller was in turn purchased by Em.V. Svitzer, a subsidiary of the Danish A.P. Moller Group (Maersk), based in Copenhagen.

Svitzer, with seventy-two vessels, provided towage and salvage in Danish and Swedish waters and barging and North Sea services. Paint hardly dry, ECTUG funnels were repainted again in Svitzer colors. Such is the effect of globalization in the world of tugs today.

Entering a New Century

As in every field of endeavour, those who go out on the waters in tugs and those who send them have had to adjust to changing times. Technology and commerce considerations also dictate to the world of tugs.

In earlier times tugs had little power and ships were very big by comparison. Water and rail transport were paramount. Tugs fussed about harbours in much greater numbers. Old pictures of New York Harbour show it dotted with dozens of tugs and rail barges. By comparison, the harbour now looks empty. Similarly, the Thames at London no longer teems with the little craft tugs and their trains of barges. On the eve of the First World War the giant German passenger liner *Imperator* (HMS *Berengaria*) had seventeen tugs

assigned to berth her at her New Jersey Pier. When the wind blew her out of the normal channel, more than a dozen more tugs came to the rescue. Now, there are berthing tugs individually producing eight or ten times the power; tugs lined four or five abreast pushing a ship are seen only in unusual circumstances.

In Canadian ports the story is similar. There are no more glamorous, express passenger ships now, but the new breed of cruise ships, container ships and tankers are as big and bulky as the transatlantic liners once were. Normally, a couple of high-powered tugs can handle them with ease and finesse because of their power and sophisticated operating capabilities. New cruise ships have arrived on the Canadian port scene that are greater in above water bulk than the old liners. But like the many large container vessels, they have their own built-in tugs in the form of bow thrusters and sometimes steering propellers. As a result of petroleum tanker disasters in recent years, tugs are now used extensively in an escort capacity for large tankers in restricted waters, exercising braking force to slow or stop them. A new breed of very large, high-power escort tugs has been designed and built for this

The environmental threat of petroleum cargoes complicates salvage operations in large tankers. Heavy ice conditions applied when, in 1979, a consortium of Smit International, McAllister Towing and Eastern Canada Towing recovered the two halves of *Kurdistan*, which broke in two near Canso, Nova Scotia. The stern half is shown being readied for tow by *Guardsman* of United Towing to Britain to get a new bow section. (John Weeks Collection)

The largest ocean towing vessels now include a few of of Dutch, Russian, South African and Japanese registry in the style of *Smit Rotterdam*. This tug and two sisterships each produce 22,000 horsepower. (Nationaal Sleepvaart Museum, Maassluis)

purpose. Recently delivered for escort duties in Norwegian waters, the 10,000hp, 90-ton bollard pull, "state of the art" VSP tug *Ajax* was Canadian-designed and built in Spain.

A strong current trend in tug design is specific for articulated barge work (ATB). The technology now permits practical operation of barges on the open ocean. One tug, with its relatively small crew, attached to a deeply-notched barge the size of a ship, is particularly effective in bulk trades and oil tanker service. Seaspan in Vancouver recently inaugurated an ATB for intermodal traffic between the mainland of British Columbia and Vancouver Island. The Chinese-built 453-foot *Coastal Express* has been mated to the modified 3600bhp tug *Seaspan Challenger*.

The implementation of this service in 2001 involved a plan illustrating the global and innovative thinking in the towing industry in the new century. The Washington Marine Group's Seaspan division ordered the barge *Coastal Express* built at Shanghai. Two chip barges were also ordered. With a view to the lengthy tow to

bring them home, the chip barges were assembled on the deck of *Coastal Express*. The stalwart veteran *Seaspan Commodore* (5750 bhp) set out on the 12,000 mile, seventy-seven day voyage. Not wasting the outgoing trip, she towed the old barge *Seaspan 271* to China for scrapping. But first, this barge was submerged in the company's floating drydock so six old tugs and an oil barge could be floated aboard. Refloated, this barge load was hauled to Victoria where a drillship tender was added to the tow in tandem for the Pacific crossing.

On the Great Lakes McAsphalt Industries, liquid barging specialists, have combined with Upper Lakes Group Inc., to build and operate a 70,000 barrel ice-strengthened, bow thruster-equipped tank barge, *Norman MacLeod*, linked by hydraulic rams to the 6000bhp shallow draft pusher type tug *Everlast*.

Competitive movement of cargoes using large barges has returned to the coasts of North America, but has been limited in the inland lakes until recently due to a season curtailed by ice. The notch tug with high auxiliary wheelhouse is tied rigidly in the notch of the barge, usually with sophisticated latching devices. This makes the two handle as one vessel. (John Weeks Collection)

Tugs have had a role in the economic life of the world that is significant beyond the small chores we see them perform. Their function at the beginning and end of the voyages of the big ships that sail the seven seas, and in moving materials on narrow inland waters is important. They also have a brave record of hurrying out to sea to rescue the bigger vessels from their own element, the ocean, when it storms.

A specialized type of vessel, with its own unique hull and massive power for its small size, the tug exudes a pretentious air. There is something about this stubby, homely vessel that promotes a sympathetic and affectionate feeling in many people. However, it would be misleading to overly romanticize the tug, or towboat, because it is always a very practical commercial vessel, even in its most glamorous role of rescue for ships and their crews in distress.

The tug has performed a variety of tasks. It has saved great liners and their passengers from disaster, or merely embarrassment, fought fires afloat and ashore, has towed and been towed by whales, and has tended mud and garbage scows. Using more sophisticated barges, it has competed worldwide, with varying success, against freighters, tankers and even passenger ships. Its main purpose, though, has been to help and expedite other waterborne traffic.

Today, the tug industry fights to meet the vicissitudes of a new era of competition and markets, from bow thrusters on large ships to the ups and downs of offshore oil exploration, pollution emergencies and intercontinental tows. It is ready to tow anything just about anywhere, wet or dry, and supply its own barges, local or ocean-going; but large self-propelled barges are coming into competition, some ready to pick up and carry drill rigs, smelters, container cranes and other very bulky loads.

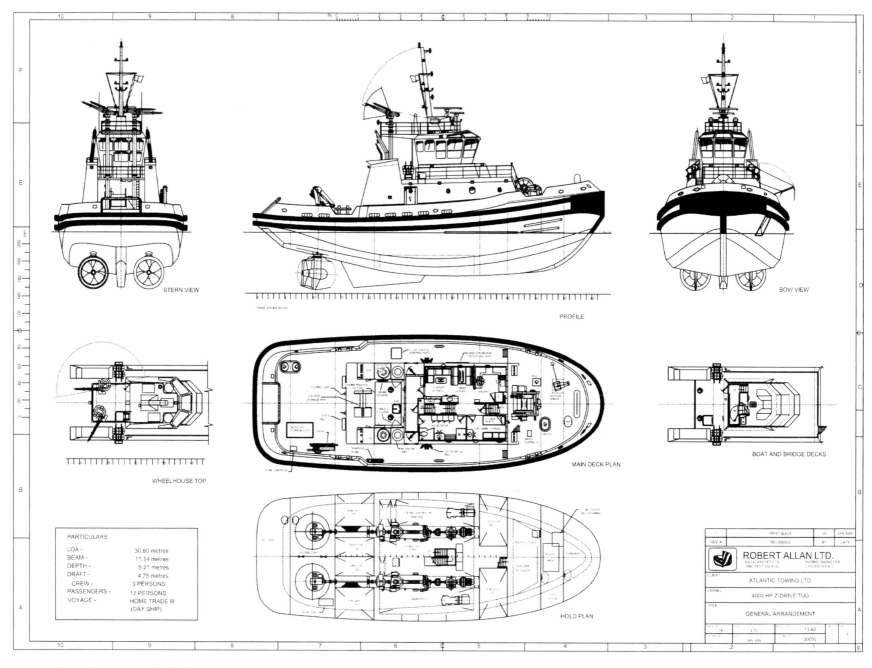

STERN VIEW

PROFILE

BOW VIEW

WHEELHOUSE TOP

MAIN DECK PLAN

BOAT AND BRIDGE DECKS

HOLD PLAN

PARTICULARS	
LOA -	30.80 metres
BEAM -	11.14 metres
DEPTH -	5.21 metres
DRAFT -	4.78 metres
CREW -	3 PERSONS
PASSENGERS -	12 PERSONS
VOYAGE -	HOME TRADE III (DAY SHIP)

ROBERT ALLAN LTD.
NAVAL ARCHITECTS   MARINE ENGINEERS
VANCOUVER B.C.

CLIENT: ATLANTIC TOWING LTD.

VESSEL: 4000 HP Z-DRIVE TUG

TITLE: GENERAL ARRANGEMENT

Atlantic Fir - An example of the popular, compact, Azimuth Stern Drive "day boat" docking tug now seen on both coasts. One of a number built on the East Coast to Allan designs, accommodating a crew of three. (Robert Allan, Ltd.)

Appleton, Thomas E. *Ravenscrag: The Allan Royal Mail Line.* Toronto: McClelland & Stewart, 1974.

Baird, Kenneth A. *Benjamin Franklin Tibbets and Saint John River Steamers.* Saint John: N.B. Historical Society, Unpublished Paper, 1962.

Baker, W.A. and Tre Tryckare. *The Engine Powered Vessel.* New York: Crown Publishers, 1972.

Barker, A.J., and D. Kirk. *The Great Escape.* Toronto: J.M. Dent & Sons, 1977.

Brady, Edward M. *Tugs, Towboats and Towing.* Centreville, MD: Cornell Maritime Press, 1967.

Brookes, Ivan S. *The Lower St. Lawrence.* Cleveland: Freshwater Press, 1974.

Bowen, Frank C. *A Hundred Years of Towage: History of William Watkins.* London: Gravesend and Dartmouth Reporter, 1933.

Calvin, Delano Dexter, III. *A Saga of the St. Lawrence.* Toronto: Ryerson Press, 1945.

Canadian Register of Ships. Vol I. Ottawa: Department of Transport, various years, notably December 1939 list.

Cree, E.H. *The Cree Journals.* Scarborough: Nelson Canada, 1981.

deHartog, Jan. *Captain Jan.* London: PAN Books, 1958.

deHartog, Jan. *The Captain.* London: PAN Books, 1968.

Divine, David. *The Nine Days of Dunkirk.* London: Faber & Faber, 1959.

Drushka, Ken. *Against Wind and Weather.* Vancouver: Douglas & McIntyre, 1981.

Fleming, Peter. *Operation Sealion.* London: PAN Books, 1957.

Flexner, James Thomas. *Steamboats Come True.* Boston: Little Brown & Co., 1978.

Forester, C.S. *Hornblower in the West Indies.* London: Michael Joseph, 1958.

Gaston, M.J. *Tugs and Towing.* Sparkford, Somerset: Patrick Stephens, Ltd., 1991.

Hannan, W.J. *Fifty Years of Naval Tugs.* Liskeard, Cornwall: Maritime Books, 1994.

Janes Fighting Ships. Various editions. Coulsdon, Surrey: Janes Information Group.

Glover, J.R. and D.D. Calvin. *A Corner of Empire, Ontario's Strand.* Publisher unknown.

Lamb, W.K. "Advent of the *Beaver.*" *B.C. Historical Quarterly*, Vancouver, July 1938.

Lawrence, Hal. *Tales of the North Atlantic.* Toronto: McClelland & Stewart. 1985.

Leggett, R.F. *Ottawa Waterway: Gateway to a Continent.* Toronto: University of Toronto Press, 1975.

Lloyds Register of Shipping. London: Numerous References over 150 years.

Lord, Walter. *The Miracle of Dunkirk.* New York: Viking Press, 1982.

Lower, A.R.M. *Great Britain's Woodyard.* McGill Press, 1961.

Mackay, Donald. *Lumberjacks.* Toronto: McGraw Hill Ryerson, 1978.

McCormick, Daniel C. *The Wishbone Fleet.* Massena, New York: D.C. McCormick, 1972.

McKay, John. *The Hudson's Bay Company's 1835 Steam Ship* Beaver. St. Catharines, Vanwell Publishing Limited, 2001.

Merrilees, Andrew. *A History of the Sincennes McNaughton Line.* Unpublished paper, undated.

Mitchell, W.H. *Empire Ships of World War II.* Liverpool: Sea Breezes, 1965.

Morison, Samuel Eliot. *Victory in the Pacific, 1945.* Boston: Little Brown, 1960.

Mowat, Farley. *Grey Seas Under.* Toronto: McClelland & Stewart, 1958.

Mowat, Farley. *The Serpent's Coil.* Toronto: McClelland & Stewart, 1961.

Musk, George. *Canadian Pacific.* Toronto: Holt, Rinehart & Winston, 1981.

Newell, George. *Pacific Tugboats.* New York: Bonanza, 1957.

Ocean Highway. Victoria, B.C: Island Tug and Barge Company. Company History. 1957.

Ocean Odyssey. Vancouver: Vancouver Tugboat Company. Company History. 1957.

O'Neill, Paul. *A Seaport Legacy.* Vol II. Erin, Ont: Press Porcepic, 1976.

Oram, H.K. *Ready for Sea.* London: Seely, Service & Co., 1974.

Penn, Geoffrey. *Up Funnel, Down Screw.* London: Hollis & Carter, 1955.

Pethick, Derek. *S.S.* Beaver*, The Ship That Saved the West.* Vancouver: Mitchell Press, 1970.

Plant, Al. *The Tugboat Book.* Detroit: W.E.C. Plant Enterprises Inc., no date.

Pratt, Fletcher. *Monitor and Merrimack.* New York: Random House, 1951.

Pullen, T.C. "3000 Mile Towing Odyssey in the Arctic." *Canadian Geographic.* Vol. 101, No. 6, 1981.

Roorda, A. *Small Seagoing Craft and Vessels.* Haarlem, Holland: Technical Publishing Co. 1957.

Roskill, S.W. *H.M.S.* Warspite. London: William Collins, 1957.

Scrapbook, Cadieux Collection. Collection MSS 782. Public Archives Vancouver.

Sevigny, Pierre-Andre. *Trade and Navigation in the Chambly Canal.* Ottawa: Parks Canada, 1983.

Shirer, William L. *The Rise and Fall of the Third Reich.* New York: Simon and Schuster, 1960.

Skalley, Michael. *Ninety Years of Towboating.* Seattle: Superior Publishing, 1981.

Sullivan, R.S. "History of Foundation Maritime, Ltd." Montreal: Unpublished Paper from Company records, 1955.

Thomas, P.N. *British Steam Tugs.* Wolverhampton: Waine Research Publications, 1983.

Troup, Ken D. (Editor). *First North America Tug Convention Proceedings.* London: Thomas Reed Industrial Press, 1973.

Fifth to Eighth International Tug Convention Papers. London: Thomas Reed Industrial Press, 1977 to 1984.

Williams, Mark. *No Cure, No Pay: The Story of Salvage at Sea.* London: Hutchinson Benham, 1978.

Wilson, James E. & S.C. Heal. *Full Line, Full Away: A Towboat Master's Story.* Vancouver: Cordillera Publishing, 1991.

Winton, John. *The War at Sea.* London: Arrow, 1970.

Woods, Shirley. *The Molson Saga.* Toronto: Avon of Canada, 1983.

INDEX OF TUGS